Alaska's Oil/Gas & Minerals Industry

ALASKA GEOGRAPHIC®
Volume 9, Number 4, 1982

The cover, clockwise from upper left: A geologist's pick marks an outcrop of volcanic breccia near Hoonah in southeastern Alaska. (Greg Fernette) / Miners use a hydraulic giant to wash dirt into their sluice in the Circle mining district. (Ron Wendt) / An old steam shovel sits abandoned at Circle City, evidence of past mining activity. (Gil Mull) / The green mineral malachite is visible in this weathered copper ore from the Ruby Creek deposit in the western Brooks Range. (Donald Grybeck) / A geologist's gear, including insect repellent, is spread out on the ground at a camp in the Circle district. (Greg Fernette) / A pan, patience, and a lot of luck are all that are necessary to find gold. (Ben Porterfield) / A mammoth oil rig operates in the Gulf of Alaska in the 1960s. (Steve McCutcheon) / Sean Hamilton watches for blockage while Kelly Adams uses a Cat to fill the sluice box. (Brian Milne)

The Alaska Geographic Society

To teach many more to better know and use our natural resources

Chief Editor: Robert A. Henning
Assistant Chief Editor: Barbara Olds
Editor: Penny Rennick
Editorial Assistant: Kathy Doogan
Design and illustrations: Jon.Hersh
Maps: Jon.Hersh and David Shott

About This Issue: To put together this issue of *ALASKA GEOGRAPHIC®*, we had to call on many experts both in Alaska and Outside. For starters, we thank Donald Grybeck; David Stone, of the University of Alaska; Greg Fernette, Riz Bigelow, Jami Fernette, and Gaylord Cleveland of WGM, Inc.; Doug Smith; W.R. Kastelic; Thomas K. Bundtzen and Gil Mull of Alaska Division of Geological and Geophysical Surveys; Cleland Conwell; Leah Madonna; Robert Sanders; Mike Hershberger, of Alaska Oil and Gas Association; G. Michael Doogan; and Earl Beistline for contributions and review of the text.

We appreciate the comments of Charles Herbert and Tom Smith on the manuscript; and we thank the fine photographers who have documented Alaska's geology and mining and shared their material with us.

Editor's note: Weights of precious metals (gold, silver, platinum, etc.) in this issue are given in troy ounces. Twelve troy ounces equal one troy pound; 14.6 troy ounces equal one avoirdupois pound.

Abbreviations which have been used in this issue are: D.G.G.S. (Alaska Division of Geological and Geophysical Surveys); U.S.B.M. (U.S. Bureau of Mines); U.S.G.S. (U.S. Geological Survey); and BLM (Bureau of Land Management).

Library of Congress cataloging in publication data:
Main entry under title:

Alaska's oil/gas & minerals industry.

(Alaska geographic, ISSN 0361-1353; v. 9, no. 4)
1. Petroleum—Alaska.   2. Gas, Natural—Alaska.
3. Mines and mineral resources—Alaska.   I. Title:
Alaska's oil/gas and minerals industry.   II. Series.
F901.A266 vol. 9, no. 4   917.98s   82-16312
[TN872.A7]   [533′.09798]
ISBN 0-88240-170-X

ALASKA GEOGRAPHIC®, ISSN 0361-1353, is published quarterly by The Alaska Geographic Society, Anchorage, Alaska 99509. Second-class postage paid in Edmonds, Washington 98020. Printed in U.S.A.

THE ALASKA GEOGRAPHIC SOCIETY is a nonprofit organization exploring new frontiers of knowledge across the lands of the polar rim, learning how other men and other countries live in their Norths, putting the geography book back in the classroom, exploring new methods of teaching and learning — sharing in the excitement of discovery in man's wonderful new world north of 51°16′.

MEMBERS OF THE SOCIETY RECEIVE *Alaska Geographic®*, a quality magazine which devotes each quarterly issue to monographic in-depth coverage of a northern geographic region or resource-oriented subject.

MEMBERSHIP DUES in The Alaska Geographic Society are $30 per year; $34 to non-U.S. addresses, U.S. funds. (Eighty percent of each year's dues is for a one-year subscription to *Alaska Geographic®*.) Order from The Alaska Geographic Society, Box 4-EEE, Anchorage, Alaska 99509; (907) 274-0521.

MATERIAL SOUGHT: The editors of *Alaska Geographic®* seek a wide variety of informative material on the lands north of 51°16′ on geographic subjects — anything to do with resources and their uses (with heavy emphasis on quality color photography) — from Alaska, Northern Canada, Siberia, Japan — all geographic areas that have a relationship to Alaska in a physical or economic sense. We do not want material done in excessive scientific terminology. A query to the editors is suggested. Payments are made for all material upon publication.

CHANGE OF ADDRESS: The post office does not automatically forward *Alaska Geographic®* when you move. To insure continuous service, notify us six weeks before moving. Send us your new address and zip code (and moving date), your old address and zip code, and if possible send a mailing label from a copy of *Alaska Geographic®*. Send this information to *Alaska Geographic®* Mailing Offices, 130 Second Avenue South, Edmonds, Washington 98020.

MAILING LISTS: We have begun making our members' names and addresses available to carefully screened publications and companies whose products and activities might be of interest to you. If you would prefer not to receive such mailings, please so advise us, and include your mailing label (or your name and address if label is not available).

I isn't quite like the "old days" when we were a kid growing up in one of the biggest gold mining towns in the world, Juneau, where we can still hear the sound of rock falling off the end of the belt stackers out on the rock dump on a clear windless night, hear the steady horn signal announcing a pending big blast in the depths of the mountain, listen to the exciting tales of roaming prospectors in the lobby of the old Gastineau Hotel . . . to know the thrill of news of a new strike . . . to hold in your hand somebody's you-know-it-was-carefully-selected piece of quartz shot through with veinlets of unmistakable pure gold. "Bullshit rich" was the expression.

Then the great wars came, again the men left the drifts and the stopes and the placers, and a quiet lay on the land. Now, in a new day we for one cannot quite yet

grasp, the pace is quickening, the claims stakes are studding the landscapes with fresh-blazed corner markers and piles of stone, "secret" men and women with science fiction diving clothes and modern plastic riffles and long toms are prowling the creeks, oil men drill in the Arctic stillness and take the stillness with them into locked lab studies to examine drill cores and little seashells. Big companies raise black glass and gleaming aluminum office buildings obviously "betting on the come."

You know Alaska again stands on the threshhold of vast riches. We thought it was a good time to take an overall look at the scene and thus this issue.

On another score, your Alaska Geographic Society has undertaken a challenging new job. Five years ago a fascinating little newssheet on news stock,

but to magazine dimensions, was launched to take basic natural marine knowledge to Alaskan school kids and their teachers . . . about the lovelife of the different kinds of shrimp, the seals, clams, the tides, octopus, etc. It was called *Alaska Tidelines* and existed on Sea Grant and Alaska Legislature/University of Alaska funding. Somebody locked the door on the vaults and the little paper, which as a free circulation thing had grown to 40,000 issues eight times a year, was about to fold. We thought saving this one was a proper function of our Society . . . "To teach many more to better know and use our natural resources" . . . so we've kept it afloat . . . and changed the title to *Alaska Earthlines/Tidelines* to broaden our opportunities to provide the kids fundamental knowledge of what makes their world tick, both in and around the waters and in the land itself as well.

We think it belongs in every kid's classroom, the world over, and we'll be interested in any suggestions or help. For starters, we're offering economical student subscriptions to anyone who orders 10 or more copies, but we're also selling individual subscriptions at bargain prices because the little paper packs a big portion of information into each issue . . . and kids of all ages should have it. Prices and how to order are at the back of this issue.

President
The Alaska Geographic Society

Cinnabar (red), a mercury sulfide, and stibnite, an antimony sulfide, occur in this specimen from the Red Devil mine.
(Donald Grybeck)

Putting the Pieces Together

The Geology of Alaska

For centuries man has wondered about the earth, about the ground on which he walks, about the earthquakes and volcanic eruptions which he endures. Geology, the study of the earth, in Alaska is made even more challenging by the land's youth, in a geologic sense, and its constantly changing geologic structure. In the last few decades, scientists have determined that the state is made up, in part, of land masses that have migrated to the northern Pacific rim from far to the south. According to current theory, the forces driving plate tectonics and continental drift have also created this unique land puzzle that is Alaska.

The theory of plate tectonics has revolutionized geology in the last two decades. Basically, the theory holds that the outer shell of the earth consists of a series of large plates, each of which moves independently. These plates are about 60 miles thick and are made up of solid material which collectively is termed the lithosphere. The solid, comparatively brittle lithospheric plates are, in effect, floating on the relatively fluid portion of the earth beneath them, the athenosphere.

Two types of crust, that portion of the earth that we can actually see, make up the upper portion of the lithospheric plates. The oceanic crust consists mainly of relatively young basalt, a dark-colored volcanic rock. Typically, the earth's plates expand outward, by extrusion of basalt, from spreading zones along mid-ocean fractures of the oceanic crust. The continental crust, in contrast, is more heterogeneous and thicker than the oceanic crust. The continental crust is made up of igneous, sedimentary, and metamorphic rocks that have progressively been welded together during the last four billion years.

If the earth's plates continually grow outward from spreading zones, indeed if the plates simply move independently of each other, they must both slide past each other and often collide and converge. This continual growth further implies that unless the earth is expanding, which is unlikely, the plates must also somehow be destroyed to balance their growth in the oceans. A convenient way to terminate plates is to have them dive under, or

subduct, another plate. Subduction zones are particularly appropriate to Alaska geology because the Aleutian Islands form a classic example of a subduction zone in action today. Also, southern Alaska and the Alaska Peninsula show many examples of subduction zones that have existed through geologic time.

There are several types of subduction zones. The diagram on page 6 is an idealized cross section, from northwest to southeast, of the geology of a hypothetical subduction zone, much like the one along the Alaska Peninsula. The oceanic plate is typically marked by a deep oceanic trench (the Aleutian Trench) which receives the sediments shed from the volcanic arc by erosion and stream action. A portion of these sediments are then carried down with the descending plate and are subject

Dirty sandstone from the Red Devil Mine northeast of Bethel is part of the Kuskokwim Group sandstone. These sediments were deposited widely in a marine basin in what is now southwestern Alaska in Cretaceous time about 100 million years ago. (Donald Grybeck)

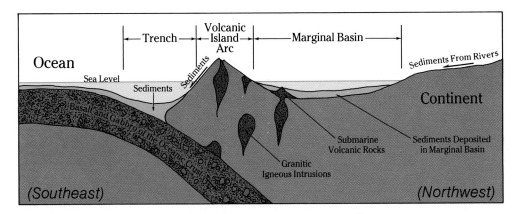

Ocean
Sea Level
Sediments
Basalt and Gabbro of the Oceanic Crust
(Southeast)

Trench — Volcanic Island Arc — Marginal Basin —
Sediments From Rivers
Continent
Submarine Volcanic Rocks
Sediments Deposited in Marginal Basin
Granitic Igneous Intrusions
(Northwest)

This diagram of a subduction zone involving an island arc is hypothetical in detail but is modeled after a section through the southern Alaska Peninsula from southeast to northwest. The oceanic crust (purple) is subducting a volcanic island arc. Sediments (green) are being deposited in an oceanic trench at the line of deflection and in the marginal basin behind the volcanic arc. Magma is being formed below the island arc as the descending plate becomes hotter at depth; the magma rises to produce plutonic igneous bodies (red) and volcanic rocks (also red) along the island arc.

to increased temperature and pressure at depth. Eventually, granitic magmas are generated which move upward to form plutonic igneous bodies if they do not reach the surface, and volcanoes and volcanic rocks if they do. Subduction zones commonly have marginal basins between the volcanic arc and the main continental mass; some geologists interpret Bristol Bay as the modern Alaska equivalent of a marginal basin. The marginal basins receive sediments both from the volcanic arc and from the continent. As is strikingly demonstrated by the Alaska Peninsula and Aleutian Islands, subduction zones are usually marked by severe tectonic activity such as earthquakes, faulting, and volcanoes.

Where the plates simply slide past each other, the motion forms very large faults known as transform faults. Perhaps the best known of these is the San Andreas fault in California. Everything east of the San Andreas fault system is part of the North American plate; everything to the west is on the Pacific plate. The Pacific plate is moving relatively north at about three inches per year. In Alaska, currently active transform faults are in southeastern Alaska, but a trace of an older transform fault can be seen in the Denali fault along the line of the Alaska Range.

(**Editor's note:** Dr. David Stone, professor of geophysics at the University of Alaska, Fairbanks, contributed most of the following text for this chapter. Dr. Stone specializes in paleomagnetic studies, in which scientists study drill core samples from the earth to determine where magnetic north was during the age of the core sample. With this information, geophysicists can tell if a certain piece of ground has shifted on the earth's surface.)

Looking at the large scale plate picture with regard to Alaska, scientists know that Alaska is part of the North American plate. In southeastern Alaska a transform fault system is active where the Pacific plate is sliding by on its way north. As the Pacific plate approaches the Gulf of Alaska, it collides with the North American plate. It seems the Pacific plate is sliding underneath southcentral Alaska, and perhaps not curving downward to plunge deep into the earth until reaching the vicinity of Mount McKinley, several hundred miles inland. This may be one reason for the abrupt rise to great heights of the central Alaska Range near Mount McKinley.

Tracing the plate boundary farther westward through the Aleutians, the Pacific plate joins another island arc-trench system in Kamchatka and the Kurile Islands, Soviet-owned territory in the western Pacific. The boundary of the Pacific plate is very clear as it continues

The pattern of earthquakes around the world clearly outlines the major plate boundaries. Each dot on the map represents a single event recorded by the worldwide seismograph network during the years 1961 to 1967. Intensely active seismic areas, such as those around the Pacific Ocean, are due to one plate sliding beneath another at a subduction zone. The thin lines of earthquakes through the oceans mark the oceanic spreading centers and faults. Though the major boundaries are clear, others, such as those through eastern Africa and Siberia, are less well defined. The arrows on the plates represent the directions in which the plates are moving relative to each other today.
(Source map: NOAA)

A field worker notes this columnar basalt at Rocky Pass west of Petersburg in southeastern Alaska. Often, cooling basalt develops into a series of columns, each of which is five- or six-sided in cross section. (Donald Grybeck)

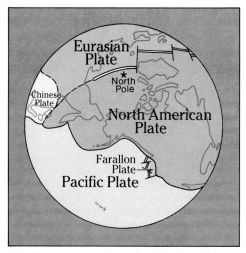

This diagram shows the major plate boundaries that surround Alaska, with the Pacific plate moving generally northwards, and thus sliding past southeastern Alaska and diving under southcentral and western Alaska. In the North, the plate boundary is the Arctic Ocean spreading center, a continuation of the mid-Atlantic system. The far western boundary is the most controversial and has been left as a dashed line. (Drawn from information developed by D.B. Stone, Geophysical Institute, University of Alaska, Fairbanks).

south along the western Pacific, but somewhere the North American plate boundary has to cut northwards to join the spreading zone of the Atlantic mid-oceanic fracture where it crosses the Arctic Ocean. Earthquakes and volcanic activity which would normally define a plate boundary are difficult to detect in this area, but scientists think that the boundary crosses eastern Siberia.

Thus, Alaska is caught between a fracture in the Arctic with the plates spreading outward trying to push Alaska to the south, and a northward-moving Pacific plate trying to push Alaska to the north. The combination of forces generated by these motions is responsible for the tectonic activity seen today — principally earthquakes and volcanoes — and traced backwards in time, may well be responsible for the large curved systems of mountains, valleys, and major faults that dominate Alaska's present landscape.

The advent of the plate tectonic concept in the 1960s helped explain some of the geology observed in Alaska, but this same theory left many questions. One of these questions revolved around the fact that rocks of similar ages were often observed near one another, but they were of types which could not reasonably have been originally formed close together. The way a rock has been assembled, the material of

Layers of chromite (gray) are exposed at Red Mountain near Seldovia on the Kenai Peninsula. (Donald Grybeck)

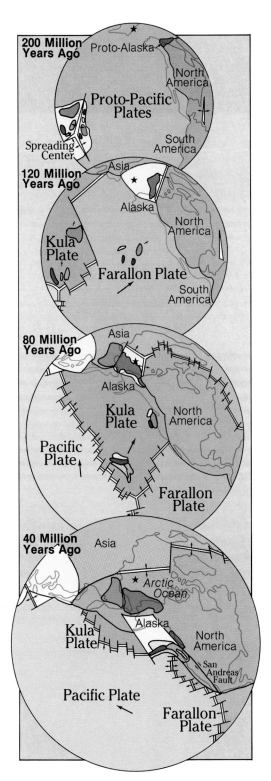

These reconstructions of plate movement and concurrent shifts in land masses for 200, 120, 80, and 40 million years ago show how land masses originated in the central Pacific Ocean may have ridden northward on crustal plates and eventually reached Alaska. These diagrams include much speculation. The data available show that the terranes were far to the south 200 million years ago, but whether they were together in the central Pacific Ocean, as we now call it, or spread out is open to debate. Timing of the northward movement is also the subject of much debate. Movement of land masses shown in these diagrams is based on steady northward motion. The changes in direction of some of the terranes are assumed to have been caused by the known reorganizations of the mid-oceanic spreading centers in the Pacific.

At 200 million years ago, a three-pronged spreading center starts to form in the Pacific. At the same time, a small area (purple) at the top of the North American continent is still attached to the main continental mass.

At 120 million years ago, movement of the Farallon plate causes land masses (orange, yellow, and red) to move toward the North American continent. The land mass (purple) at the top of the continent begins its swing to the west.

By 80 million years ago, land masses destined to reach North America continue their movement, only now they are riding on the Kula rather than the Farallon plate. The northernmost land mass (purple) has nearly completed its swing to the west and now bridges the North American and Asian continents across the Arctic Ocean.

At 40 million years ago, the land masses moving eastward across the Pacific Ocean have collided with the North American continent and, through transform or lateral faulting based on the San Andreas fault system, have slid northward along the west coast of North America and are about to collide with southcentral Alaska. Note that the Farallon and Kula plates have subducted beneath the North American plate. And the land mass that broke off from the top of the North American continent now forms much of northern Alaska and a part of northeastern Siberia.

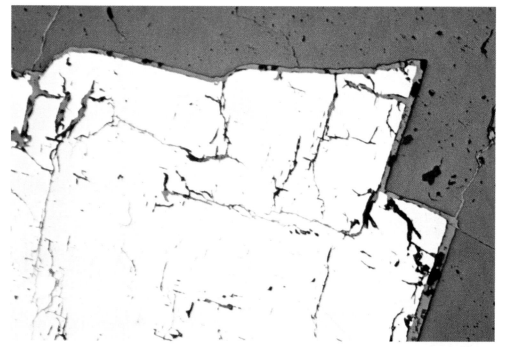

This polished ore specimen from Fairbanks is magnified under a microscope about 160 times. The gray mineral is arsenopyrite, an iron-arsenic sulfide; the yellow mineral is native gold.
(Donald Grybeck)

which it is made, the fossils the rock may or may not contain, the rock's chemistry and other properties may all be interpreted in terms of the ancient environment in which the rock was formed. For instance, the sharpness or roundness of the grain of a sandstone indicates how far the grain has traveled before being trapped. Similarly, deep ocean sediments are easily distinguished from shallow water sediments.

The recognition that rocks from different geological environments can be seen close together, but usually separated by faults, led to the concept of tectonostratigraphic terranes. These are defined as areas that are fault (tectonically) bounded and have internally consistent sequences of rocks (stratigraphies), the latter indicating a coherent geologic history within a block. Because some of these terranes are so different from their neighbors, it is obvious that considerable relative motion has to have taken place between them. An example of one of these exotic terranes is the Chulitna terrane in southcentral Alaska. According to the geologists who described it, the Chulitna terrane ". . . contains a distinctive suite of rocks found nowhere else in Alaska or, for that matter, in North America."

Alaska has currently been subdivided into more than 50 of these tectonostratigraphic terranes by U.S. Geological Survey geologists, but some of these terranes may be subdivisions of larger, major terranes. Some terranes are very large and distinctive, such as

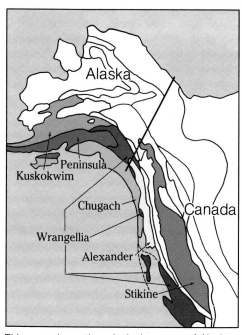

This map shows the principal terranes of Alaska and western Canada. Each labeled terrane defines an area in which the rocks indicate an internally consistent geologic history. The terranes are generally separated from one another by tectonic boundaries such as faults. All the terranes making up southern Alaska are interpreted as having been considerably farther south early in their geologic history. Note how some terranes, such as Wrangellia, appear to have been fragmented.
(Source map: D.L. Jones, U.S.G.S.)

Wrangellia forming the Wrangell Mountains area, which includes thick sequences of submarine lava flows and limestone. Others, such as the Chulitna terrane, are small but equally distinctive.

Alaska is not unique in being divided into these terranes; most of the western United States is now thought to be made of terranes also, as can be seen in the figure at left. This figure clearly shows that some of these terranes have been fragmented into several pieces. The most notable of these is Wrangellia, which is centered in the Wrangell Mountains, but which has fragments as far south as Idaho.

Paleomagnetic studies — the study of the earth's magnetic force as recorded by rocks when they were formed — on rocks from a number of Alaska's tectonostratigraphic terranes have shown that southern Alaska was far to the south, near the equator, about 200 million years ago. Between that time and the present,

the terranes of southern Alaska have migrated northward, perhaps riding on the plates that made up the ancient Pacific, in the same way that all the rocks currently sitting on the eastern parts of the Pacific plate today will probably end up in Alaska.

The big questions that are being worked on in Alaska today are how much of Alaska was involved in the plate movement, when did this land arrive in Alaska, and what made up ancient Alaska. None of these questions have been answered yet. The speculations presented here in terms of possible reconstruction should be looked upon as being just that, speculations.

Whether these speculations are correct or not in detail, it is certain that the geologic processes involved in the collisions of the various pieces of today's Alaska were also important to the generation and concentration of Alaska's mineral deposits.

Origin of Mineral Deposits

Many theories have been proposed to explain the origin of mineral deposits. Undoubtedly, the main reason for the numerous theories of deposition is that ore deposits do indeed form in various ways. And research during the last two decades has clarified the origins of several principal types of mineral deposits.

A description of the major rock types and their origins must precede a detailed account of the origin of mineral deposits because the formation of rocks is directly or indirectly tied to the formation of ore deposits. Indeed, ore deposits are exceedingly rare varieties of rocks.

Rocks fall into three major families: sedimentary, igneous, and metamorphic. Igneous rocks are formed by solidification of molten magma. The depth of solidification is important. Plutonic igneous rocks generally cool slowly at depth and consequently consist of a distinct mosaic of discrete mineral grains fractions of inches in size. In contrast, volcanic igneous rocks cool quickly at or near the earth's surface, and individual grains often do not have sufficient time to grow to significant size.

Volcanic rocks typically are made up entirely of grains too small to distinguish by sight, or contain large crystals, which grow early in the magma, scattered in a dense matrix of tiny indistinguishable crystals. The latter is often called a porphyry. Light- to medium-gray plutonic igneous rocks characteristically are found on the continents and commonly form the core of mountain ranges. They include such varieties as granite and diorite; their volcanic equivalents are rhyolites and andesites. Dark-colored igneous rocks are widely scattered on the continents, but in particular form the rocks beneath the oceans. Basalt is by far the most common dark-colored, volcanic, igneous rock; its plutonic equivalent is gabbro.

Sedimentary rocks are deposited layer by layer at the surface of the land or on the ocean floor by mechanical or chemical processes. Clastic sedimentary rocks — sandstones, shales, and conglomerates — form by accumulation of rock fragments that were produced by erosion of preexisting rocks and transported by water or wind.

Chemical sedimentary rocks are formed by precipitation of minerals in an aqueous, usually marine, environment; the most common variety is limestone. Limestone forms either by direct chemical precipitation of calcium carbonate in sea water or by accumulation of the remains of marine organisms that extract calcium carbonate from sea water to produce their shells.

Metamorphic rocks are formed from preexisting igneous, sedimentary, and metamorphic rocks by heat and pressure. The effects of the heat and pressure combine to change the mineralogy and texture of the original rocks often to the point that their identity is obscured. Some common metamorphic rocks are slate which forms from shale; schist and gneiss which can form from a variety of preexisting rocks including shale,

---

This is a microscopic view — magnified about 100 times — of a porphyritic volcanic rock from the Alaska Range. The gray mineral is feldspar, the brown mineral, pyroxene. (Donald Grybeck)

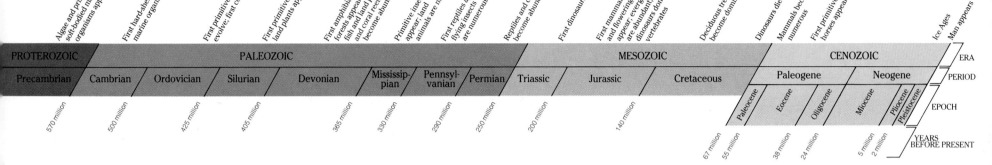

This time scale traces geologic time from the Precambrian period, which ended 570 million years ago, through the present. Figures represent ages in millions of years before the present.

sandstone, and various igneous rocks; and marble which is the metamorphic equivalent of limestone. The conditions of metamorphism vary. The effects of low temperature and pressures usually result in relatively minor changes in the parent rock. However, extremes of metamorphism involve temperatures and pressures so high as to produce entirely new rocks and can even result in melting, which produces magma.

The origin of some of the prominent theories of ore deposition is lost in history. Placer deposits and lode deposits have been distinguished since antiquity. Placers, most commonly gold placers, occur in the sands and gravels of streams and rivers throughout the world. Typically, they are

relatively simple deposits that probably furnished some of the earliest metals used by man. Lodes, however, occur in solid rock as veins and disseminated deposits. Lodes of gold, silver, and copper have been mined since at least Biblical times. The need to excavate them from solid rock, often in underground workings, quickly set them apart from placers.

Some of the current theories of ore deposition are surprisingly old. For instance, in the mid-16th century, George Bauer, better known as Agricola, wrote several classic books on the geology of mineral deposits, mining, and metallurgy that were to remain influential texts for centuries. Agricola ascribed the origin of mineral deposits to juices that flowed

along cracks in the ground. In other words, mineral deposits formed from solutions, and the metals were introduced into the rocks rather than being native to them. His ideas persist as one of the most prominent of present-day theories, the hydrothermal theory of ore deposition, i.e., some mineral bodies are deposited from hot water that carried the metals.

There are numerous subtypes of hydrothermal ore deposits. One of the best known types is veins adjacent to small bodies of plutonic granitic rocks. The molten magma which eventually solidified to form the plutonic rocks originally had water and small amounts of various metals distributed through it. As the magma crystallized, the water and metals progressively segregated into a water-rich phase at the top of the magma chamber. This metal-rich hydrothermal fluid was then injected out along cracks and joints above and adjacent to the igneous body. The metals and other elements carried in the fluid precipitated as planar bodies or veins as far as several thousand yards or more away from the plutons. Commonly these veins consist mainly of quartz and ore minerals. Most common precious and base metals occur in veins; but usually certain suites or associations of elements occur together, such as gold-quartz veins, lead-zinc-silver veins, mercury-antimony veins, and others. Commonly the mineral associations vary away from the igneous body, implying that the elemental associations are a function of change in temperature and pressure away from the cooling igneous body. Numerous examples of hydrothermal veins occur in Alaska; for instance, the gold-quartz veins of the Willow Creek district, or the silver-lead-zinc veins of the Kantishna district.

Hydrothermal fluids may form deposits other than veins. As they move away from their source, the fluids often preferentially replace certain types of rocks to form large, irregular masses of ore minerals. Classical examples of replacement deposits are flat-lying, lead-silver-zinc ore bodies in limestone.

Alternately, as the plutonic body crystallizes, the metals are deposited as a multitude of thin, disseminated veinlets near or just above the top of the body. The best known of these disseminated

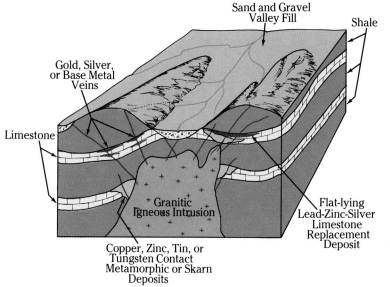

This diagram shows a model of hydrothermal mineral deposits associated with the apex of a granitic igneous body. Ore veins (red) radiate out from the top of the igneous body (orange) as the hydrothermal fluids move along cracks and joints in the rocks. Flat-lying replacement bodies (also in red) form when the hydrothermal fluids encounter reactive rocks such as limestones. Locally, contact metamorphic (skarn) deposits (green) form near the igneous body in response to the heat and pressure of the intruding body and diffusing hydrothermal solutions. Note that only a few of the veins are exposed at the surface; the full extent of the mineralization can only be determined by subsurface exploration. Lowering of the surface topography by weathering and erosion will progressively expose the different types of mineralization and the igneous body.

This diagram shows a porphyry copper-molybdenum deposit (red) that has formed at the apex of a granitic igneous body (orange). Note that the outer shell of altered rocks associated with the deposit (green area) is a much larger exploration target than the zone of copper-molybdenum veinlets. In this diagram the outer shell (green area) is all that is exposed at the surface.

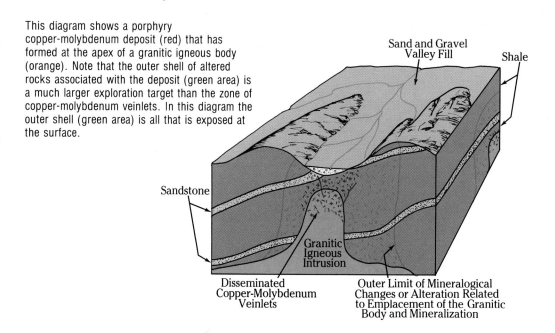

— 15

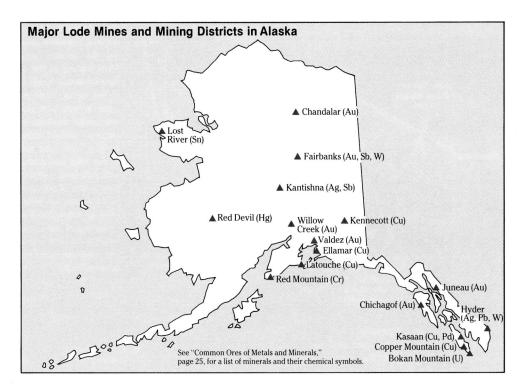

Major Lode Mines and Mining Districts in Alaska

▲ Chandalar (Au)

▲ Lost River (Sn)

▲ Fairbanks (Au, Sb, W)

▲ Kantishna (Ag, Sb)

▲ Red Devil (Hg)

▲ Willow Creek (Au)

▲ Kennecott (Cu)

▲ Valdez (Au)

▲ Ellamar (Cu)

▲ Latouche (Cu)

▲ Red Mountain (Cr)

▲ Juneau (Au)

Chichagof (Au) ▲

Hyder (Ag, Pb, W)

Kasaan (Cu, Pd) ▲
Copper Mountain (Cu) ▲
Bokan Mountain (U) ▲

See "Common Ores of Metals and Minerals," page 25, for a list of minerals and their chemical symbols.

should be remembered that there are vast areas of plutonic igneous rocks and many igneous bodies that have no discernible mineral deposits associated with them.

If veins and porphyry deposits result from solidification of magma at depth, what happens if the igneous rocks are emplaced near the surface or vent their hydrothermal fluids to the surface? In the last two decades, these massive sulfide or volcanogenic massive sulfide deposits have been recognized as an important type of deposit. Generally they occur in marine sedimentary rocks, often associated with rhyolite or basalt flows.

The model for these deposits is that the rhyolitic or basaltic magma and associated hydrothermal fluids flow from submarine vents. The magma quickly solidifies and forms rhyolitic piles on the ocean floor near the vent; shortly after or concurrently, the metals are deposited near the vent on the sea floor as the hydrothermal fluids react with the sea water. Probably the best-known example of an Alaska massive sulfide deposit associated with rhyolite volcanics is the large Arctic deposit in the southern Brooks Range near Ambler. A good example of a deposit associated with basaltic volcanics is the Beatson Mine on Latouche Island in Prince William Sound. However, the hydrothermal fluids may not react with the sea water near the submarine vent but flow outward along the sea floor, in some cases for great distances, before precipitating in ocean troughs. They flow along the sea floor because they are heavy

deposits are the porphyry copper and stockwork molybdenum deposits. Alaska examples include the copper porphyries at Orange Hill, Bond Creek, and several other locations in the Wrangell Mountains, and the U.S. Borax molybdenum deposit near Ketchikan. Porphyry deposits are usually large in volume but of relatively low grade compared to veins. Porphyry copper deposits now being mined often contain less than 0.8% copper and molybdenum deposits less than 0.4% molybdenum. Usually, porphyry orebodies are outlined by a much wider

shell of rocks that has been altered mineralogically by the heat and pressure of the cooling igneous body; various elements are added to the shell or subtracted from it by hydrothermal fluids. These zones of alteration, while devoid of ore minerals, are an important guide to the discovery of porphyry deposits and are avidly studied by exploration geologists. Vein deposits and disseminated deposits often occur together associated with an igneous body.

But while many vein and porphyry deposits can be related to igneous rocks, it

Layers of coal mix with granite on the beach near
Deep Creek just south of Ninilchik on the
Kenai Peninsula. (John and Margaret Ibbotson)

Layers are easily distinguished in this sedimentary deposit of shale near Pet Lake, 50 miles northwest of Wiseman in the Brooks Range. (George Wuerthner)

fluids that move downslope by gravity faster than they mix with the surrounding sea water or react chemically with it. The result is metal-rich layers interbedded with normal marine rocks in sedimentary basins.

Many mineral deposits lack nearby igneous rocks that might reasonably be their source even though the ore minerals were clearly deposited later than the rocks in which they occur. Data indicate that many of these deposits formed from hydrothermal fluids 120°F to 390°F. One answer to the origin of these deposits is that they were deposited from hydrothermal fluids derived from granitic igneous rocks, but the fluids have moved such great distance that their igneous source is deeply buried or cannot now be identified.

Increasingly, however, scientists recognize that hydrothermal fluids with significant metal content can be generated other than as part of igneous processes. In general, the steps in the formation of hydrothermal deposits consist of first generating the hot water, charging it with metals, then moving the water to a site where the physical and/or chemical conditions are favorable for deposition of the metal from solution. One of several environments in which this can occur is in marine basins where clastic sedimentary rocks are accumulating. Subsurface water is readily available in sedimentary basins. At depth, this water is certainly hot. The general rule is that temperature in sedimentary basins increases at about

2° to 3°F per 100 feet of depth. The water in drill holes in sedimentary basins is typically 120°F to 212°F at a depth of 10,000 feet, and water at 490°F has been measured at about 20,000 feet below the surface of the Gulf Coast.

That water circulates at depth is not easy to document, but such waters are subject to thermal and chemical gradients and structural forces — for instance, the increasing weight of overlying rocks as the basin develops, or tectonic forces related to earthquakes — that indicate subsurface waters should indeed move. What might seem to be an insurmountable problem, a source for the metals for these circulating waters, is probably almost universally present. The source is almost any common rock through which the hydrothermal fluids may move. The rationale is that all rocks contain minute quantities of the common metals; for instance, the average shale contains about 0.005% copper. Although the percentage is extremely small, the total amount of copper available in the large volume of shale in the earth's crust is immense. One cubic mile of average shale — and most other common rocks have similar values — contains more than 700,000 tons of copper, or about one-half of the yearly United States production. If even a part of the copper could be extracted from several cubic miles of shale and concentrated, a very substantial deposit would result.

Most water found in deep sedimentary rocks is a brine, and the high salt content would undoubtedly aid in charging what is essentially a hydrothermal fluid with metals. A plausible sequence of events is that a marine basin gradually fills in with sediments. As the sediments pile up, the basin sinks, either from the weight of the sediments themselves or from larger tectonic forces. As these water-rich muds and sands accumulate and sink, the water is gradually expelled, and the sands and muds consolidate into coherent rocks, with sufficient connected pore space to transmit fluids.

As deposition continues and the rocks sink to greater and hotter depths, the remaining water, which is continually being expelled, takes on the characteristics of a hydrothermal fluid and picks up metals from rocks through which it is moving. This process is taking place in geologic time; a million years or more may have been consumed by the processes described. Precipitation of the metals occurs when the hydrothermal fluids reach a zone of favorable physical or chemical conditions: for instance, if the solutions become cooler or encounter reactive rocks such as limestone.

To reiterate, once the metals are deposited, determining that they were indeed developed as part of a sedimentary process as opposed to an igneous process is difficult, and many low-temperature deposits have been the subject of intense controversy for years. The Kennecott

Conglomerates make up this beach face along the Alaska Peninsula. (John and Margaret Ibbotson)

mines in the Wrangell Mountains are an example of a low-temperature deposit. These copper sulfide deposits were certainly introduced into massive limestone at a relatively low temperature. It is impossible to say whether the source of the copper is the sedimentary rocks of the area, the copper-rich Nikolai basalt which underlies the limestone host of the deposit, or several nearby granitic bodies.

Clearly not all deposits are formed by hydrothermal fluids. Several well-documented types form directly from igneous magma. Chrome deposits — there are several Alaska examples, notably at Red Mountain near Seldovia — almost invariably form as the result of the cooling of certain types of basaltic magma at great depth. In the early stages of solidification, the heavy mineral chromite forms as the magma crystallizes and sinks to create irregular pods and layers of chromite crystals near the bottom of the magma chamber.

Related processes form nickel-copper-cobalt deposits that often contain significant platinum-group elements; the Brady Glacier deposit in Glacier Bay

Contorted by intense heat, this radiolarian chert lines the shore of China Poot Bay near Homer. The chert was built up, layer by layer, by tropical microorganisms called radiolarians which sank to the bottom of a tropical sea. Radiolarians only survive in warm climates, and thus geologists believe rocks of the Kachemak Bay area migrated north from warmer climates by continental drift and plate tectonic movement. (Jan O'Meara)

National Park and Preserve is a typical example. In this type of deposit, the metals in the magma segregate into an immiscible liquid consisting mainly of iron, copper, nickel, cobalt, and sulfur as the rock-forming minerals crystallize at high temperatures. This metal-sulfur liquid either fills in the interstices of the mush of rock minerals formed earlier, settles as a discrete phase, or is injected into adjacent rocks.

Mineral deposits subjected to heat and pressure of metamorphism are sometimes only changed in mineralogy and texture without a major movement of elements. However, most metals are relatively mobile under elevated temperature and pressure and often move to areas of different temperature, pressure, or chemical conditions to form concentrations of ore minerals.

It is often difficult to recognize the origins of deposits that are concentrated by metamorphism, at least partly because the origin of the rocks in the vicinity may be obscured by the metamorphism. Several deposits affected by metamorphism occur along the Canadian border in southeastern Alaska. These include the Alaska-Juneau and Treadwell mines near Juneau, the Sumdum copper deposit on Endicott Arm, and lead-zinc deposits in Groundhog Basin near Wrangell. If metamorphism reaches a sufficiently high temperature and pressure, the rocks will melt to produce a granitic magma. Several of these deposits may be part of an even larger process which includes metamorphism, igneous activity, and subsequent hydrothermal mineralization.

Conversely, the temperature, and to a lesser degree the pressure, effects of the placement of an igneous magma often produce a pronounced metamorphic halo around the body. This effect, with hydrothermal mineralization from the cooling magma, often results in a specific type of mineral deposit known as a contact-metamorphic deposit, which often consists of one or more of the elements copper, zinc, tin, and tungsten. The effect is often particularly striking when granitic igneous rocks invade a limestone to produce a diverse and colorful group of minerals. The tin-tungsten-fluorite deposit at Lost River on the Seward Peninsula is a classic contact-metamorphic deposit that formed when a granite invaded a thick limestone about 75 million years ago.

Some very large mineral deposits result from direct precipitation of minerals in sea water, usually in shallow marine basins. An obvious example is salt. Salt is produced commercially today in many areas by allowing sea water to flow into shallow basins or evaporating pans. These are then sealed off to allow the water to evaporate and eventually leave a layer of salt. A similar process has operated geologically to produce salt beds hundreds of feet thick in many areas of the United States. These beds resulted from slightly more complicated processes than in commercial salt pans; the salt was formed in shallow bays that once covered large areas of what is now the North American

A dike of rhyolite (under the grass) has intruded limestone in the York Mountains of the Seward Peninsula. Limestone's high alkaline content and tendency to dissolve rather than break down into soil hinder the growth of vegetation over the exposed limestone shown here. (Donald Grybeck)

—21

A gold placer forms when erosion of a gold vein and downslope movement of gold eventually creates a concentration or paystreak of gold beneath the stream channel.

Former Stream Pattern

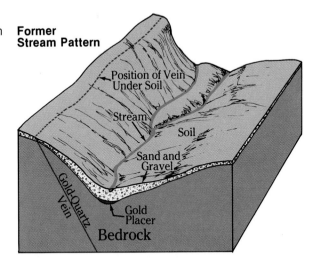

Position of Vein Under Soil

Stream

Soil

Sand and Gravel

Gold-Quartz Vein

Gold Placer

Bedrock

Subsequent development of the topography shows that the stream drainage pattern has shifted significantly, and the gold placers are now forming in entirely different positions. Note, however, that remnants of paystreaks formed under the former position of the streams are preserved on the hillsides as bench deposits.

Present Stream System

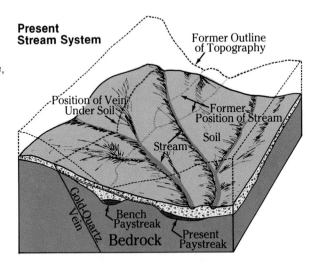

Former Outline of Topography

Position of Vein Under Soil

Former Position of Stream

Soil

Stream

Gold-Quartz Vein

Bench Paystreak

Present Paystreak

Bedrock

continent. The basins had relatively restricted inlets, and the inflow of sea water was matched by the loss of water from evaporation. Thus, the basins became progressively saltier. Productive gypsum deposits near Iyoukeen Cove on Chichagof Island in southeastern Alaska were formed in this way.

Another example of marine precipitation is the marine phosphate deposits which formed when phosphorous-rich, cold sea water circulated up onto marine shelves adjacent to the continent or onto shallow marine basins on the continent and precipitated phosphates in thick beds. Some of the largest of these deposits are in the Phosphoria Formation of Idaho, but marine phosphate deposits occur for more than 200 miles along the northern flank of the Brooks Range.

Several types of deposits form as a result of weathering and erosion; by far the best-known deposits of this type in Alaska are placers. Formation of a placer first requires that the mineral involved be heavy and resistant to weathering. Among the minerals that form placers are those of the platinum-group elements, tin, and titanium, but gold placers are by far the best known in Alaska.

The principles of placer formation are relatively straightforward. Most form in streams, although beach placers are not uncommon. Beach placers were the source of the gold during the early stages of the gold rush at Nome. Gold-quartz veins, such as those at Fairbanks, are usually the source for placer deposits of gold. As the land weathers and is carried away by stream action and creep of soil downhill, the gold lags behind because of its high specific gravity and eventually concentrates along stream beds. Even in streams with relatively thick gravels, gold generally forms concentrations or paystreaks just above bedrock; the gold works down through the gravels by agitation and stream action just as it does in the gold pan.

In detail, however, the paystreaks are often not continuous or predictable. Gold is often caught in potholes, ledges, or cracks on the surface of the bedrock. Most importantly, the paystreaks do not necessarily follow present stream courses. In many cases, they are some distance away or are even perched on the sides of hills as in the famous White Channel at Dawson in the Klondike. These paystreaks were formed when the topography was hundreds, perhaps thousands, of feet higher, by streams that have now long since shifted elsewhere in the valley. Placers require considerable time to develop and once formed, they can be destroyed by other geologic processes. Thus, gold placers are rare and relatively small in southeastern Alaska, even near gold lodes, because recent glaciation has largely scoured out the valleys in which placers might have formed. Placers that have not been moved much by the action of water, but rather formed almost in place near their hard rock lode sources by mechanical erosion and concentration processes, are known as residual placers.

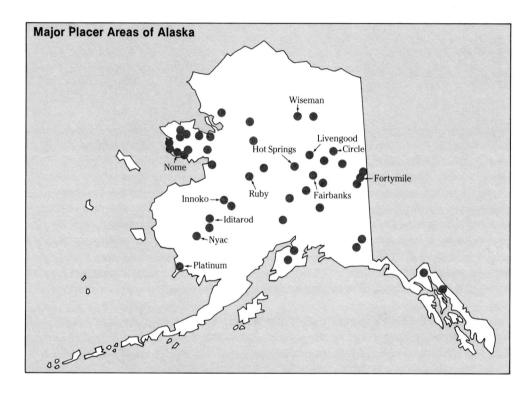

Major Placer Areas of Alaska

Examples in Alaska include the rich paystreaks of the Iditarod district.

To reiterate, ore deposits form in various and complex ways. Geologists are now able to explain the origin of many deposits with some confidence, but many remain an enigma. Ore deposits are only a very small part of the exceedingly complicated and lengthy processes that have affected the earth. Except in the broadest terms, predictions about the location of undiscovered ore deposits are essentially impossible based on theories of deposition alone. The theories must be accompanied by hard work, imagination, physical exploration, money, and luck.

—23

A substantial amount of gold ore has been blocked out at the Mikado Mine in the Chandalar area of the Brooks Range. A near vertical fault trends up the center of the picture; it can best be seen passing between the two saddles in the mountains in the distance. (Donald Grybeck)

Common Ores of Metals and Minerals

Metal or mineral	Chemical symbol	Common ore mineral
Aluminum	Al	Bauxite (hydrated aluminum oxide)
Antimony	Sb	Stibnite (antimony sulfide)
Asbestos		Chrysotile (hydrous magnesium silicate)
Barite		Barite (barium sulfate)
Chromium	Cr	Chromite (ferrous chromic oxide)
Cobalt	Co	Cobaltite (cobalt sulfarsenide, 35.5% Co)
		Smaltite (cobalt, nickel, iron triarsenide, 21% Co)
Columbium	Cb	Now called Niobium
Copper	Cu	Native copper
		Chalcopyrite (copper iron sulfide, 34.5% Cu)
		Chalcocite (copper sulfide, 79.8% Cu)
Fluorine	F	Fluorite (calcium fluoride)
Gold	Au	Native gold
Gypsum		Gypsum (hydrous calcium sulfate)
Iron	Fe	Hematite (iron oxide, 70% Fe)
		Magnetite (iron oxide, 72.4% Fe)
		Siderite (iron carbonate, 48% Fe)
Lead	Pb	Galena (lead sulfide, 86.6% Pb)
Magnesium	Mg	Dolomite (calcium magnesium carbonate)
		Magnesite (magnesium carbonate)
Manganese	Mn	Pyrolusite (manganese dioxide, 63.2% Mn)

Metal or mineral	Chemical symbol	Common ore mineral
Mercury	Hg	Cinnabar (mercury sulfide, 86.2% Hg)
Mica		Muscovite (potassium aluminum silicate)
		Biotite (potassium, magnesium, iron aluminum silicate)
Molybdenum	Mo	Molybdenite (molybdenum disulfide, 60% Mo)
Nickel	Ni	Pentlandite (nickel iron sulfide, 22% Ni)
		Niccolite (nickel arsenide, 43.9% Ni)
Niobium	Nb	Columbite (iron manganese niobate, 77% Nb_2O_5)
		Pyrochlore (complex oxide of varied composition)
Palladium	Pd	Native platinum-group metals
Potash	K_2O	Sylvanite (potassium chloride, 63.2% K_2O equivalent)
Salt	NaCl	Halite (sodium chloride)
Silver	Ag	Native silver
		Argentite (silver sulfide, 87.1% Ag)
Tin	Sn	Cassiterite (tin oxide, 78.6% Sn)
Titanium	Ti	Ilmenite (iron titanium oxide, 31.6% Ti)
Tungsten	W	Scheelite (calcium tungstate, 80.5% WO_3)
		Wolframite (iron manganese tungstate, 76.5% WO_3)
Uranium	U	Uraninite (uranium oxide, 50%-85% U_3O_8)
		Pitchblende (uranium oxide, 50%-58% U_3O_8)
Zinc	Zn	Sphalerite (zinc sulfide, 67% Zn)

Adapted from "Ores of Metals and Industrial Minerals," courtesy of Northern Miner Press, Limited

Significant Alaska Minerals

Gold

Many of the events that have filled Alaska history during the past century have been interwoven with the lives and dreams of seekers of the precious yellow metal, gold.

Among the 50 states, Alaska ranks in the top four in total gold production. So far, about 30.5 million troy ounces of gold have been produced from lode and placer deposits in the state.

Indians, Eskimos, and Aleuts knew of gold early in Alaska's history and used it and other metals — especially copper —for ornamental beadwork and jewelry as well as for some functional purposes such as utensils and weapons. The first Westerners to learn of gold in Alaska were members of a party of Russian-Americans who reported gold on the Russian River

---

Editor's note: *This material is excerpted from "Historic gold production in Alaska-A 'minisummary' " by M.S. Robinson and T.K. Bundtzen, published in* Mines & Geology Bulletin, *Division of Geological & Geophysical Surveys, September, 1979.*

drainage on the Kenai Peninsula in 1834; no production was reported from these initial discoveries.

Gold was mined at Windham Bay on the Southeast mainland and at Sitka in the late 1860s and early 1870s, but the first major gold mining activities in Alaska began in southeastern Alaska near Juneau during the early 1880s. Initial discoveries in the Juneau area were gold placers in the Silver Bow Basin. Later, large, low-grade deposits of gold quartz were discovered on Douglas Island and at other areas on the east side of Gastineau Channel.

By 1887 the Treadwell mining complex on Douglas Island was one of the largest underground gold mines in the world. When production ceased in 1922, more than three million ounces of gold had been won from 28.8 million tons of ore. Until a disastrous 1917 cave-in, almost 2,000 miners worked in the four mines within the several-mile-long lode line. The cave-in flooded the Treadwell, 700 Foot, and Mexican mines; the Ready Bullion continued to operate until 1922.

The Alaska-Juneau Mine was consolidated in 1897 and remained in almost continuous operation until 1942 when the federal government closed all mines not necessary to the war effort. Alaska-Juneau was later reopened on a reduced basis by special permit because of its importance to the economy of Juneau. The mine ceased operation permanently in 1944. At the end of World War II, increased operating costs and other pitfalls put an end to any hopes of reopening what was once one of the lowest-grade gold mines ever successfully operated with a profit. During full-scale operations, more than 1,000 workers were employed by the Alaska-Juneau Mine.

Aleutian Islands Region

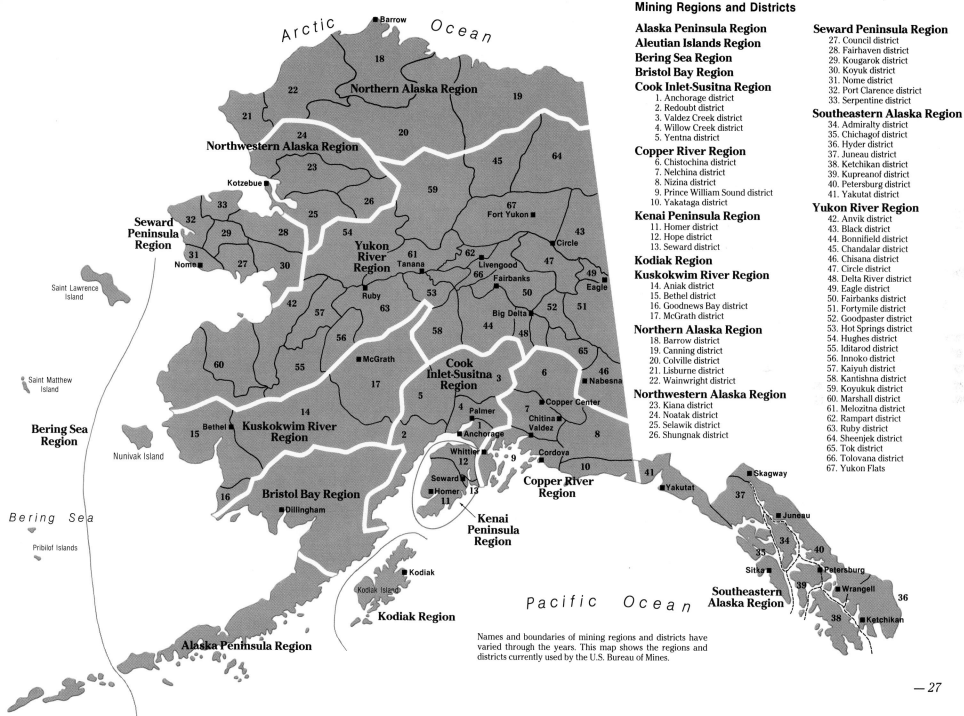

Mining Regions and Districts

Alaska Peninsula Region

Aleutian Islands Region

Bering Sea Region

Bristol Bay Region

Cook Inlet-Susitna Region
1. Anchorage district
2. Redoubt district
3. Valdez Creek district
4. Willow Creek district
5. Yentna district

Copper River Region
6. Chistochina district
7. Nelchina district
8. Nizina district
9. Prince William Sound district
10. Yakataga district

Kenai Peninsula Region
11. Homer district
12. Hope district
13. Seward district

Kodiak Region

Kuskokwim River Region
14. Aniak district
15. Bethel district
16. Goodnews Bay district
17. McGrath district

Northern Alaska Region
18. Barrow district
19. Canning district
20. Colville district
21. Lisburne district
22. Wainwright district

Northwestern Alaska Region
23. Kiana district
24. Noatak district
25. Selawik district
26. Shungnak district

Seward Peninsula Region
27. Council district
28. Fairhaven district
29. Kougarok district
30. Koyuk district
31. Nome district
32. Port Clarence district
33. Serpentine district

Southeastern Alaska Region
34. Admiralty district
35. Chichagof district
36. Hyder district
37. Juneau district
38. Ketchikan district
39. Kupreanof district
40. Petersburg district
41. Yakutat district

Yukon River Region
42. Anvik district
43. Black district
44. Bonnifield district
45. Chandalar district
46. Chisana district
47. Circle district
48. Delta River district
49. Eagle district
50. Fairbanks district
51. Fortymile district
52. Goodpaster district
53. Hot Springs district
54. Hughes district
55. Iditarod district
56. Innoko district
57. Kaiyuh district
58. Kantishna district
59. Koyukuk district
60. Marshall district
61. Melozitna district
62. Rampart district
63. Ruby district
64. Sheenjek district
65. Tok district
66. Tolovana district
67. Yukon Flats

Names and boundaries of mining regions and districts have varied through the years. This map shows the regions and districts currently used by the U.S. Bureau of Mines.

The Denali Mining Company runs a large placer gold operation at the confluence of Valdez Creek and Susitna River, on the south side of the Alaska Range. The photo at left shows Denali's sluicing operation at the old drift mine on Tammany Channel, a buried glacial channel which runs underground for about one mile, at depths of up to 200 feet. At right is one of the company's sluices on the south side of Valdez Creek. Earth from the excavation is dumped into the box, then washed down the riffles of the sluice to separate the gold. The gold is removed from the riffles during the cleanup, yielding the final reward — a pan full of nuggets, shown below. (All photos by James Gill)

On July 24, 1914, Jay Livengood and N.R. "Teddy" Hudson discovered gold in an unnamed tributary of the Tolovana River, 50 miles northwest of Fairbanks. The creek was later named after Livengood, as was the village that grew there during the winter of 1914-1915. By 1916 the Livengood camp had 250 residents, including 48 women. The population began declining in 1920, and the post office which opened in 1915 was closed in 1957. This photo, probably taken in the early 1930s, shows Teddy Hudson with a pan of gold, at the time worth $2,200. Little is known about Hudson, who died in Fairbanks in 1952, at the age of 86. (R.L. Frost, U.S. Weather Bureau)

Other mineralized areas were discovered along the coast in southeastern Alaska near Ketchikan and Hyder. Additional finds in Prince William Sound; on Chichagof Island and on Prince of Wales Island, both in southeastern Alaska; on the Kenai Peninsula; and in the Aleutians resulted in significant gold production.

Hard-rock gold mining has taken place at many localities throughout the state. Mines that have produced a significant amount of lode gold include the Independence Mine in the Willow Creek district, the Nabesna Mine in the northern Wrangell Mountains, the Apollo Mine on Unga Island, the Cliff Mine near Valdez, the Nixon Fork Mine near Medfra, the Cleary Hill Mine north of Fairbanks, and the Big Hurrah Mine near Solomon on the Seward Peninsula. Small, hard-rock mines scattered throughout the Fairbanks, Yentna, Kantishna, Chandalar, Kenai Peninsula, Ketchikan-Hyder, and Glacier Bay districts also produced significant amounts of gold.

Interest in gold placers of the Yukon basin in both Alaska and Canada's Yukon Territory began as early as 1870, when rugged explorers and pioneers ventured into the interior and brought back tales of gold. The first significant strike in interior Alaska occurred in the Fortymile camp in 1886. Other discoveries made in the region include Circle (1893) and Seventymile (1895). But the gold find that captured the imagination of people from all over the world was the Klondike strike of 1896 in Yukon Territory. After the Klondike rush, more than 34 back-to-back stampedes occurred in Alaska, including such notable strikes as Koyukuk (1893), Nome (1898), Council (1898), Fairbanks (1902), Innoko (1906), and Iditarod (1908), culminating with the Livengood or Tolovana discoveries of 1914.

About two-thirds of Alaska gold production has come from placer deposits, most of which were located in the state's interior. Here the general absence of extensive late Pleistocene glaciation allowed development of extensive heavy mineral placers. Such deposits also occurred in recently glaciated terranes such as Yentna-Cache Creek, Chistochina-Chisna, Koyukuk-Nolan, and districts of the Kenai Peninsula.

The patterns of development in each of the gold mining districts were similar. The initial discovery of high-grade pay dirt in both lode and placer form resulted in early exploitation by individuals and small companies. Exhaustion of the initial rich deposits led to consolidation of mining ground by larger companies and the subsequent exploitation of the lower-grade deposits.

After World War II, the price of gold remained fixed at the 1934 standard —

This 1939 photo shows the great Alaska-Juneau Mill on a mountainside above Gastineau Channel just south of Juneau. The mine operated almost continuously for nearly 50 years and was at one time one of the lowest-grade gold mines ever operated with a profit. (M. Peter Vogel)

These two photos, probably taken in 1912 or 1913, show workers at the Cameron-Johnson Gold Mining Company's site, 14 miles northwest of Valdez. In the photo at left, a barge carrying supplies and materials for constructing the mine's stamp mill and aerial tram is being unloaded near the terminus of Shoup Glacier. Cameron-Johnson, later known as the Valdez Gold Company, worked 17 claims on the ridge between Shoup and Columbia glaciers. A five-stamp mill and lower camp were built in 1913, at an elevation of 2,400 feet — 900 feet above the surface of Shoup. During the summer a pack train was used to transport supplies from Shoup Bay to the lower camp. In 1914, a 3,850-foot aerial tram was built between the lower camp and a point 3,700 feet up Mount Cameron; a smaller camp consisting of a bunkhouse and cookhouse was then built near the terminus of the tram. The photo at right looks down the Cameron-Johnson trail to Shoup Bay. The signal tower is located at the crossing of the trail from the adjacent Gold King Mine. Milling began at the Cameron-Johnson Mine on July 20, 1913, and the mine employed an average of 30 workers during the summer months.
(Both photos from Mary Whalen Collection, University of Alaska, Fairbanks)

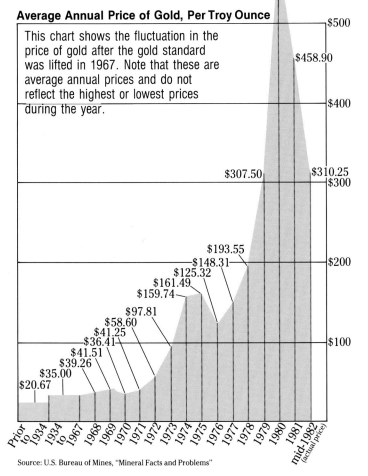

Average Annual Price of Gold, Per Troy Ounce

This chart shows the fluctuation in the price of gold after the gold standard was lifted in 1967. Note that these are average annual prices and do not reflect the highest or lowest prices during the year.

$569.73
$500
$458.90
$400
$307.50 $310.25
$300
$193.55
$148.31
$125.32
$161.49
$159.74
$200
$97.81
$58.60
$41.25
$36.41
$41.51
$39.26
$100
$35.00
$20.67

Prior to 1934 · 1934 to 1967 · 1968 · 1969 · 1970 · 1971 · 1972 · 1973 · 1974 · 1975 · 1976 · 1977 · 1978 · 1979 · 1980 · 1981 · mid-1982 (actual price)

Source: U.S. Bureau of Mines, "Mineral Facts and Problems"

1981 Placer Gold Production in Alaska, By Region*		
Region	**Number of Major Operators** **	**Production, in Troy Ounces**
Northern	18	10,500
Western	40	21,000
Eastern Interior	104	63,900
Southcentral	26	22,500
Southwestern	16	16,500
Southeastern and Alaska Peninsula	3	unknown
TOTAL	**191**	**134,400**

*Regions listed here are those used by the Alaska Division of Geological and Geophysical Surveys.
**Total placer mines statewide, major and minor, exceeded 400. (Prepared by Alaska Division of Geological and Geophysical Surveys for the Office of Mineral Development under RSA Contract 10-46-9-142.)

$35 per ounce — which caused a decline in the industry. Inflation and the buildup of a large government infrastructure — especially military bases which paid high wages to workers and thus drew the cream of the labor force away from the mines — in Alaska competed with gold mining activities. By the early 1960s, most of the great bucketline gold dredges had been shut down.

The recent rise in the price of gold has revitalized Alaska's gold mining industry. In the early 1980s, several hundred individual mechanized placer mines were operating, and six floating dredges had been reactivated. Despite the rapid decline of gold prices after the $800-per-ounce peak in spring, 1980, the approximately $310-per-ounce price of summer, 1982, could sustain the present high levels of activity. However, this optimism must be balanced with several factors, including the high cost of petroleum fuels and equipment, inflation, and recognition that many of the best placers and obvious lode deposits have already been worked.

A man operates a hydraulic giant at the Speaker Mine, southwest of Circle. The giant is used to push gravel and overburden up and through a sluice box, which separates out the gold. (Fred Wilkerson)

Miners wash gravel down a sluice box at a placer claim off the Steese Highway north of Fairbanks. Walter Roman, who runs this claim, washes down banks of ice and gravel with high pressure hoses called giants. He then scrapes the gravel over to his sluice box with an old bulldozer. Walter, his son, and a small crew use equipment to lift the gravel to the top of the sluice. As the water runs down the sluice, the gravel and lighter material washes off the end, and the gold settles to the bottom of the box. (Kris Valencia, staff)

—35

George Pearce operates a high-pressure hose, called a giant, at Gilmore Mining Company's placer mine on Gilmore Creek near Fairbanks in this 1939 photo. (M. Peter Vogel)

Copper

From 1911 until 1930, the territory of Alaska ranked with the top 10 copper-producing states. During peak production, from 1916 to 1920, copper had the highest dollar value of any Alaska mineral product.

Mining copper in Alaska for regular commercial shipments started in 1900 in southeastern Alaska on Prince of Wales Island. During the early years from 1900 to 1906, the copper-iron-zinc deposits of Niblack, Khayyam-Mammoth, and Copper City mines produced most of the ore. After 1906, deposits on the Kasaan Peninsula, particularly the Mount Andrews, Mamie, and Stevenstown mines, overshadowed the earlier producers. Two copper smelters were constructed in 1905: a 400-ton-per-day plant at Hadley on the Kasaan Peninsula and a 250-ton-per-day installation at Coppermount on Hetta Inlet. The smelters were operated intermittently for three years. By 1908, however, both smelters were closed because of declining ore quality, a falling copper market, and the difficulties in obtaining good coking coals. The overall grade of the copper deposits mined in Southeast was 3.1% copper, 0.038 ounces per ton of gold, and 0.316 ounces per ton of silver.

The mill at Kennecott processed a staggering amount of ore from the great copper mines of the Wrangell Mountains. The mines were on the hillside above town. Ore was shipped down to the mill by a tram. (John and Margaret Ibbotson)

Between 1900 and 1930, 214 million pounds of copper were produced in the Prince William Sound area. Of that, more than 200 million pounds came from just two mines — the Beatson-Bonanza on Latouche Island, and the Ellamar, on Virgin Bay, 20 miles southwest of Valdez. The photo on the left shows miners in one of Ellamar's stopes. The orebody was discovered in 1897 by M.O. Gladhaugh and C. Peterson, and the first shaft was begun in 1901. The Ellamar Mining Company was formed in 1902, and by April, 1905, when the photo on the right was taken, the mine was in full production. The buildings included a power plant, bunkhouse, and ore bunkers. There was also a loading tram to carry the ore from the bunkers to ships at the dock. The Ellamar Mine closed in 1919, not because the deposit was exhausted, but because the ore mined in later years was of such low grade that its extraction became unprofitable. The buildings were later converted to a salmon cannery.
(Both photos from Mary Whalen Collection, University of Alaska, Fairbanks)

Two mines operated on the west side of Latouche Island in the early part of this century. The Beatson-Bonanza Mine (later known simply as the Beatson after the deposit's discoverer, A.K. Beatson) produced copper ore from 1904 to 1930. While one company worked the Beatson Mine, another company staked claims about one-quarter mile to the north and called their mine Blackbird. The companies were mining the same orebody, and after a while the Beatson owners bought out the Blackbird company and connected the two mines through underground tunnels.

In its heydey, the town of Latouche boasted a population of about 400 mine workers. The long building in the center of this photograph housed the mine elevator of the Blackbird Mine and the mill. Crushed ore was taken by conveyor (the long, low building running from the mine building to the left) to the 1,500-ton-per-day concentrator built by Kennecott Copper Company in 1914. The power generator for the mine and town were also located in this building. After being concentrated, the copper continued by conveyor to the ship loading dock, far left. Housing for workers can be seen scattered throughout the complex and to the far right. Houses in the right foreground were on a spit which was destroyed in the March, 1964, earthquake. (Courtesy of Pete Robinson)

Later, copper production shifted to Latouche Island in Prince William Sound. Here the Beatson Mine became the largest producer in terms of tons per day when 435,826 tons of ore were extracted from the mine in 1918. Average grade for this great mass of ore was 2.4% copper, and much of the operation's success depended on the use of flotation (see *The Mining Process*, page 120) in concentrating the ore.

Possibly one of the first shipments of copper to come from Alaska left Latouche Island in 1899. At the turn of the century, there was a flurry of claim-staking on the island, and at one time mining claims covered all of Latouche. The Beatson Mine was staked in 1897, and began shipping ore on a regular basis in 1904. Production increased dramatically in 1914 when Kennecott Copper constructed a 700-ton-per-day concentrator which was later enlarged to handle 1,500 tons per day. The Beatson operated as a tight, isolated, island community employing nearly 400 men until production ceased in 1930.

Overriding all other copper mines in the territory was the great Kennecott complex in the Wrangell Mountains. Most famous of the Alaska copper mines, Kennecott was one of the richest copper mines in the world. By today's standards, Kennecott probably would not be considered a world-class mine. However, when the mine was worked out and abandoned in November, 1938, the total tonnage mined was 4,626,000 tons containing an average grade of about 13% copper. Total production was 591,535 tons of copper and about 9 million ounces of silver. The total value of this production was $200 million with a net profit of about $100 million, based on an average of each year's production applied to the average copper and silver prices for those years. Kennecott used the profits from its Alaska mines, in part, to gain control of large, low-grade copper mines in New Mexico, Nevada, and Arizona. These acquisitions enabled Kennecott to become one of the largest copper mining companies in the world; a major multi-metal producer by 1980; and, in turn, to be purchased by Standard Oil Company of Ohio in 1981.

The history of the Kennecott development in the Wrangells dates back to April, 1885, when Lt. Henry T. Allen made his way up to Dan Creek where he met Chief Nikolai. The chief had samples of ore that assayed at 60% copper, and he and his people used native copper nuggets for utensils and bullets.

Chitina Mining and Exploration Company opened up the Nikolai deposit in 1899; in 1900 came the Bonanza claim. By 1909 Kennecott Mines Company (Kennecott Copper Company) had gained control of the area, and the real push for production began. Moving the ore from the great Kennecott mines required a railroad, and by 1911 the Copper River & Northwestern Railway was busy hauling the bounty from the Kennecott operations to Cordova for shipment to the Lower 48.

The Kennecott mines produced a staggering amount of high-grade ore; at one time in 1916 the aerial tramway which carried material from the hillside mines to the mill transported 175 tons per day of crude ore averaging 70% copper.

Operators at Kennecott had to perfect several leaching and flotation processes to extract the maximum amount of copper from the ore. After 1916, by gravity concentration, ammonia leaching, and froth flotation (see *The Mining Process*, page 120) workers at Kennecott could recover 96% of the copper.

Although the operation closed in 1938, the Kennecott Copper Company never stopped its efforts in Alaska. In the 1960s, Kennecott explored and partially developed a copper mine near Bornite in northwestern Alaska. In the 1970s, they explored a deposit at Arctic, also in the Brooks Range (see *Prospecting Alaska*, page 88). With the Picnic Creek deposit in the Brooks Range, which Anaconda Copper Company explored, these prospects have a gross discovered metal value of not less than $7 billion on the 1981 market.

Silver

More than 85% of the 20.1 million ounces of silver recovered from Alaska deposits has been derived as a by-product of copper mining from the Kennecott mines in the Wrangell Mountains, and as secondary recovery from placer and lode gold bullion statewide. However, the Omilak area on the Seward Peninsula north of Golovin, the Kantishna, Fairbanks, Ruby, and Kaiyuh districts of the Interior, and the Riverside Mine in southeastern Alaska have been the source of primary silver ores.

Virtually all of these silver ores occur as complex minerals of lead, zinc, antimony, and silver in fractures cutting a variety of metamorphic, sedimentary, and igneous rocks. One important exception is the Greens Creek silver base metal lodes on Admiralty Island. Normally this stratiform deposit would be considered a copper-lead-zinc mine, but the silver content exceeds all others in value.

The first known exploration of hard-rock ores north of Southeast took place at the Omilak Mine on the Seward Peninsula in the late 1880s.

The largest producer of primary silver ores in Alaska has been in the Kantishna District on the north flank of the Alaska Range. Following high silver price levels after World War I, approximately 1,450 tons of ore yielded 260,000 ounces of silver and by-products of gold, lead, and zinc. Sporadic production and development of Kantishna's Quigley Ridge lodes continues to the present. Similar lodes in other parts of Alaska were developed just after World War I.

Exploration of the relatively small ore-bodies statewide that contain silver has required expensive underground mining methods; hence, production has been limited to times of high silver demand.

High-grade lead-silver ores were stockpiled and awaiting shipment at the Red Top Mine near the base of Quigley Ridge in 1922. From 1919 to 1924 more than 1,000 tons of ore were taken from the eight small deposits on Quigley and Alpha ridges in the Kantishna district north of Denali National Park and Preserve.
(John Brooks Collection, University of Alaska Archives; reprinted from *The ALASKA JOURNAL®*)

The Apollo Mining Company produced nearly $3 million worth of gold, silver, and other metals from its two mines on Unga Island, south of the Alaska Peninsula. The photo at left, taken in 1980, shows the remains of the 60-stamp mill used to crush the ore (the ruins have since burned). Both mines were operated by the same company and shared the mill, but ore processing was segregated: the 20 stamps on the left processed ore from the Sitka Mine; the 40 stamps on the right were used for ore from the Apollo Mine. The mines were active from 1891 to 1904, and were reopened briefly in 1908 to process ore which had been previously mined. The rusted wheels and compressor pistons below were used to run the mine's machinery eight months of the year: water from a dam three miles upstream was piped to the wheels, which returned compressed air to the mine. A coal-fired boiler provided power during the winter months.
(Both photos by Charles B. Green)

Iron

Iron, an abundant element, makes up about 5% of the earth's crust. The two most important ore minerals are the iron oxides, magnetite and hematite. Probably the most distinctive and common iron mineral is the iron sulfide, pyrite. Pyrite is found in almost every geological environment, but rarely has any value except to produce sulfuric acid at favorable locations if available in quantity.

The United States is a major iron ore producer, chiefly from the iron ranges near Lake Superior. Alaska has almost innumerable occurrences of iron minerals, but none of sufficient grade, tonnage, and accessibility to have been mined in the past. It is unlikely that Alaska will generate sufficient local demand for steel to sustain a steel mill in the foreseeable future. Thus, production from Alaska's iron deposits is probably dependent on the markets of the Pacific rim countries. Consequently, transportation costs will figure predominately in marketing iron ore from known Alaska deposits or others still to be discovered.

For at least 20 years, there has been interest in several iron deposits in southeastern Alaska. These deposits, at Klukwan and at Snettisham south of Juneau, consist of magnetite disseminated through a dark-colored igneous rock; the high titanium content of the magnetite poses technical problems during smelting. Japan is frequently mentioned as a possible market for these deposits, but no decision to develop them seems imminent.

Geologists examine a red gossan zone in the Brooks Range. Iron-stained, pyritic rocks are often associated with sulfide mineral deposits. (Mark McDermott)

Lead

The principal ore mineral of lead is galena, the lead sufide. Galena and other lead minerals are widely distributed in Alaska, but nearly all Alaska lead production has been as a by-product from deposits that have been mined primarily for other minerals. The major Alaska source of lead was the Alaska-Juneau Mine which produced more than 40 million pounds of lead. Although the lead content of the Alaska-Juneau ore was minor, the galena could be conveniently recovered from the immense tonnage of gold ore that was put through the mill.

Lead also occurs in numerous deposits in Alaska associated with silver and zinc materials, as in the Kantishna and Hyder districts. Galena often has a substantial silver content, and commonly the silver content of galena ore is more valuable than the lead content.

The Alaska-Juneau Mine, from which more than 40 million pounds of lead were taken, was the major Alaska source for this mineral. Galena, the lead ore, was a minor component of the material produced at the mine, but was easily recovered from the immense amount of gold ore processed at the mill, shown here. (Bruce Molnia)

Molybdenum

The only molybdenum mineral of economic interest is molybdenite, the greasy, gray molybdenum sulfide. Molybdenum is a critical component of many alloy steels; its importance is diminished only by the unusual situation that the United States is a net exporter of molybdenum and dominates world production.

Molybdenum occurs throughout Alaska, but until recently none of the deposits seemed destined to be mined. In 1974, U.S. Borax and Chemical Corporation found a porphyry molybdenum deposit 45 miles east of Ketchikan at Quartz Hill; the deposit has since been determined to contain about 1.5 billion tons of mineable ore, making it one of the world's largest molybdenum deposits.

By spring, 1982, U.S. Borax had decided to go into production at Quartz Hill; the first phase of construction will be to build a 10-mile access road from the mine site to tidewater. Construction of a processing plant is scheduled for 1984, with production beginning in 1987. The predicted production rate of the mine is 40 million pounds of molybdenum per year, or about 12% of world demand, throughout the 70- to 100-year life of the mine. When full production begins, the mine will require 800 employees. If families of the workers are added to the mine's population, the number of mine-site residents could approach 3,000, which would make it the ninth-largest city in the state.

The entrance to one of the tunnels blasted at Quartz Hill is topped by a clean air intake pipe.
(Rollo Pool, staff)

This aerial view shows the work camp and exploration base of U. S. Borax and Chemical Corporation's Quartz Hill molybdenum mine, 45 miles east of Ketchikan. With estimated reserves of 1.5 billion tons of mineable ore, Quartz Hill is one of the world's largest molybdenum deposits. (Rollo Pool, staff)

A-frame construction is standard for living quarters and work stations at the Quartz Hill Mine, where winter snowfall may reach a depth of 20 feet. (Rollo Pool, staff)

Uranium

The search for uranium in Alaska has correlated directly with high demand associated with peaceful and military nuclear energy applications. There was a flurry of prospecting during the early- to mid-1950s when the Atomic Energy Commission stockpiled radioactive materials for nuclear weapons. Later, during the energy crisis of the 1970s, investigations were again intensified.

Probably the best known and most common uranium mineral is the black uranium oxide, pitchblende, which is found in a variety of types of deposits. The only commercial uranium deposit found to date in Alaska was discovered by two amateur Ketchikan prospectors, Don Ross and Kelly Adams. They staked radioactive deposits in the early 1950s at Bokan Mountain, near Kendrick Bay on Prince of Wales Island.

The Bokan deposit occurs as a breccialike accumulation of radioactive minerals and rare earth elements in a sodium-enriched (or alkaline) granite. Being the first of its type to be recognized, uranium geologists look for Bokan-type radioactive occurrences worldwide. Although small by most standards, the Bokan deposits of Southeast are of high grade, and easily accessible because they are near the water. Approximately 120,000 tons of ore were mined by various operators intermittently from 1955 to 1971. Further exploitation of the reserves at Bokan Mountain will depend on improvement in the depressed uranium market.

In Alaska uranium has been found in the westcentral part of the state, on the Seward Peninsula, in the Yukon-Tanana uplands, and in the Alaska Range.

Below—Scott MacInnes explores for uranium in the Alaska Range by measuring radiation from uranium, potassium, and thorium with a spectrometer.
Right—Tom Dunn tests the water of upper Cook Inlet for uranium. (Both photos by Mark McDermott)

Zinc

Of the several zinc materials, only sphalerite, the zinc sulfide, is now commercially important. Sphalerite occurs widely in Alaska, but zinc was not produced in the territory until 1947. Little has been produced since then. Zinc ore has relatively low value per unit and is unfavorably affected by high transportation costs. In the last decade, large, zinc-bearing deposits have been found in northwestern Alaska and exploration continues there. The best known deposits are the copper-zinc, massive sulfide deposits of the copper belt along the southern flank of the central Brooks Range and the zinc-lead deposits of the De Long Mountains, notably the Lik and Red Dog deposits, in northwestern Alaska.

Shiny sphalerite, the ore mineral of the great Red Dog deposit in the De Long Mountains of northwestern Alaska, lies in the right foreground in this photo of Red Dog Creek. (Gil Mull)

Sphalerite, the zinc sulfide, is the only zinc mineral of commercial importance. Although sphalerite was known to occur in many areas of Alaska, not until 1947 was zinc produced commercially. Little zinc has been produced since then. (Gil Mull)

Jade

Jade — a hard, greenish-white to dark green material — was used for ornaments and as a cutting tool by Alaska Natives at the time of the earliest explorers. Much of the jade came from the Jade Mountains of Kobuk country in northwestern Alaska.

In the first half of the 20th century, successive miners tried to exploit the jade. Chief drawback to their making a profit, however, was the large size of the boulders, which prohibited transporting them from the remote mountains to commercial centers. Eskimos and others who gathered the smaller nuggets were able to sell them in Fairbanks, but they, too, found no great bonanza in the green gem.

In 1952, Archie Ferguson, long-time resident of the Kotzebue area, developed a portable wire saw which could slice the boulders in the field. This device did much to solve the transporting problem.

Gene Joiner, who owned several claims in the Jade Mountains, sought foreign markets for his jade. Sometimes successful, sometimes not, Joiner continued to push for markets for the green gem until 1976 when he sold his claims to NANA, the Native regional corporation for northwestern Alaska.

NANA expanded the Jade Mountains operation and built a modern shop in Kotzebue for cutting and polishing jade. By far the largest jade mining enterprise in Kobuk country, NANA's holdings include significant deposits on Cabin and Jade creeks and at two peaks in the Jade Mountains. Their modern equipment can handle boulders weighing 50,000 to 75,000 pounds.

Ivan Stewart, Anchorage businessman, operates Stewart's Jewel Jade Mine on Dahl Creek in the Kobuk area. He welcomes visitors to inspect his powerful saws that slice green slabs off the huge boulders.

In Girdwood, south of Anchorage, Ray Heinrichs, formerly of Kotzebue, runs Kobuk Valley Jade. Heinrichs exploited the German jade market and displays many fine pieces carved by German craftsmen.

Above—Ivan Stewart poses with a jade boulder from his claims at Dahl Creek in the Kobuk Valley. The boulder rests on a pallet awaiting shipment to Anchorage. **Left**—A powerful saw cuts a jade boulder at Ivan Stewart's Jewel Jade claims. (Both photos by John Nicholson)

Alaska's Strategic Minerals

By Thomas K. Bundtzen

Since the turn of the century, Alaska has added significant amounts of "strategic" and "critical" materials to United States domestic mineral production. Alaska's contribution includes tin, tungsten, platinum-group metals, antimony, mercury, and chromium.

Strategic minerals are those commodities essential to the national defense for the supply of which, during war, we are wholly or in part dependent upon sources outside the boundaries of the United States, and for which strict measures controlling conservation and distribution are necessary.

Critical minerals are those essential to the national defense, the procurement of which in war, while difficult, is less serious than that of strategic minerals (because they can either be domestically produced or obtained in more adequate quantities from reliable foreign sources) and for

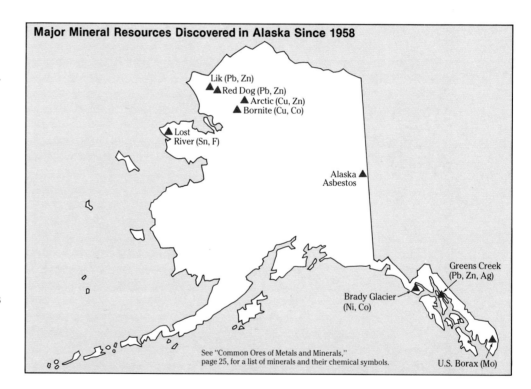

Major Mineral Resources Discovered in Alaska Since 1958

Lik (Pb, Zn)
Red Dog (Pb, Zn)
Arctic (Cu, Zn)
Bornite (Cu, Co)
Lost River (Sn, F)
Alaska Asbestos
Greens Creek (Pb, Zn, Ag)
Brady Glacier (Ni, Co)
U.S. Borax (Mo)

See "Common Ores of Metals and Minerals," page 25, for a list of minerals and their chemical symbols.

Editor's note: *Thomas K. Bundtzen is employed by the Alaska Division of Geological and Geophysical Surveys.*

Production, reserves, and resources of selected strategic minerals in Alaska

Mineral	1980[1]	Major foreign source	Production	Proven reserve	Indicated resource	Major Alaska deposits
Niobium (columbium) and tantalum	96	Brazil, Canada Thailand, Malaysia	—	—	—	Bokan Mt., Rapid River, Ruby, Manley
Manganese	98	Gabon, Brazil, South Africa, Australia	—	—	—	Yukon-Charley, Sinuk, Central Alaska Range
Cobalt	90	Zaire, Zambia	—	9 million pounds	63 million pounds	Brady Glacier, Yakobi Island, Mirror Harbor, Mertie Lode, Bornite
Chromium	90	South Africa, U.S.S.R., Turkey	36,849 tons	300,000 tons 28% Cr_2O_3	Millions of tons low grade ore	Seldovia, Eklutna, Bernard Mt., Union Bay
Platinum group metals	89	South Africa, U.S.S.R.	567,500 ounces	350,000 ounces	600,000 ounces	Goodnews Bay, Brady Glacier, Salt Chuck
Tin	81	Canada, South Africa, Malaysia, Bolivia	5 million pounds	125,973,000 pounds	5,046,000 pounds	Western Seward Peninsula, Manley, Rapid River, Sithylemenkat
Fluorine	81	Mexico, South Africa, United Kingdom, Italy	—	4.94 million tons	—	Lost River
Nickel	77	Canada, Norway, New Caledonia	—	1.123 billion pounds	.950 billion pounds	Brady Glacier, Yakobi Island, Mirror Harbor, Mertie Lode, Emericks
Mercury	62	Algeria, Spain, Italy	2,500,000 pounds	—	.25 million tons potential ore grade rock	Red Devil, Cinnabar Creek, DeCoursey Mt., White Mt.
Tungsten	59	Canada, Korea, Bolivia	286,000 pounds WO_3	—	19,345,560 pounds WO_3	Gilmore, Bear Mt., Hodzana, Chulitna, Lost River, Hyder, Chichagof, Golden Horn
Antimony	13	China, Bolivia, Mexico, Yugoslavia	10,493,360 pounds	10,500,000 pounds	110 million pounds	Fairbanks, Kantishna, Wiseman, Nome, Tok, Red Devil

[1]U.S. net import reliance from U.S. Bureau of Mines Commodity Summary, 1981.

A mineralized nunatak protrudes through Brady Glacier in Glacier Bay National Park and Preserve. Nickel, cobalt, copper, and platinum are found in this area. (U.S.B.M.)

which some conservation measures may be necessary for nondefense uses.

Past Production and Established Reserves of Strategic Minerals

Since World War II, private industry and limited federally subsidized exploration have delineated economic or near-economic reserves of 9 of the 15 strategic minerals evaluated here: cobalt, nickel, tin, platinum-group metals, mercury, fluorine, tungsten, antimony, and chromite. Commercially viable reserves of bauxite (aluminum), manganese, niobium, graphite, tantalum, and mica are not found anywhere in Alaska although resources of many of these exist in mineralized regions of the state.

Cobalt and Nickel

There has been no production of cobalt or nickel in Alaska. Resources of cobalt metal contained within four deposits in the southeastern panhandle — Brady Glacier, Yakobi Island, Mirror Harbor, and Funter Bay — amount to about 63 million pounds, or about three years of annual United States cobalt consumption. Of this, eight to nine million pounds contained within the Yakobi Island deposits are considered proven reserves, should those deposits be mined. No production schedules have been announced by their owners — Inspiration Development Company. Another important cobalt resource exists at the Bornite copper deposit in northern Alaska, but estimates of cobalt in these rich copper lodes are lacking partly because the cobalt resource was not recognized until recently. The same four southeastern Alaska deposits contain an estimated 1.12 billion pounds of proven reserve of nickel, equal to 2.1 years of current United States consumption.

The bulk of the cobalt and nickel resources and reserves are contained in the large Brady Glacier sulfide deposits in Glacier Bay National Park and Preserve. The Brady Glacier deposit contains from 24 to 54 million pounds of cobalt, but the deposit has not been sufficiently studied to determine success of cobalt recovery.

Platinum

Alaska has been the largest producer of platinum metals in the United States. More than 98% of the total production of 567,500 ounces has come from two regions — the Goodnews Bay district in southwestern Alaska and the Salt Chuck copper-platinum metal mine near Ketchikan. Platinum at Goodnews Bay was discovered in 1926, 25 years after gold discoveries in the region, by Walter Smith, an Eskimo prospector. Although Smith did not recognize the metal as platinum, he sent a sample of the suspicious steel-gray metal in concentrated form to the Territorial Department of Mines, who confirmed his find. By 1937, large scale dredging operations commenced and through 1981, 545,000 ounces of platinum metals have been won from the placer deposits in the Salmon River drainage.

The hard-rock platinum deposits at Salt

Chuck near Ketchikan were originally mined for copper, but in 1918 samples from various Southeast lodes were run for the platinum metals and nickel. No nickel was found at Salt Chuck, but platinum metals, mainly palladium, turned up in the assays. Eventually by 1941, 19,000 ounces of palladium and 2,500 ounces of platinum were produced as a by-product of the copper mining from the Kasaan Peninsula lode. Several thousand ounces of the platinum metals have been recovered as a by-product of extensive placer gold mining activities in various Alaska mineral districts since 1902, most notably from the Cache Creek, Chistochina, and eastern Seward Peninsula areas.

The largest resources of platinum metals remaining in Alaska, about one million ounces, are found at Goodnews Bay and in the Brady Glacier nickel-copper deposits. The former are being mined today and are contained in complex placers. Successful recovery of the bulk of the remaining reserves will depend on modifications to the eight-cubic-foot bucket line dredge and better recovery methods of clay-rich paystreaks from which only 40% of the platinum metals were originally recovered.

Metallurgical research conducted by the U.S. Geological Survey in cooperation with Newmont Mining Corporation has discovered a resource of approximately 580,000 ounces of platinum metals in the Brady Glacier deposits. However, specific metallurgical characteristics of this important nickel reserve have not been

Left—Alaska is the largest producer of platinum metals in the country. These nuggets of platinum and gold come from the Goodnews Bay Mining Company's operation in southwestern Alaska. (Jerry L. Hout)
Below—A dredge works the placers of the Salmon River. By 1981, 545,000 ounces of platinum metals had been won from placer deposits near Goodnews Bay. (Jerry L. Hout, reprinted from ALASKA GEOGRAPHIC®)

delineated; hence platinum recovery may or may not take place should nickel mining commence on the property. The U.S. Bureau of Mines concluded that the Salt Chuck deposit contains the best metallurgical characteristics for platinum metal recovery.

Despite significant past production, platinum metals have been Alaska sleepers. Most important deposits have been discovered by accident, and new occurrences continue to turn up today. Until the mid-1970s, accurate platinum assays of ores were expensive and difficult to obtain in this country. Prime areas of future prospecting for these important metals will be mineral belts in southwestern Alaska, and modern exploration of igneous complexes of southeastern Alaska.

Chromium

Chrome mineralization is found in a variety of deposits in at least six major mineral belts in Alaska, but has only been mined on the Kenai Peninsula where production was largely subsidized by the federal government. During critical shortages of World War I, approximately

Upper left—Jeff Foley examines an outcrop bearing layers of chromite, the ore of chromium, in the Kanuti River area of central Alaska. (Mark McDermott)
Left—This chromite ore (gray) comes from Red Mountain near Seldovia on the southern Kenai Peninsula. Deposits in the Red Mountain body may be some of the largest low-grade chrome reserves in the nation. (U.S.B.M.)

2,000 tons of metallurgical-grade chrome was mined from the Claim Point Mine near Seldovia. During World War II and the Korean War, chrome shortages occurred again, and production commenced from chrome deposits at Red Mountain about 12 miles east of Claim Point. Between 1943 and 1957, a total of 28,849 tons of ore was produced from numerous lenticular orebodies within the Red Mountain body. Production was subsidized under a Defense Minerals Exploration Administration price support which expired in 1958. Most United States domestic production ended in 1961. Reserves of chromite on the Kenai Peninsula, according to the U.S. Bureau of Mines, amount to approximately 300,000 tons of 28% Cr_2O_3, equivalent to about six weeks of United States consumption. However, the Red Mountain deposits may represent one of the largest, low-grade chrome reserves in the nation.

Other chromite belts in Alaska include deposits on the Kanuti River north of Fairbanks, Eklutna near Anchorage, Bernard Mountain near Chitina, eastern Chichagof Island, and in the De Long Mountains of northwestern Alaska. Because chrome is a low unit value ore, only those deposits near existing transportation systems should be considered to have economic potential.

Tin

Alaska, unlike the rest of the United States, has been endowed with promising tin resources. As early as 1902, placer tin

Extensive exploratory diamond drilling at the Lost River Tin Mine, on the Seward Peninsula, and other nearby deposits have indicated an inferred reserve of 124 million pounds of tin, the largest single reserve of this mineral in North America. Some work is done each summer at Lost River's present campsite, shown here. (Ron Sheardown)

As early as 1902, placer tin deposits were successfully mined on the Seward Peninsula. This placer tin operation is at Cape Creek, near the western end of the peninsula. (U.S.B.M.)

deposits on the western Seward Peninsula near Nome were successfully mined. Although total state production of about 5 million pounds has been very modest compared to other world sources, it still constitutes America's largest primary source of the metal.

The strategic importance of tin in Alaska has long been known. Both lode and placer deposits of the Lost River area near Nome eventually became the focus of national concern. By late 1942, two-thirds of the tin resources and three-fourths of the world's tin smelter capacity had been taken over by Japanese occupation of Malaysia. The War Production Board immediately approved government construction of a 500-ton-per-day mill at the Lost River tin deposit, but construction depended on the U.S. Navy's ability to keep open shipping lanes in the area. Because of the Japanese invasion of the Aleutian Islands, the United States military establishment decided, after lengthy debate, that the Lost River mine did not constitute enough comparative importance to justify a significant diversion of critically important cargo and naval strength in the area, and the construction project was cancelled. However, government exploration of the Lost River deposits commenced in 1942, and by the end of the war a significant tonnage of high-grade tin ore had been successfully delineated.

Finally, with the onset of the Korean War, the government, under the 1950 Defense Production Act, advanced funds to the United States Tin Corporation for construction of mine infrastructure and production facilities. By 1956, 51,000 short tons of ore averaging 1.13% tin had been won from the deposits. When government participation ended after the Korean War, the mine closed down and remains so today.

Extensive exploratory diamond drilling of the Lost River Mine and nearby deposits continued, and by the mid-1970s, an inferred reserve of 124 million pounds of tin had been blocked out, the largest single reserve of tin in North America. This reserve equals about one year of present United States consumption. The other major area in Alaska that has sustained tin production has been the Manley district northwest of Fairbanks where more than 600,000 pounds of cassiterite has been recovered as a by-product of gold mining. Today, Alaska produces about 120,000 pounds of tin concentrate annually from small placer operations on the western Seward Peninsula and in the Manley area — the only primary source of tin in the United States.

Tungsten

Modest amounts of high-grade tungsten concentrate were shipped from Alaska mines during World Wars I and II and the Korean War. Early Fairbanks-area gold prospectors found tungsten deposits, and with the tungsten requirements of World War I came modest production from several small deposits on Gilmore Dome.

Likewise the same pattern was followed

during World War II in the Hyder district of southeastern Alaska. Primarily a gold-silver base metal mine, the Riverside Mine reopened after several years of dormancy and shipped tungsten concentrates from 1941 to 1945 for the war effort.

During the Korean War, the pattern changed because the 1950 Defense Production Act essentially subsidized exploration and production of tungsten throughout Alaska, resulting in tungsten mining on the western Seward Peninsula, in southeastern Alaska, and the Fairbanks area. Total tungsten output, about 286,000 pounds, has been very modest compared to national requirements; but significant tungsten resources have now been delineated at the Lost River tin deposits, the Stepovich Lode near Fairbanks, and at scattered sites throughout Alaska.

Antimony

Antimony is plentiful in Alaska and exists in many mining districts throughout the state, often associated with gold mineralization. Antimony ores from at least 16 deposits were shipped to markets during 1905, 1914 to 1916, 1926 to 1927, 1936 to 1944, 1951 to 1953, 1969 to 1972, and 1978 to 1979, usually coincident with high demand for war and related industries. During the Korean War, some production was subsidized by the federal government in the Fairbanks, Livengood, and Kantishna districts. Alaska's total yield of 10,493,360 pounds of antimony

Abandoned buildings of the Riverside Mine stretch along the bank of the Salmon River, near Hyder, in this 1967 photo. Production of gold, silver, copper, lead, and zinc continued here intermittently from 1924 to 1950. A small amount of tungsten was also mined at Riverside during World War II. (Steve McCutcheon)

— 59

amounted to about 8% of domestic production through the early 1970s. During actual wartime needs, Alaska's contribution figured even more importantly. For example, the Scrafford property in the Fairbanks area supplied a large percentage of the country's antimony needs during World War I. Likewise, during 1936 to 1942 the Stampede Mine in the Kantishna district is credited with about three-fourths of United States domestic production of the metal.

Although large resources remain in the Fairbanks and Kantishna areas, antimony mines in Idaho, Montana, and Nevada now overshadow Alaska's contributions. Moreover, the strategic value of the metal has decreased with substitutions for past uses in tracer bullets, Babbitt (tin alloy), hardening agents in storage batteries, and paints. However, increased usage of antimony-oxide-based fire retardants suggests that this metal could again be mined in Alaska during times of high demand.

Mercury

Mercury vapor and certain mercury compounds — particularly the organic ones — are toxic. Although common mercury sulfides such as cinnabar are relatively stable, any person using mercury should be aware of the potential hazard.

Because of cumulative toxicity, mercury's use in many pesticides, fungicides, and other industrial products have been prohibited. Despite the undesirable effects of mercury pollution, its

Increased demand in recent years has renewed interest in mercury production. The photo above shows an old milling and ore crushing device at a mine in the Kilbuck Mountains, about 100 miles east of Bethel. The mine was reopened during the summer of 1981 after having operated intermittently since 1946. The photo at right shows samples of cinnabar, the principle ore of mercury. (Both photos by Third Eye Photography)

safe use in batteries, lab apparatus, and control instruments makes substitution impractical. Demand has begun to rise, and mercury prices have been climbing in the last few years.

A large mercury district in southwestern Alaska extends from Marsh Mountain near Dillingham to the Cripple Mountains north of McGrath. A dozen mines have recovered more than 40,000 76-pound flasks of mercury intermittently since World War I. The principal producer has been the Red Devil Mine near Sleetmute on the Kuskokwim River which was developed intermittently between 1942 and 1972 with continuous mine operation occurring from 1954 to 1963. During high prices of the 1950s, Alaska mercury mines supplied the nation with from 10% to 20% of its mercury requirements. Reserves of this metal are difficult to block out, and development could resume on Alaska deposits should prices continue to rise.

Other Strategic Minerals

Fluorite is often associated with tin deposits statewide. The only viable Alaska reserve is contained within deposits at Lost River previously described for their tin and tungsten content. One estimate made in the early 1970s infers that approximately 4.94 million tons of fluorite are contained in both high- and low-grade ores at Lost River — equivalent to about 25% of the stated United States reserve base. Demand for fluorite is currently low because of the sagging steel industry, which uses fluorite as a fluxing agent, but

exploitation of Alaska's reserves could go a long way in reducing dependence on foreign sources should economics warrant their development.

Niobium, tantalum, manganese, and titanium are all known to occur in Alaska, but no reserves of any of these commodities have been published. Niobium and tantalum do exist in small quantities in some Alaska tin deposits, and by-product production seems possible should tin recovery commence. Large sedimentary manganese deposits such as those mined in the U.S.S.R. are unknown in Alaska, but smaller lodes are known to exist in the Alaska Range and Yukon-Tanana uplands. Titanium occurs in enormous low-grade, lode iron deposits and in some rich beach placers in Southeast, but economic extraction of either metal has not been considered in recent years.

There are no indications of commercially viable bauxite (aluminum) deposits in Alaska.

In past years, graphite was regarded as a strategic element and looked for in Alaska. Some production occurred on Uncle Sam Mountain near Nome during World War I. When German U-boats successfully blockaded our principal sources of graphite in Madagascar and southern Africa during World War II, the War Production Board instituted a policy of encouraging domestic graphite production. This directly resulted in further development and shipment of more than 500,000 pounds of graphite

from the high quality deposits of Uncle Sam Mountain. The strategic needs of graphite are substantially less today than they were 40 years ago even though virtually all domestic needs are still met by foreign imports.

Sheet mica and oscillator-quality quartz crystals have been crucially important materials in times of war. In fact, both were at times considered the country's top strategic mineral procurement problem during World War II because of their unique electrical properties. The desire to develop domestic reserves spurred prospecting in Alaska during the 1940s. A number of pegmatite deposits were examined, particularly in southeastern Alaska and the Seward Peninsula, but no production of either material ever took place.

The Future for Strategic Minerals in Alaska

Those commodities that would appear to have a healthy future in terms of price will certainly have a better chance of exploitation. But it's really more complicated than that. In Alaska, land status, minerals policy, transportation, labor, availability of energy, climate, and proximity to urban areas all play an important role in deciding whether mineral ores of any type will be mined. Certain high-unit-value concentrates such as tin, tungsten, and platinum could be successfully shipped by aircraft while materials such as chrome or titanium need cheap transportation facilities. With the

A tractor pulls a container of drilling equipment from the hold of a cargo plane at the Lost River Tin Mine in May, 1971. (Ron Sheardown)

exception of gold, it is no puzzle that most Alaska large-scale mineral developments have occurred proximal to railroads or the sea. Deposits near cheap and available energy sources will definitely have an advantage over deposits without such sources. The length of shipping seasons will also play an important role along Alaska's northern coastline.

Land status has had a substantial effect on mineral exploration and development in Alaska (see *Who Owns Alaska?*, page 86). Prior to statehood, almost all of Alaska was in the federal public domain and except for national park or military withdrawals, most of the territory was open to mineral entry and development under liberal mining laws. Since statehood, the complexity of land ownership has increased. In 1971 the Alaska Native Claims Settlement Act permanently changed land use patterns in Alaska by awarding 11.7% of the state to Native Alaskans as part of their legitimate aboriginal rights; section 17 (d) (2) mandated that at least 83 million acres be placed into four conservation units for unique and valuable natural heritage. In December, 1980, the U.S. Congress placed approximately 100 million acres of Alaska into various conservation units, many of which are closed for further mineral entry.

Mineral price trends of selected strategic minerals			
	1974	*1978*	*1981*	*1981 Net Import Reliance (%)*
Niobium	$1.28/lb	$3.18/lb	$11/lb	100
Tantalum	$6.88/lb	$21/lb	$104/lb	100
Cobalt	$2.87/lb	$5.60/lb	$25/lb	90
Mica	$1.66/lb	$2.80/lb	$7.30/lb	100
Chromium (SA)	$34/mt	$59/mt	$55/mt	90
Platinum	$150/oz	$162/oz	$439/oz	89
Tin	$2.27/lb	$5.29/lb	$8.56/lb	81
Fluorine	$85/mt	$115/mt	$150/mt	81
Nickel	$1.53/lb	$2.40/lb	$3.45/lb	77
Tungsten	$44.22/stu	$157.21/stu	$131/stu	59
Mercury	$286/f	$145/f	$400/f	62
Antimony	$68.50/lb	$177/lb	$200/lb	43
Titanium	$1.42/lb	$2.98/lb	$6.75/lb	W

Abbreviations: lb = pound; mt = metric ton; oz = ounces; stu = short ton unit; f = flask; W = information withheld

The relative importance of strategic minerals will continue to be debated at the national level. There seems to be a high interest in Alaska chrome, tin, tungsten, nickel, cobalt, and platinum metals potential, judging from the recent increase in industry development and exploration efforts. Exploitation of such commodities seems possible during the next 10 to 20 years; platinum was recovered at Goodnews Bay in 1981.

Alaska's Industrial Minerals

By Thomas K. Bundtzen and Thomas E. Smith, D.G.G.S.

Territorial assayer Art Glover wrote in 1948, "non-metallic minerals can ill afford to be overlooked if there is to be an orderly development of Alaska . . . the very existence of new industry in the territory may well depend on local development of minerals previously deemed valueless."

This farsighted prophecy has come true. Surprisingly, while many Alaskans are aware of Alaska's contributions toward supplying metals and energy, they are nearly totally ignorant of the existence and importance of domestic suppliers of such commodities as building stone and sand and gravel. Additionally, chemical and structural grade limestone, gypsum, garnets, graphite, asbestos, barite, pumice, and clay have all been mined in the 49th state. The largest single component of the mineral extractive industry — excluding oil and gas — is the sand and gravel industry, with about a dozen operations active statewide. Nationally significant reserves of fluorite and asbestos have recently been discovered, and development is possible for both

commodities. If Alaska agriculture is to expand, it may require the development of domestic lime and phosphate fertilizers.

A summmary of those industrial mineral resources judged to be most important to the 49th state follows.

Sand and Gravel

Gravel is one of the most important commodities in Alaska, ranking third in value behind oil and gas. Since 1948, more than 709 million tons of aggregate have been mined. Gravel figures importantly in development of urban areas where much of the total state production is consumed. In Anchorage, for example, a chronic shortage of gravel created by urban growth has necessitated importation of aggregate from the Matanuska Valley. Gravel mine tailings derived from past gold dredging and modern floodplain deposits serve as important local sources in the Fairbanks area. River deposits on the North Slope supply aggregate for development of the northern oil fields.

The gravel deposits of southcentral Alaska formed as a result of meltwater

streams deposited on or adjacent to Pleistocene glaciers; those mined in interior Alaska are ancient to modern river and stream deposits covered by reworked and windblown silt.

Gravel is either processed by washing and sizing for use as concrete aggregate, road metal, and petroleum-base paving, or as unprocessed fill and base material. Because gravel and sand continue to be important building materials in urban areas, large amounts will continue to be mined. Additionally, proposed hydroelectrical developments may require concrete aggregate for building dams.

Marble and Building Stone

Alaska marble was used before the coming of Russians by Tlingit Indians of southeastern Alaska for carved utensils, art ornaments, and religious objects. The

---

Gravel ranks third in value, behind oil and gas, of commodities extracted from Alaska's earth resources. This sand and gravel plant operates on the Tanana River immediately south of Fairbanks. (M.S. Robinson, D.G.G.S.)

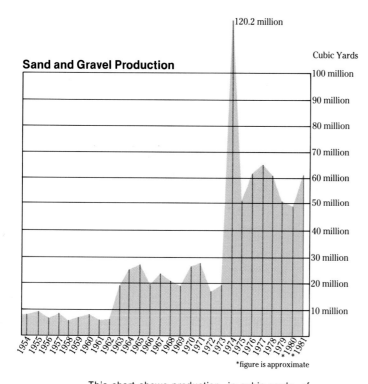

Sand and Gravel Production

120.2 million

Cubic Yards

100 million
90 million
80 million
70 million
60 million
50 million
40 million
30 million
20 million
10 million

1954 1955 1956 1957 1958 1959 1960 1961 1962 1963 1964 1965 1966 1967 1968 1969 1970 1971 1972 1973 1974 1975 1976 1977 1978 1979 1980 1981

*figure is approximate

This chart shows production, in cubic yards, of sand and gravel in Alaska from 1954 to 1981. Construction of the trans-Alaska pipeline haul road in 1974 caused a sharp increase in production. High levels of production were sustained following that construction by sand and gravel use for ice island construction on the North Slope and recent development of urban areas around the state. (Source: U.S. Bureau of Mines Annual Statistical Summaries; 1973, 1974, and 1975 Division of Geological and Geophysical Surveys Annual Report; Division of Geological and Geophysical Surveys Annual Summaries, 1977-1980)

Russians themselves largely ignored this resource, but potentially viable marble and limestone on Prince of Wales Island were some of the first mineral resources mentioned in late-19th-century geological reports of the U.S. Geological Survey.

In the 1890s, some marble, from Ham Island near Wrangell, was worked by Natives for tombstones. This skill locally replaced crudely carved wooden totems after westerners introduced their burial culture to local Natives.

Around 1900, the rapid growth of urban areas on the west coast created a demand for ornamental and building stone. Beginning in 1902, shipments of high quality ornamental marble commenced from quarries at Tokeen. By 1949, at least 2,150,000 tons of chemical-grade stone and 450,000 tons of structural-grade limestones were won from a dozen quarries on Prince of Wales and Dall islands, but the principal workings remained in the Tokeen-Calder area. Through 1920, more than 72 buildings in Washington, Oregon, California, Idaho, Utah, Montana, Minnesota, Massachusetts, and Pennsylvania used Alaska marble (principally from Tokeen) for interior work. The beautiful exterior of the Isaacs Building in Los Angeles, California; the old Federal Post Office in Fairbanks; and the corridor of the Admissions Building at the University of Utah in Salt Lake City are long lasting monuments to the Alaska marble industry. The State Capitol in Juneau was built in 1930 with four big exterior columns of Tokeen marble, plus marble wainscoting and trim inside. During and subsequent to World War II, inflation, changes in building styles, marketing, exploitation of marble in the western states, and other complex factors ended the southeastern Alaska industry.

The measured reserves of high quality marble in southeastern Alaska — should demand warrant development — amount to more than 800 million tons.

Small quantities of limestone have been quarried in other parts of the state. Marble was quarried by the U.S. Corps of Engineers at Gray Cliff about two miles north of Seldovia. The amount of rock quarried is unknown, but considerable quantities were used as riprap on a sea wall.

Chemical-grade limestone deposits suitable for concrete have been investigated and drilled by the U.S. Bureau of Mines along the Alaska Railroad near Cantwell. Several hundred million tons of reserves are known from three deposits. Such deposits could become important for large scale hydroelectric power development. During the last several years, the Delta barley project has renewed some interest in establishing

The building boom that began on the west coast in the late 1890s spurred the demand for building stone from Alaska. As a result, marble quarries opened in several areas of southeastern Alaska. The Alaska Marble Company operated this quarry at Calder, on Kosciusko Island west of Wrangell.
(Alaska Historical Library; reprinted from *The ALASKA JOURNAL*®)

The late Al Ritchie of Wrangell inspects marble from the quarry at Tokeen on Marble Island off the west coast of Prince of Wales Island in southeastern Alaska. Tokeen, largest of Alaska's marble quarries, operated from 1909 to 1932. (Mike Miller; reprinted from *The ALASKA JOURNAL®*)

Four large exterior columns of marble from the Tokeen quarry on Marble Island, off the west coast of Prince of Wales Island, dominate the entrance to the state capitol building, built in 1930 in Juneau. Between 1910 and the early 1930s, marble from Tokeen was used to ornament many major buildings in the lower 48, including the Washington State Capitol at Olympia, the Southern Pacific Railroad passenger station at Los Angeles, and the Orpheum Theater in Boston.
(Lael Morgan, staff; reprinted from *ALASKA GEOGRAPHIC®*)

domestic reserves of agricultural limestone and phosphate. The search continues for deposits proximal to cheap transportation.

Basalt building and ornamental stone is currently being mined at the Yutan Construction Company basalt quarry on Badger Road near Fairbanks. In the last decade several million tons of high quality basalt have been produced for crushed rock in septic-leach fields; as fill for the Moose Creek diversion dam; D-1 asphalt road metal; and ornamental stone. About 650,000 tons have been produced in the last three years. Up to 22 individuals drill, blast, and transport the stone to various consumers in the area. The quarry operates intermittently, based on contract awards for specific construction projects.

Building stone has been used on other construction projects statewide, such as the sea wall at Nome, and bridge fill reinforcement.

Barite

Barite has more than 2,000 industrial uses; more than 85% of world consumption is applied to well-drilling, mud-weighting properties, especially in high-pressure petroleum exploration efforts. Deposits of commercial significance occur in southeastern Alaska. Minimal development of a lode on Prince of Wales Island resulted in a large 1915 bulk shipment which tested satisfactorily as a drilling agent. Since 1963, a lode cropping out in the Castle Islands near Petersburg has been exploited. Development initially took place onshore, but after 1967 mining

Workers load barite in this 1966 photo of the Chromalloy operation near Petersburg. More than 85% of the world's consumption of this mineral results from its use as a mud for drilling in the petroleum industry. (Steve McCutcheon)

was offshore; the orebodies were drilled, blasted, and retrieved underwater with a barge-mounted clamshell — a large scoop shaped like a shell. Production reached highs of 100,000 tons annually in the 1960s, but since 1974 a smaller tonnage of ore was processed and bagged as a drilling mud for Alaska oil fields. Chromalloy, the principal operator for the last decade, announced in late 1980 that the operation would be closed down, and there was no Alaska barite production in 1981.

Pottery and Brick-Quality Clays

Structural-grade clay deposits have been the subject of investigations in the southcentral railbelt near Anchorage for many years. After World War II, Clay Products, Inc., established a kiln and brick plant in Anchorage utilizing Bootlegger clay as their prime material source. More than 200,000 bricks were formed in the kiln — 25,000 of these derived from clay mined at Sheep Mountain on the Glenn Highway — but structural imperfections such as exfoliation gave the company's bricks an inferior reputation, and the project failed in late 1948. It is unclear whether Bootlegger clay has unfavorable physical characteristics, or if improper burning techniques caused the severe exfoliation in the product.

The feasibility of producing bricks, ceramic tile, sewer pipe, flue tile, and clay molding from clay horizons in the Healy coal field south of Fairbanks was tested by a University of Alaska student, Robert Sullivan. The proposed extraction envisions the mining of clay partings in coal seams simultaneous with the present coal mining. The clay itself, after undergoing preparation, is adequate for structural-grade products, but the main constraint in exploiting of the resource is economics. Sullivan believed that the present or projected consumption of brick and other clay products in the railbelt could not sustain the Healy-based industry. Nevertheless, a future clay-based product industry seems possible in a state where bricks are imported at high prices.

Today, Alaska's potters create functional containers and objects of beauty from clay deposits statewide. One estimate, for example, places wet clay consumption in the Anchorage area at 150 tons annually. In the Fairbanks area, at least 20 studio and one production potter use roughly 40 tons of raw material a year. Value of production is difficult to estimate because of the art value of the products. Interior Alaska potters work clays from the coal-bearing section at Healy. For years, Joe Usibelli of Usibelli Coal Mines has supplied railroad carloads of clay for interior potters.

An independent researcher, David Stannard, has studied the possibility of creating high quality porcelain out of kaolinite-based clays — derived from interior Alaska sericitic schist. Beautiful porcelain containers have been created from kaolinitic clays near Tenderfoot, in interior Alaska, but sample preparation makes significant utilization of the resource prohibitive at present.

Liz Berry of Fairbanks throws a pot made from clay from the Healy coal fields. Estimates place clay consumption in the Fairbanks area at about 40 tons annually. In the Anchorage area, clay consumption reaches about 150 tons annually.
(Thomas K. Bundtzen)

— 69

Gypsum

Beginning in 1902, the Pacific Coast Gypsum Company developed high-grade gypsum beds near Iyoukeen Cove on eastern Chichagof Island. By 1926, when the mines closed, more than 500,000 tons of high quality blue gypsum had been won from folded and tilted beds of Late Paleozoic age (350 to 280 million years ago). During World War II, Kaiser Industries acquired the property for possible exploitation in war industry construction, but the project never went beyond an initial feasibility study.

Gypsum demand fluctuates with the housing industry, which utilizes gypsum in sheetrock and Portland cement. The economics of developing gypsum deposits in Alaska today are tough, and it is not clear whether Alaska's future has a place for gypsum mining.

Asbestos

During World War II, the War Production Board declared chemical- and friction-grade asbestos fiber a strategic mineral and recommended policies conducive to the development of domestic reserves. In 1942, bulk sampling of small high-grade deposits of tremolite and chrysotile asbestos in the Kobuk Valley commenced, and by 1943 small shipments of selected ores were freighted to the coast via winter trails. One hundred thousand pounds of tremolite asbestos eventually found its way to a buyer. Indicated reserves of 2,600 tons of tremolite asbestos remain in the Kobuk deposits.

Gypsum deposits add to the color on the hillsides of the Sheep Mountain area along the Glenn Highway northeast of Palmer. Today, development of Alaska's gypsum deposits faces an uncertain future; in the early 20th century, however, more than 500,000 tons of gypsum were extracted from beds near Iyoukeen Cove on Chichagof Island in southeastern Alaska.
(Steve McCutcheon)

This camp near Slate Creek in eastern Alaska houses workers exploring a major discovery of asbestos. According to late-1981 drilling records, reserves here amount to 55 million tons of 6.35% chrysotile asbestos, one of the country's largest asbestos deposits.
(Robert Rogers, courtesy of Riz Bigelow)

In 1980 Doyon Regional Corporation announced the discovery of a major asbestos deposit at Slate Creek in the Yukon-Tanana Upland southwest of Eagle. According to their drilling results, indicated reserves amount to 55 million tons of 6.35% chrysotile fiber, one of the largest asbestos deposits in the United States — probably the most important discovery of its type in North America in more than 30 years. Bulk sampling of the deposit is in progress, but no development plans have been announced. The health problems related to unwise asbestos use in our industrial society has caused permanent losses in domestic markets, but many substitutions in friction products are still inferior. Depending on marketing, the Slate Creek deposit could substantially reduce the 85% net import reliance for asbestos in this country.

Other Industrial Minerals

From 1912 to 1920 high quality almandine garnets were selectively mined from schist and migmatite near Wrangell. In addition to their value as museum-quality specimens, the garnets' physical characteristics of hardness, specific gravity, and uniform and equidimensional fracturing make them suitable for abrasive applications — which is what they were

Garnets, such as these from the Stikine River Mine near Wrangell, are valuable as museum-quality specimens, but also were mined for industrial applications because of their abrasive characteristics. (Steve McCutcheon)

marketed for. Although more than 11,000 tons of contained garnet are believed to be proven in the Wrangell deposits by exploration, there has been little interest (except to the collector) for quite some time. Even so, Fort Wrangell garnets can be found on display in museums worldwide.

Zeolites, perlite, diatomaceous earth, sulfur, and pumice have been examined for production potential in southcentral Alaska and on the Alaska Peninsula. Promising resources of all these commodities are known, but only small amounts of pumice have been exploited for use in the Anchorage area.

The Future for Alaska's Industrial Minerals

Most industrial minerals are low-unit-value minerals worth only a few tens of dollars per ton. With Alaska's high labor and operational costs, it is difficult to envision exportation of these minerals to foreign or lower 48 customers. Exceptions are asbestos, fluorite (as a by-product of tin mining near Nome) and possibly a limited market for something like abrasive-quality garnet. In southeastern Alaska, an ideal shipping situation could make the difference and allow for exploitation of low-unit-value materials.

The real importance of most of these commodities lies in local utilization and needs. No matter how fast or slow we grow, the people of Alaska will need increasing amounts of these materials to sustain an increasingly complex society.

This sample of antimony and tungsten is exposed to ultraviolet light: the bright blue mineral is scheelite, the principal ore of tungsten; the dark gray mineral is stibnite, the principal ore of antimony. (M.S. Robinson, D.G.G.S.)

The brassy-colored mineral scattered through this specimen is chalcopyrite, an ore mineral of copper. The gray-to-brown sulfides are a fine-grained mixture partially made up of pentlandite, an important ore of nickel. Recoverable cobalt occurs in the other sulfides. (Jim Barker, U.S.B.M.)

Cinnabar, the red mineral in both of these specimens, is the principal ore of mercury. The dark gray mineral on the left is stibnite, the principal ore of antimony. (Thomas K. Bundtzen, D.G.G.S.)

The dark gray mineral in this specimen is chromite, the principal ore of chromium. The brown mineral is dunite, the host rock. (Thomas K. Bundtzen, D.G.G.S.)

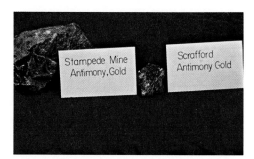

Stibnite, the dark gray mineral in both of these specimens, is the principal ore of anitmony. (Thomas K. Bundtzen, D.G.G.S.)

The dark brown pebbles in this specimen are cassiterite, the principal ore of tin. The other minerals are not identifiable, but the concentrate contains anomalous niobium, uranium, and thorium. (Jim Barker, U.S.B.M.)

Pyrolusite, the dark brown mineral in the specimen on the left, is an ore of manganese. On the right, the purple mineral is bornite, a copper ore mineral. The pen is pointing toward the light steel gray mineral carrollite, a cobalt-nickel-copper sulfide. (J.Y. Foley, U.S.B.M.)

The specimen on the left is primarily made up of the dark gray mineral magnetite, an iron oxide. The titanium, in the form of ilmenite and rutile, is not visible in the specimen. On the right, the purple mineral is bornite, a copper ore; the gold and palladium values are tied up in the bornite and other unidentifiable minerals.
(Jim Barker, U.S.B.M.)

The steel gray mineral making up most of this specimen is galena, the principal ore of lead. The lighter gray spot in the upper part of the specimen is a mixture of tetrahedrite and polybasite, which accounts for the high silver, antimony, and copper values. The gold found in assays cannot be seen. (Thomas K. Bundtzen, D.G.G.S.)

This specimen of chrysotile asbestos comes from the Slate Creek deposit near Eagle. Chrysotile is a serpentine group mineral and an important component of asbestos. (Thomas K. Bundtzen)

The brassy mineral in the left and right specimens is chalcopyrite, a copper mineral. The gold and silver values are tied up in the other sulfides and are not identifiable. The gray mineral in the center specimen is molybdenite, the principal ore of molybdenum; however, the deposits were never exploited for this metal.
(Thomas K. Bundtzen, D.G.G.S.)

Galena, the steel gray mineral in this specimen, is the principal ore of lead. The brown mineral is dominantly sphalerite, an ore of zinc. Silver values are tied up in the galena and cannot be seen. (Jim Barker, U.S.B.M.)

Exploration

By Greg Fernette

Since reserves of ore in any mine will eventually be depleted, the search for new deposits and extensions of known deposits is vital to assure continuity of mineral production and to supply demands. Acquiring additional reserves can be likened to adding to a store's inventory. The process of searching for, finding, and developing new reserves is the process of mineral exploration. Exploration in mining is like research and development in other industries, as there is no guarantee of success for any single effort. This risk is a fundamental element of mineral exploration. Mining is a risky business, but exploration risk is even higher. The prospect of a reasonably high return is what motivates exploration.

There are a variety of approaches to exploration, depending on the size of the

---

Editor's note: Greg is a senior geologist with WGM, Inc., an Anchorage based geological consulting firm active in minerals exploration and development in Alaska.

venture. We will deal mainly with exploration as it is practiced by mining companies in Alaska.

Exploration Techniques

Before describing how and why exploration is done in a particular way, we will first review the techniques and tools used to search for mineral deposits. Several factors should be kept in mind. Most mineral deposits are small. Even the large porphyry copper or stockwork molybdenum deposits may cover less than a square mile. Massive sulfide deposits are even smaller, and vein-type deposits containing high-grade concentrations of valuable minerals are relatively tiny. Further, deposits do not always crop out at the surface. Most often little or none of the deposit is exposed. Surface debris — glacial till, stream gravel, soil, and vegetation — obscure mineral deposits near the surface.

In many areas outcroppings and near-surface deposits have been discovered, so the search must be extended to find concealed deposits. The following

questions must first be asked:
— Where do we look?
— How do we narrow down the area of search so we can concentrate our efforts?

There are three principal methods of exploration — geology, geochemistry, and geophysics; each of these methods in turn covers a variety of individual techniques.

Geology

An understanding of the nature and habit — the geologic setting of mineral deposits — is basic to exploration. Geologists and prospectors know the characteristics of the deposits they are searching for, and the kind of rocks in which these deposits occur. The first step in any exploration program is usually to locate favorable geologic environments.

Helicopters have been a great boon to mineral exploration in the state by providing access to remote and rugged areas, thus maximizing the amount of time that can be devoted to actual exploration. This chopper, flown by Bob Tow, is dropping off geologist Peter Dea for a traverse near Pybus Bay on Admiralty Island. (Greg Fernette)

This photo shows exceptionally high-grade molybdenite mineralization (the silvery streaks in the center of the picture) in copper skarns which were mined from 1907 to 1923.
(Thomas K. Bundtzen, D.G.G.S.)

For example, porphyry copper and stockwork molybdenum deposits are associated with certain types of intrusive igneous rocks. Lead and zinc deposits tend to occur in carbonate rocks and shales. The favorable environment can often be recognized through a review of literature and by geologic reconnaissance.

Although modern exploration employs a variety of techniques to search for mineralization, prospecting is one of the oldest and most effective approaches. One simply walks an area, looking for mineralization or clues to its existence. Many prospectors without formal scientific training become very good geologists.

In the more advanced stages of exploration when a mineral deposit or prospect is evaluated in detail, geologic mapping and interpretation are fundamental in determining the relative importance of the prospects, many of which will not be of economic interest. Understanding of geology is aided by topographic maps, aerial photographs, and, in recent years, satellite photos. But the ultimate understanding comes from careful geologic mapping. Geologic mapping involves constructing a map which shows the surface distribution of different rock types and mineralization. The map is then used to formulate an interpretation of the geologic history of the region — including how and in what order each rock type was formed and subsequent structural events which may have deformed the rocks by folding or faulting. The goal of such mapping in

exploration is to extrapolate the various rock units and mineral occurrences into the area below the surface, and predict the location and relative value of mineralized bodies. The use of geologic extrapolation is becoming more important as the emphasis in exploration shifts to concealed deposits.

Geochemistry

Geochemistry has become a powerful and widely used technique in the past 25 years and has been instrumental in several of the major mineral discoveries in Alaska.

The basis of geochemical exploration is that the mineral deposits are geochemical anomalies, i.e., they represent unusual accumulations of elements in the earth's crust. Mineral deposits also exhibit geochemical haloes which extend over larger areas than the deposits themselves. This has the effect of making the target larger.

The most valuable halo in terms of exploration is known as the secondary, or dispersion, halo. This is formed by the action of weathering and erosion on mineral deposits. As a deposit weathers — including both chemical and physical breakdowns — the weathering products are dispersed by erosion. By sampling the products of weathering and erosion, dispersion haloes can be detected and traced to their source.

The most commmonly used geochemical sampling methods in mineral exploration are stream sediment and soil surveys. Since the stream sediments in a particular drainage are formed by the breakdown of the rocks in the valley, the metal content of the sediments reflects the metal content of the rocks from which they are derived. In stream sediment surveys two media are sampled depending on the target sought. For base metals such as copper, lead, zinc, and molybdenum, the fine sediment is sampled, i.e., the mud and clay. When base metal sulfides weather, they break down into metal ions. These ions become attached to clay particles, silt grains, and oxide coatings on grains. In practice, samples of stream mud are collected and the fine portion is removed by sieving. This sediment is dissolved in acid, and the resulting solution is analyzed for the target elements.

For metals such as gold, tin, tungsten, and chromium, a different approach is used. These metals occur in minerals which resist chemical weathering and as a result are transported as discrete mineral grains in the sand-sized stream sediment. These minerals are heavier than most others and can be concentrated by gravity methods. In heavy mineral surveys, large samples, five pounds or so, of sand and gravel are collected and concentrated using a gold pan. Many of the minerals sought will, if present in the stream drainage, be visible in the panned concentrate. The concentrate may also be dissolved in acid and analyzed for the target elements at a laboratory.

Soil sampling follows much the same principle. Residual soils are formed by the weathering of the underlying rocks, and the metal content of the soil is related to the metal content of the rocks. Soils are typically composed of mixtures of organic and mineral material. Soil samples are collected from small pits, sieved, and analyzed in the same manner as stream sediments. In some cases, heavy minerals can be detected by panning the soils.

Since stream sediments are transported away from their source, the dispersion haloes can be quite large. The size of the halo is determined largely by the size of the source area of the sample. The further downstream the sample is taken from the source, the weaker the anomaly. In the case of soil samples there is comparatively little transport, so soil anomalies occur very close to their source. For this reason stream sediment sampling is commonly used as a reconnaissance technique whereas soil sampling is used mainly as a follow-up technique to pinpoint the location of a covered deposit within a drainage basin.

As with everything, there are complications. In many areas the sediment being carried by streams is not locally derived, so its metal values do not reflect those in the drainage. This is particularly true in areas that have been glaciated and in large stream valleys. In these cases locally derived anomalies are masked or diluted. This means many areas are not suited to standard geochemical exploration and more refined and complex approaches must be used.

This geologist's loot — samples of rocks, silts, and panned concentrates — was collected in one day of following up a tin anomaly near Candle on the Seward Peninsula. (Greg Fernette)

Geophysics

Geophysical techniques provide an indirect method of viewing the subsurface. Basically, geophysics is used to measure some physical property which creates a contrast between mineralized and barren rock. The most commonly used geophysical techniques are magnetic, electric/electromagnetic, gravity, seismic, and radiometric surveys. These techniques measure the density and electrical, acoustic, and radioactive properties of rocks. One advantage of geophysics is that some techniques can be used with airplane- or helicopter-mounted instruments. This makes geophysics a valuable tool for reconnaissance as well as detailed work.

In magnetic surveys a magnetometer is used to measure local variations in the earth's magnetic field which are caused by differences in the magnetic susceptibility of the rocks in the area. Rocks containing the mineral magnetite or certain sulfide minerals have a high magnetic susceptibility. Magnetometer surveys can be used to outline the extent of rocks containing these minerals even if they are not exposed at the surface. Magnetic methods are used in the exploration of iron deposits such as those on the Kasaan Peninsula in southeastern Alaska, contact metamorphic copper or tungsten deposits, and in outlining rocks containing asbestos mineralization.

Magnetic methods are also readily adaptable to airborne use and are a valuable aid in interpreting geologic

Instruments used in magnetic and electromagnetic prospecting hang from a helicopter flying over the Alaska Range. State and federal geological surveys conduct regional airborne magnetic surveys because this method provides valuable information about geologic structures in areas with little outcrop.
(Mark McDermott)

structure in areas of little outcrop. For this reason both state and federal geologic surveys conduct regional airborne magnetic surveys.

Electrical methods are some of the most important geophysical techniques currently in use by the mining industry. There are two major techniques: electromagnetics (EM) and induced polarization (IP).

Electromagnetic methods basically measure the conductivity of rocks in the ground. Certain minerals such as graphite and many sulfides are highly conductive whereas most other rock-forming minerals have only low conductivity.

Electromagnetic methods are used to explore for massive sulfide deposits in areas of little outcrop such as in central and northwestern Alaska. Airborne EM techniques are used for regional reconnaissance of tundra and forested areas. EM anomalies can also be caused by graphitic rocks, fault zones, or even saline groundwater, and many false anomalies have been drill tested. However, the technique does narrow the search to an identifiable target. EM techniques have been valuable in exploring for several major Alaska deposits including Greens Creek, Arctic, Sun, and Lik.

The induced polarization method does not measure conductivity to detect sulfides but instead measures secondary currents generated by conductive minerals after an inducing electric current applied at the surface is turned off. The technique is expensive and time consuming, but is

Two geophysicists use a horizontal loop — wire coils wrapped in plastic for waterproofing and protection — to conduct an electromagnetic survey for massive sulfides in the Brooks Range. One geophysicist carries a transmitter, the other a receiver. Together these instruments measure electrical currents. When the scientists encounter mineralization, their instruments will record currents given off by the metallic body. (Mark McDermott)

A worker empties diamond drill core samples into boxes at mining claims in central Alaska.
(Mark McDermott)

more selective than EM techniques with metallic minerals. Unlike EM, which can only detect relatively massive metallic mineral concentrations, IP can detect disseminated minerals as well. Therefore, IP is often used in exploring for porphyry copper and stockwork molybdenum deposits in which the metallic mineral constituents are widely dispersed in the rock.

A gravity meter measures very small changes in the earth's gravitational field. Because the field is proportional to the mass of the earth below the measurement point, bodies of heavier-than-normal rock, such as massive sulfide deposits, can be detected using this method.

In seismic surveys, a small shock wave is sent through the earth, and measurements are taken of the energy which comes back to the surface by reflection and refraction from boundaries between layers of different rock types. Seismic methods are used primarily in petroleum exploration to map potential hydrocarbon-bearing layered rocks, but are also used to a lesser extent in placer gold and coal exploration.

Radiometric methods are used to detect radioactive minerals. The products of uranium decay are alpha, beta, and gamma rays. The most penetrating are gamma rays, which are best detected by scintillometers. Geiger counters are less sensitive to gamma radiation than scintillometers. Selectivity and sensitivity are needed because several elements, e.g., potassium and thorium, also give off radiation which can be confused with that given off by uranium. A gamma ray spectrometer can distinguish between uranium, potassium, and thorium.

Radioactive particles can travel only a short distance through rock or air. The scintillometer is sensitive enough for airborne use, but the Geiger counter is not. Both methods can only detect radioactivity near the surface, as the rays will not pass through more than five feet of soil or rock.

The Exploration Process

With a background in the techniques used to look for mineral deposits and some understanding of the risk involved, we can now discuss how exploration is conducted in Alaska. The discussion will mainly cover exploration by mining companies because this represents the majority of the exploratory effort in Alaska. It should be noted, however, that a significant proportion of the important discoveries in Alaska have been made or contributed to by individual prospectors and government geologists.

Mineral exploration begins in the office with the development of a target concept. This may be conducted either before or after the decision by a company to explore for a particular type of deposit in Alaska. Why look for mineral deposits in Alaska, with its harsh climate, scant road system, scattered population centers, and large areas of environmentally sensitive land? There are three reasons. First, the drawbacks to exploration in Alaska mean that it is relatively unexplored, and there is the potential to discover major deposits near the surface. Second, the geology of Alaska is highly favorable for the occurrence of many types of mineral deposits. Third, Alaska has a number of recently discovered world-class mineral deposits — Quartz Hill, Arctic, and Red Dog, in particular — and the reasoning goes that where there are some, there may be more.

The target concept is developed by geologists through a review of published geologic reports and maps, comparison of descriptions of areas in Alaska with those of known mining districts, and visits to mineral prospects and potential exploration areas. This is known as the compilation period. It involves an extensive and detailed review of all the known literature on a particular area. The majority of the published geologic information in Alaska is from the U.S. Geological Survey and the Alaska Division of Geological and Geophysical Surveys. From all of this information an idea is developed that a particular area would be a good place to look for certain types of mineral deposits. The concept must then be sold to company management. An estimate of the cost of the program is made, and the funds are obtained.

In areas which have been poorly explored or have only a few known prospects, such as most of Alaska, the first stage of exploration is reconnaissance. In this stage large areas are covered in a short period of time at a relatively low cost

per unit area. Reconnaissance represents the highest risk in exploration since there is no guarantee of discovery. The most commonly used method of reconnaissance in Alaska is a combination of regional geochemical sampling, prospecting, and geology.

The helicopter has revolutionized mineral exploration in Alaska in the last 20 years. Previously, geologists spent most of their time on the logistical aspects of exploration, getting to and from the area, camp chores, etc. The helicopter maximizes the amount of time spent in actual exploration. Even though a helicopter is expensive, it results in lower exploration costs in terms of the amount of data collected and the area covered. The crew works out of tent camps which are moved from place to place throughout the season as the area is covered.

A typical crew consists of five or six geologists, a cook, and a helicopter pilot. The project supervisor is a geologist with eight or more years of experience. The other geologists on the crew will have varying levels of experience, and several may be college students majoring in geology who have been hired for the summer field season.

On reconnaissance programs stream sediment samples are collected over large areas, generally one sample for every square mile or so. Each geologist will collect 20 to 30 samples per day. At each site the sample location is plotted on a map, and observations are made of the stream's characteristics and geology. In

particular, boulders in the stream are examined for mineralization. The more experienced personnel participate in the geochemical sampling to a lesser extent and devote most of their time to examining the regional geology and looking for indications of mineralization. It is not unusual for a reconnaissance crew to cover several hundred square miles in a single season.

In the evenings after each day's work, the geologists plot their sample locations and geologic data on maps and make short reports. It is necessary to pull together the observations of the entire crew into a picture of the region. It is this picture which will be used to decide whether to continue exploration in the area. The geochemical samples are shipped off to a laboratory for analysis. When the analyses are complete, the data are sent back to the field as quickly as possible, usually in about two to three weeks. The geochemical data are plotted on overlays of maps of the area with the values coded either by colors or symbols so that anomalous areas can be identified. In some cases the crew has moved to another area by the time the analytical data have returned, so immediate follow-up is not possible. The identification of target areas, be they geochemical anomalies, favorable geology, or mineral showings, is the objective of reconnaissance.

The next phase of exploration, known as evaluation, begins with the identification of targets. Evaluation takes place in two stages: initial and follow-up, and detailed. Target areas identified during reconnaissance are followed up as soon as possible, often in the same field season. The initial evaluation consists of geologic mapping of the area, prospecting for mineralization, and detailed stream sediment sampling to localize geochemical anomalies. The results of the initial follow-up are generally unfortunate — no mineralization may be found, or the geochemical anomaly may turn out to be from an anomalous rock unit or a small mineral occurrence. In the process of exploration only 1% to 2% of the targets identified during reconnaissance prove to be worth detailed evaluation after the initial follow-up. This is one of the facts of mineral exploration — large areas of favorable ground yield relatively few good prospects.

The evaluation phase differs in many respects from reconnaissance. It is much more intensive, and much labor and money is spent on a small area, making the cost-per-unit-area high. The risk is lower than in reconnaissance, but still there is little guarantee of success.

Evaluation begins with detailed geologic mapping, in which surveyors lay out a grid over the prospect to provide location control for mapping and for soil sampling and geophysical surveys. Soil samples are collected on lines across the trend of the rocks. The first geophysical surveys are typically EM or magnetics. Outcrops are examined and carefully sampled to give an idea of the grade (richness) and thickness

Geologist Opal Adams gathers soil samples at the HP claims on Madman Creek on Admiralty Island. (Greg Fernette)

of the mineralization. Trenches are dug or blasted to expose unweathered rock for sampling. Prospect pits are dug on soil anomalies to locate mineralization. All of this work serves to localize the area of the search and to refine the target.

A most important refinement occurs at this stage. In the reconnaissance stage the target concept is geologic and may be very broad, e.g., volcanogenic massive sulfide deposits like those which occur in similar rocks in other parts of the world. After the initial evaluation, the geologist begins to talk about the potential size of the deposit which might occur at each prospect. The initial evaluation is designed to give an idea of the geologic setting, the type of mineralization, and, if possible, its thickness, length, and grade. From all of these, the probable deposit type, range of potential tonnage, and grade can be inferred. From this inference the decision is made to either proceed with further evaluation or drop the prospect. Again, more prospects are dropped than are pursued.

The key decision to be made, based on the initial evaluation, is whether or not to drill. Drilling gives a direct view of the subsurface and provides a means to go from a target to an actual testing of the grade and thickness of various portions of a deposit. Drilling is very expensive, often costing more than $100 per foot. As a result, considerable effort is put into refining the drill targets so that they can be tested in the most economical manner.

The first drill test, often known as

scout drilling, is done using lightweight drills which are moved into the prospect by helicopter if no roads exist. Several shallow holes are drilled to test the best targets or the strongest geochemical and geophysical anomalies. Many times the results of the drilling are different than expected, especially in areas of little outcrop, and the geologic interpretation must be changed. The first phase of drilling concentrates on establishing the validity of the target concept, that is, whether significant mineralization is present below the surface showings or anomalies. In most cases the results are not favorable, and the project is dropped. If the results are positive, however, additional drilling is recommended.

The second stage of drilling involves more holes and generally larger drills. In Alaska the drills are usually still moved by helicopter in the absence of roads, so that the environmental impact is minimal. The drilling steps out from the first few holes, as the objective now is to assess the size of the deposit. Holes may be drilled 200 to 800 feet apart. The work at this point is becoming very expensive, so it is necessary to determine if the deposit's potential makes it worth pursuing.

By now the target has gone from concept to reality. The tonnage and average grade are the two numbers which matter most in mining. The potential economic viability must be assessed. Samples of drill cores are sent to a laboratory for metallurgical testing to determine if there could be problems in

the separation of the mineral from the worthless material. Using the inferred grade and tonnage (ore reserves at this point are not proven) and the metallurgical data, a preliminary economic feasibility study is completed. A study of this type is done by using analogies with similar deposits.

The preliminary feasibility study is a major step in the evaluation of a prospect, for it is here that company financial goals exert their strongest influence. All companies require a certain minimum rate of return. If the prospect cannot meet the goal, it is rejected.

The amount of money expended to this point is relatively small, although the risk is still fairly high. A typical reconnaissance program as described here and covering a relatively large area may cost $300,000 to $800,000, including pre- and post-field season costs. A preliminary drilling program involving 2,000 feet of drilling takes about one month and costs $150,000 to $300,000. Bear in mind that this amount is spent on a small area. A larger-scale drilling assessment, with metallurgical tests and a preliminary feasibility study, may cost several million dollars. The next step, final evaluation, is considerably more expensive.

If the preliminary feasibility study shows that the prospect will meet the company's investment criteria, the program proceeds to a full-scale evaluation. The final evaluation consists of several major elements. First the ore reserves must be

Drenched by the notorious rains of southeastern Alaska, a geologist carries on with his sampling of the Tracy Prospect at Tracy Arm south of Juneau. (Greg Fernette)

— 83

proven. This involves sampling the deposit with regularly spaced drill holes, so that the tonnage and grade can be accurately estimated. The sampling density must be such that a major part of the reserves can be classed as proven.

Proving reserves by drilling involves some problems. A drill core is only a few inches in diameter, and in some cases may not give a reliable estimate of the average grade of the surrounding rock, particularly for irregularly mineralized rock. Bulk sampling is done to check the grade and to provide a large sample for metallurgical testing. Bulk samples are collected by driving underground workings or large trenches into the deposit. The rock removed is sampled, and the bulk grade compared with the drill hole grade.

The bulk samples are also used for metallurgical testing. Large samples are sent to laboratories with scaled-down processing plants, known as pilot plants. The results of the pilot plant work will be used to design the mill (processing plant) which may be built at or near the mine site. The size of the bulk sample varies with the type of deposit. Bulk samples from massive sulfide deposits are generally 10 to 200 tons. Much larger samples, up to 20,000 tons, are needed from porphyry copper and molybdenum deposits because of their low grade and disseminated

Dr. Charles Hawley examines granite with a scintillometer at Serpentine Hot Springs on the Seward Peninsula. (Mark McDermott)

mineralization. The key factor is that the bulk sample must be representative of ore that will be mined.

While the ore reserves are being proven and the bulk samples collected, engineering data, site surveys, and environmental baseline studies are conducted; and the process for obtaining the government permits necessary for mine development is begun.

The cost of exploration to this point may be $5 to $40 million for a large deposit. The next step is the final feasibility study. All of the technical data gathered so far are used to produce a mine design. Definitive cost estimates are made by obtaining actual bids. Marketing surveys are made to see if the product is salable. The technical and cost data are then used to estimate the capital outlay (the start-up cost to put the mine into production), the operating costs, and the rate of return. Such a study takes six months to a year and costs $1 to $2 million. Based on the results of the study, the company may or may not proceed with mine development.

Even with a favorable feasibility study it may not be possible to obtain the money necessary for the project. Putting a mine into production is very expensive. A small underground mine and related facilities may cost from $2 to $20 million; larger underground mines cost $50 to $100 million; and large open-pit or block cave operations cost $500 million or more. As stated previously, the risk is high. The experience of numerous companies has shown that out of every 1,000 prospects less than five will eventually go into actual production.

Alaska is in the decision-making stage.

Several deposits, among them Quartz Hill, east of Ketchikan, and Greens Creek, on Admiralty Island, have had positive feasibility studies and are apparently proceeding toward production. Several others have had preliminary feasibility studies and are being explored further — Lik, in the De Long Mountains; Yakobi Island, in southeastern Alaska; and Alaska Asbestos, near Eagle. Still others, such as Lost River, northwest of Nome, and Arctic and Sun, both east of the Lik deposit, have had full feasibility studies and are awaiting development of other nearby deposits, improvement in accessibility or changes in market factors to proceed.

Given the importance of the deposits discovered already and the potential for additional discoveries, Alaska is certainly on the verge of becoming a major mining state.

Geophysicist Chris Hrabak explores for minerals in the Alaska Range with this Hughes 500-D helicopter, the workhorse of Alaska mineral exploration. (Mark McDermott)

Who Owns Alaska?

Land Status and Mineral Exploration

Prior to statehood, the federal goverment owned and controlled virtually all the land and waters in Alaska — some 375 million acres. With passage of the Alaska Statehood Act in 1958, the state was granted the right to select approximately 104 million acres of land during the following 25 years. The state chose its land slowly and by 1968 had selected only about 26 million acres. In 1971, the Alaska Native Claims Settlement Act (ANCSA) granted a land entitlement of almost 44 million acres to Alaska's Natives. ANCSA also provided, in Section 17(d)(2), for the withdrawal of up to 80 million acres of unreserved public land for possible addition to or creation of units of the national park, forest, wildlife refuge, and wild and scenic rivers systems. After nine years of controversy, most of these

---

Editor's note: *This excerpt is from* Permit Guidelines for the Mineral Industry in Alaska, *prepared by Jami Fernette of WGM Inc., for the State of Alaska.*

(d)(2) lands, plus an additional 25 to 30 million acres, were ultimately included in the Alaska National Interest Lands Conservation Act (ANILCA) of 1980, as conservation units closed to mineral entry. This act also provided for an additional 10-year period for the state to select its Statehood Act entitlement.

Knowledge of land status prior to commencement of an exploration program is necessary not only to avoid loss of time and money incurred by exploring on closed lands, but also to determine which laws or regulations apply to mineral rights which may be acquired by discovery or under prospecting or exploration permits and licenses. Land status is also important when researching the title of a mineral interest held by another party.

Despite the controversy surrounding the Alaska lands issue, approximately half of the area of the state, including various federal, state, and native lands, totaling roughly 180 million acres, may be available for mineral development. Most state public lands, administered by the departments of Natural Resources, Environmental Conservation, and Fish and Game, are available for leasing and/or claim location. Some federal lands administered by the Bureau of Land Management (BLM) and U.S. Forest Service are open to location of metalliferous minerals, and are gradually being made available for mineral leasing. Native lands may become available for development through private arrangements with the appropriate native corporation(s). However, as a result of ANCSA and the final settlement in ANILCA, a considerable amount of land with high mineral potential and known deposits remains closed to exploration.

Lands in Alaska which are closed to mineral exploration include: (1) federal withdrawals for units of the national conservation system, including parks, refuges, monuments, and wild and scenic rivers; (2) military reservations; (3) National Petroleum Reserve-Alaska; (4) various utility withdrawals for pipelines, hydroelectric dams, etc; and (5) withdrawals for native selection either not selected or not yet identified for conveyance. All of the land withdrawals in Alaska must take into account prior existing rights, such as valid mining claims staked while the land was in another classification.

Laws and regulations governing mineral location vary with the status of the land. Rights to metalliferous minerals on open federal lands are acquired by staking of mining claims according to the same general mining laws applied to federal lands in other states. These laws, covering metals such as gold, copper, and zinc, are specified in Title 30 of the U.S. Code, Title 43 of the Code of Federal Regulations, and Title 27 of the Alaska Statutes. Solid fuels, such as coal, lignite, and oil shale, and industrial minerals, e.g., limestone and sand and gravel, must be leased or purchased according to methods prescribed in Title 43 of the Code of Federal Regulations.

Mining rights on Alaska state lands for minerals which, in 1959, were subject to location under the general United States mining laws are governed mainly according to provisions in Title 38 of the Alaska Statutes and Title II, Chapter 86, of the Alaska Administrative Code. Provisions for leasing are provided in Chapters 84

and 85 and for salable minerals in Chapter 76 (or 71 for draft revised regulations).

Patented and tentatively approved state selections are transferred by BLM to the state for administration, and state mining claims may be staked on these lands. Lands which have only been selected by the state but not tentatively approved are still under BLM jurisdiction, and are, in the view of BLM, closed to mineral entry. Nevertheless, the state has indicated that it will honor state mining claims staked on selected lands when, and if, tentative approval is eventually received. Thus, despite the element of risk, the mineral exploration community in Alaska is conducting reconnaissance, staking, and advanced exploration programs on state selected lands. The risk element on state selected lands is generally considered to be small, except in areas where state selections are in conflict with other withdrawals (e.g., for native selection or new conservation units). If a state selection is disallowed or relinquished as an overselection, BLM will consider any state mining claims staked on the ground in the interim to be invalid.

Exploration and development activities on native selections prior to conveyance or interim conveyance are under BLM jurisdiction. BLM does not approve access by non-Natives to these lands without concurrence of the appropriate native corporation(s). Many native corporations made substantial overselections and have used the subsequent years to prioritize the lands before the Department of Interior forces relinquishment of the overselections. Following conveyance, development activities are governed by the native corporations. As with all private landowners, the state and federal agencies and municipal or borough governments retain their influence where development may impact air and water quality, socioeconomic conditions, or planning for infrastructure.

Further information on land status can be obtained from the Bureau of Land Management (P.O. Box 13, Anchorage, Alaska 99513 or P.O. Box 1150, Fairbanks, Alaska 99707) or from the State of Alaska, Division of Land and Water Management (Pouch 7-005, Anchorage, Alaska 99510).

Prospecting Alaska

The Story of Riz Bigelow

Red Dog Comes of Life

In February, 1982, the press announced a historic agreement between Cominco, the north's premier mining company, and NANA, Inc., one of the 12 Alaska Native regional corporations. The objective of the agreement is to evaluate and develop the great Red Dog deposit in the new Wulik River mineral district above the Arctic Circle in northwestern Alaska, and it is with this most recent great minerals event that I propose to start my journey through time.

Indicated reserves based on 39 Cominco drill holes are reported at 85 million tons of 17% zinc, 5% lead, and 2.4 ounces per ton silver, and the deposit is open for additional reserves. I can think of no

Editor's note: *In any discussion of minerals exploration in Alaska, a few names always come to mind. C.G. (Riz) Bigelow is one of those names, and this is his account of his involvement for three decades in exploring for Alaska's mineral wealth.*

comparable deposit in the world. Reaction has varied from labeling Red Dog the best lead-zinc discovery ever to the most significant discovery of the last 20 years. The discovery's value, calculated at winter 1981-1982 prices, has been estimated at $15 to $20 billion.

As with most major mineral discoveries, many people were involved in the evaluation, acquisition, and successful negotiation of an agreement regarding Red Dog. While recognizing this, the person who comes immediately to my mind is John Schaeffer, current president of NANA. When I first met John in the early 1960s, he was involved in another mining venture under entirely different circumstances. John was a young worker at the B&R Tug and Barge dock in Kotzebue, while I was with Kennecott Copper Corporation. The occasion was the first major mine plant mobilization up the Kobuk River to Bornite. Ten years later, I would work for John on a rapid minerals reconnaissance of withdrawn lands from which NANA would eventually select its land entitlement. Unfortunately, the

withdrawn land boundaries stopped short of Red Dog, and the massive lead-zinc sulfides remained undiscovered.

The seeds of discovery were planted in the 1960s by Irv Tailleur of the U.S. Geological Survey. An inveterate wanderer of the Brooks Range, Irv discovered barite and a lead-zinc anomaly in a creek bed loaded with red-to-orange, iron oxide-stained gravels. He apparently named the creek after a red dog owned by Bob Baker, highly respected bush pilot out of Kotzebue. Bob had been curious about the gaudy red-staining in the creek.

The Tailleur anomaly was described in a 1970 U.S. Geological Survey Open File Report, but industry response was hardly enthusiastic. The only major mining company active in the western Brooks Range at the time was my employer, Bear Creek Mining Company. As an employee of the exploration subsidiary of

Drill core samples taken from the Arctic deposit in 1967 show brass-colored high-grade copper-zinc mineralization. (Riz Bigelow)

Kennecott, the world's greatest copper mining company, lead and zinc were not on my approved shopping list. Additionally, Bear Creek was retrenching, and my resources were committed to the newly discovered Ambler district, 200 miles to the east. No company in the state was interested in following up a remote lead-zinc anomaly, at least to the point of staking.

The failure of prospectors to respond almost led to dire consequences for in March, 1972, the federal government included the deposit in its Brooks Range withdrawal. Subsequent events would remove the withdrawal restriction at Red Dog itself.

Senator Ted Stevens managed to pry a miniscule $300,000 loose from the government in 1974 for a U.S. Bureau of Mines program to evaluate the entire 19-million-acre withdrawal. John Mulligan, pioneering head of the Alaska division of the Bureau of Mines, set the parameters for my company, WGM, the consulting firm selected to execute the field program. I worked with John and his staff on establishing priorities, an exercise which placed Red Dog near the top of the list.

In 1975, Clint Degenhart and Bob Griffis, WGM project geologists, finally discovered the spectacular Red Dog massive zinc-lead-silver sulfide mineralization responsible for the metallic poisoning and coloration of Red Dog Creek. Based on a rapid surface examination, our guesstimate was 15.6% zinc, 5.4% lead, and 2.2 ounces per ton silver for the massive sulfides, with 768,000 tons per vertical foot. Assuming a thickness of 100 feet, the tonnage would be more than 70 million.

All Things Alaskan Start with Gold

If memory fails me on some dates as I regress to the beginning of my personal mining adventures in Alaska, the events nevertheless happened. Some of the recollections relate to significant mining adventures, and others are people oriented. So many people have helped and shared in my accomplishments or pleasures, that all I can do is mention a few, perhaps as examples. Many others could as appropriately have been mentioned.

Fairbanks in June, 1952, presented the aura of a new gold rush. The streets were full of wealth-seeking newcomers, many recently arrived from depressed areas in the Lower 48. However, the 1952 rush to Fairbanks was not to the nearby gold

A triumphant Riz Bigelow stakes a claim in the Brooks Range in 1975. (Paul Skyllingstad)

fields, but to government construction projects purportedly paying windfall wages. In 1952, as in the great gold strikes of an earlier time, the vast majority of hopefuls found to their dismay that the excitement in the streets didn't pay the bills.

Like many of the cheechako job seekers, Jack Wood and I arrived on bald tires with a residual cache of hardtack and peanut butter, empty billfolds, and high hopes for big bucks. The prospects offered me the promise of being able to complete college while feeding a growing family.

With no idea of where the jobs were being dispensed, our first stop was the Fairbanks Bar, where we traded our last cash for a celebration toast and information. There, we learned that hiring hall doors were jammed by a cast of thousands. With the other cheechakos, we arrived in the midst of a prolonged construction union strike. The helpful bartender said our best chance was to haunt the Fairbanks Exploration Company hiring hall out on the Steese Highway, since they paid bottom dollar, and accordingly were least popular among the restless throng.

With no delay, we joined the maddening crowd at the company's office which to this day closely resembles a cement blockhouse or jail. Periodically, a guy in the cage would shout, "No jobs today!" Some would then move on while others lingered around just in case, ourselves included. Rarely, the shout would come out for a catskinner, welder, or electrician, immediately resulting in a scramble to be first in line. Jack and I took so much of this, and finally agreed that one of us was an expert at whatever they wanted next time around, as long as it wasn't an electrician.

The next time came after we had been in the throng for about three days. The shout was "Catskinner-shoreman!" Jack was first to the cage, and a new catskinner was born. After successfully parrying the more intense questions, he signed up, and we were on our way up the Steese Highway, across Cleary Summit, and on to the El Dorado Creek placer. With one job in hand we could both eat, buy tires, and wait it out for my job to come.

While Jack was being briefed by Ralph Strom, the dredgemaster, I chatted with a winchman (dredge captain), Bob Owen. Conversation revealed that his folks were neighbors of my folks in the country north of Bellingham, Washington. His father, being down on his luck with a bad heart, had written him about a neighbor kid who was mowing the lawn, doing chores, and visiting over iced teas. The kid turned out to be me. Owen pushed the dredgemaster to put in a request for an additional employee to the hiring hall. Within three days I also became a fledgling shoreman on the Goldstream dredge.

Varied experiences during the first seven months on a gold dredge crew fixed my resolve to complete college, and embark on a mining career, in Alaska I hoped.

Geologists drill hole number 7 at Lik, a massive zinc-lead-silver deposit named for the nearby Wulik River. (Gaylord Cleveland, courtesy of Riz Bigelow)

The complex dredging operations were fascinating. The hydraulicking crew came first to blast the frozen muck off mineralized gravels, to be followed by the thawing crew who drove hollow points into the gravel through which water or steam was circulated to thaw the ground. The dredge, weighing 1,300 tons or more came next, floating in its own pond as its buckets chewed their way across and ahead into the now-thawed pay dirt. The water, upon which all else depended, was released into the dredge ponds from a supply ditch many tens of miles long, and maintained by a permanent ditch crew. Electricity to power the dredges was transmitted by lines connected to a coal-fired power plant near Fairbanks. The coal, in turn, was supplied by the Usibelli family from their Healy mine.

The gold-bearing gravels were dug out of the thawed bank by a continuous bucket line, and dropped into the dredge trommel to be broken up by high pressure water jets. The dislodged coarse material (waste) then traveled along an endless belt up the stack at the back of the dredge, to be dropped as high gravel ridges or tailings piles. The tailings piles in many areas subsequently were leveled off and used for roads, homes, gardens, etc., in areas formerly covered by worthless muck and swamp. The gold-bearing, finer-

The massive Lik deposit crosses this photo from right to left, between the water tank in the extreme right foreground and the camp.
(Gaylord Cleveland, courtesy of Riz Bigelow)

grained sediment broken loose in the bowels of the dredge passed over riffled tables where the gold flakes would drop out. The lighter sand and silt continued over the top of the tables and into the pond.

Periodically there would be a cleanup, during which employees would be exposed to the glitter of the quicksilver coating. The amalgam (gold-mercury) collected was put in small, stout boxes, and transported by pickup to Fairbanks where the gold was liberated from the mercury. The cleanups, once every two weeks, produced up to $250,000 or more in gold at the 1950s price of $35 per ounce.

The mechanics of the operation were strong stuff, but no more so than exposure to the many oldtimers finishing out their working lives on dredges. The dredges themselves were soon to be shutting down for good. The last big Fairbanks dredge closed in the 1950s because of increasing costs in the face of the artificially low fixed gold price.

Many of the oldtimers on the dredge crews had been among the original cast of characters who prospected, panned, and sluiced for gold wherever the latest strike was reported in the early days of the century. They recalled wide-open shantytowns, gold dust on the bars and counters, pleasure shacks (which were still common to Fairbanks in 1952), stores, new strikes, and broken dreams interspersed with periods of optimistic anticipation. Colorful names were still in

vogue, such as Paddy, Old Crow and Whiskey Bob (both aptly named), Blacky, Scotty, the Finn, California, and Shake-em-up, so-named for his propensity for pan, the traditional card game of Fairbanks saloons. To the best of my knowledge, many had no other names, and their origins were forgotten. Each possessed his own unique style or character, a placer about to make him rich in some remote valley, and fascinating tales of days long since gone.

The tales they reminisced about were inexhaustible, and chronically fortified with embellishments. Feats of remarkable endurance, often verified, formed a mainstay, as did wistful stories of being beaten out on the big one. Typical of the former was one of many stories about Ralph Strom, the bearlike dredgemaster at El Dorado. On a night in the early 1920s, with the temperature at -40°F and falling, he took off from a Fairbanks district saloon or store laden with a 120-pound pack. His objective was to ski to his Circle district placer some 90 miles distant. Bets were taken, with odds against his pulling through. The longshot players, of course, wound up winners. His only payoff was to still be alive since the placer was a bust. He told me later that he made it to Circle simply by not stopping, and if he'd known the odds being given, he would never have left.

Among the storied old districts were placers on the south slope of the Brooks Range, some still active but many long since abandoned. With few exceptions, such as Wiseman and Chandalar, most proved too lean to provide sustenance for long, and more commonly provided little sustenance at all. But descriptions of the great mountain range to the north suggested the possibility of mineral riches never seen. The only metal sought to the north was gold; any others remained untouched and mainly unsought up to the early 1950s. There were vague reports of something happening at a new copper prospect far to the west in the Kobuk valley, but little other news came from the north. I had no inkling when listening to these stories that one day I would carry out the first systematic multi-minerals exploration across hundreds of miles of the Brooks Range.

I returned to Washington at the end of the winter overhaul of the dredges in early 1953. However, by the mid-1950s, freshly armed with a geology degree, I was back in Alaska on the first biogeochemical nickel-copper research program in the southeastern Alaska rain forest. The major accomplishments of my senior partner and I were learning the Latin names for the conifers we sampled, picking out devil's club barbs, falling down slippery moss-covered slopes, discovering that the prospect area we were investigating had been staked by others, and maintaining sufficient civility to survive chronically wet clothes and sleeping bags without meting out bodily harm. We also learned something about geochemistry. Lessons learned during these years were to prove of value years later when I would be involved in what were destined to be major northern discoveries, including the nearby Greens Creek deposit on northern Admiralty Island.

The Brooks Range Calls

By spring, 1959, I counted myself among the herd of dispossessed mining geologists, and I was marking time in Bellingham selecting dam and tunnel locations in the Cascades for the city water supply. The cause of my plight was the demise of the great uranium boom of the 1950s, a bust which put hundreds of geologists out of work. Like many others, I bought lots of stamps, and mailed hopeful letters to many companies. Fortune smiled on me when my old Bear Creek Mining Company boss, Russell Chadwick, called. (Bear Creek is the minerals exploration division of the Kennecott Copper Corporation.) In about five minutes, he told me about a temporary assignment at some deposit called Ruby Creek (later called Bornite), 15 miles north of a village called Kobuk, in the Brooks Range. Before he could ask, I accepted. I was finally on my way to that mysterious range the oldtimers had described some years before.

My instructions were to meet a miner-catskinner named Al Stout. He was waiting for the go-ahead to open a road from the Dahl Creek airstrip to the Ruby Creek camp, to pave the way for the pending Bear Creek mobilization. I was to pass on the message confirming that Al should open the road, and assist or keep out of the way on the snow plowing venture, whichever was appropriate.

As the ski-equipped Cessna continued its weekly mail run eastward from Kotzebue to villages along the Kobuk River, the seemingly endless snow-covered slopes of the Brooks Range were etched against the clear March sky. They appeared as the most beautifully severe backdrop imaginable, an impression which remains to this day. I wondered about the treasures they might yield. The partial answers to come in the next two decades would prove startling.

The Brooks Range I first viewed some 23 years ago held the promise of satisfying a variety of needs for adventurers from all walks of life. The land withdrawals which would end mineral entry in the area were years away, but unbeknownst to us, powerful forces were girding for action. Time was even then running out on the miners, prospectors, trappers, guides, local entrepreneurs, and homesteaders in various other mountain regions like the Brooks Range. Geologists, who are more at home in wilderness than in the corridors of Washington, D.C., would prove to be meat for the grinder when matched up against the professional lobbyists and politicians destined to carve up the wilderness.

Piloted by the late John Cross, one of that storied group of early-day bush pilots, the plane settled on the river ice before Kobuk, the end of the line and my destination. The small picturesque village is nestled between the Kobuk River on the south and an oxbow lake marking an old river channel on the north.

I disembarked, clad in loafers, sport coat, and slacks. The temperature was -20°F. Tony and May Bernhardt, the Eskimo couple who ran the local store, hustled me into their home for local introductions, comments on Arctic attire, food, drink, and conversation. Tony in the years to come would contribute substantially to the success of my exploration programs. He would subsequently become an expert bush pilot, guide, and Alaska's champion wolf hunter.

My first impression of the Kobuk region was that it must have looked about the same as it always had, aside from a truck seen at Kiana, and the mail plane. However, there was a radio at each village, albeit unreliable. Nurses, dentists, and missionaries periodically visited the villages, or waited in Kotzebue for the villagers to come to them. Each village had an elementary school. Kotzebue boasted a regional hospital, Standard Oil dealership, B&R Tug and Barge, and other facilities common to a regional supply center. A few placer and jade miners were scattered around the hinterland. The local National Guard headquarters at Shungnak was ably led by Levy Cleveland who was to become proficient at surveying as well as other occupations on the Ruby Creek project. Each village had a private or cooperative general store.

Hunting and fishing were mainstays, as they are today. Seal oil was brought upriver in skins on the annual supply barge, with staples and other general merchandise. Many people still burned wood in their stoves, with stove oil phasing in. The dog sled reigned supreme in the winter, and narrow river boats provided transportation in the summer. There were boats with outboard motors on the river, but few in number compared to future years. Snowmachines were yet to come. People still lounged and visited on the high cutbanks on quiet evenings, and neighbors traveled ten to hundreds of miles by dog team or boat to renew acquaintances.

The literature of 1959 contained no references to a Prudhoe Bay oil bonanza, or a road to the Arctic Ocean. Texas accents were conspicuous by their absence, and there was a paucity of Sierra Clubbers or anyone else in the Brooks Range. Once in a while a state official would appear in a camp, but normally they stopped at the villages. I recall seeing no Bureau of Land Management personnel in my early Brooks Range years.

The history of the Kotzebue Basin, including the turn-of-the-century gold rushes, has been amply reviewed in the literature, most recently in *ALASKA GEOGRAPHIC®* (Vol. 8, No. 3). According to Al Stout, gold did not exactly ooze out of most upper Kobuk placer gravels. Many were lean, and the digging conditions of at least some vere dreadful. Lacking heavy equipment, the oldtimers had no chance to maximize gold recovery in many basins because of the presence of large boulders intermixed with the pay dirt.

Clint Degenhart stands on a discovery outcrop of massive lead-zinc mineralization at the Red Dog deposit, which he and Bob Griffis, WGM project geologist, discovered in 1975.
(Gaylord Cleveland, courtesy of Riz Bigelow)

— 95

Harry Brown, local fur trader since pre-1920 days, reminisced to me about the problem of the early miners, including those who went out to the bush never to return. For example, one early miner tried placer and lode gold mining in the Ruby Creek area. Tailings piles along the Jay Creek tributary remain as a monument to his prodigious hand-tool efforts before and during the Great Depression. (At one time I also tried working the Jay Creek placer with two companions. Four all-night sessions of sluicing yielded a total of $1.70 in gold, and two of us attribute the disappearance of even this modest payoff to our partner. We later paid him back by salting gravel with brass which he worked for a short period of time.)

The oldtimer who finally gave up on the Jay Creek placer may have been the miner who dug tunnels and shafts into the bedrock at and near Ruby Creek and Pardner Hill, searching for hypothetical lode gold deposits. In due course, he gave up entirely on the Ruby Creek basin, packed his meager belongings and trudged several miles east to the Kogoluktuk River to work placers not already taken up by others. Harry Brown and local Eskimos began to worry when he failed to come in for resupply, and finally one of them went out to the camp to see if he needed help. The finding was grim. The miner had

cashed it in by his own hand, with a farewell message in his hand: "I'm moving west." Harry said, "None of us could ever figure out why he wanted to go west; he knew there was no gold over there."

Going to Ruby Creek (Bornite)

In the late 1940s, the basis for the modern era of Brooks Range minerals exploration was laid by Rhiny Berg, a man with grit, imagination, and hope. With his traveling companion, Joe Sun, from the nearby village of Shungnak, Berg explored various portions of the southwestern Brooks Range, and most significantly the Cosmos Hills outlier, where Ruby Creek is located. While following up a minor uranium anomaly in a rock fracture which is still exposed, Berg investigated the old Ruby Creek shafts noted above. Instead of uranium he found gaudy blue and green copper minerals coating the rocks. The oldtimer who gave up decades before had found the prospective riches he was after, but unfortunately either failed to recognize copper, or considered the area too remote to exploit for anything but gold. If the latter was the reason, he may well have been right, for the time was the 1930s. Further exploration by Berg led to additional Cosmos Hills discoveries, and he soon had claims at the nearby Pardner Hill, Aurora Mountain, and Lone Mountain copper occurrences, as well as Ruby Creek.

After further work with hand tools, Jack Bullock of B&R Tug and Barge sent up a decrepit D-7 Cat and diamond core drill to

help Rhiny, his old World War II compatriot. Bullock became a partner in the process. Others who contributed to the project were also given interests in one of the properties. Joe Sun became the catskinner, and Rhiny reportedly walked beside the old Cat to advise Joe when the tracks were falling off. By 1956, a substantial outcropping of copper mineralization uncovered by Rhiny was shown to Russell Chadwick, dynamic senior geologist for the Bear Creek Mining Company. In time, an agreement was struck, and Rhiny and friends received their just payment.

The Bear Creek involvement marked the third event on the road to recognition of world-class base/precious metals occurrences in the western Brooks Range, the first two being provided by the early gold miner and Rhiny Berg.

By 1958, Chadwick concluded that the copper was in some kind of ancient coral reef complex and dreams of favorable reef facies (environments) enriched with copper were being entertained. Norm Lutz, who replaced Chadwick as project manager for 1959, was no newcomer to Alaska, being fresh off Wrangell Mountains exploration on the eastern side of the state. It was at this late date that I appeared on the scene.

Tony and May Bernhardt had pretty well filled me in on the local background towards evening, when Al Stout arrived in Kobuk with his Cat, picked up grub, and pronounced me fit to ride on the back of the Cat or walk the four miles to Dahl Creek. Aside from minor frostbite,

The rolling De Long Mountains, at the western end of the Brooks Range, are the site of two major lead-zinc-silver deposits — Red Dog and Lik. (Gaylord Cleveland, courtesy of Riz Bigelow)

the trip was uneventful, except for the scenery of the sweeping valley and surrounding hill-country spectacularly displayed in brilliant sunshine.

Stout was to be called on increasingly in years to come by Bear Creek, and later the Kennecott mining division, for cattraining, road construction, and trenching. He came into the Kobuk not to work for others, but to work the boulder-strewn Dahl Creek placer with a D-8 bulldozer and sluice box setup. The project led to significant gold production, albeit at the cost of a constant physical battering and high maintenance expenses. Al came across the state from the famed Fortymile district to which he had emigrated in the late 1920s. His past is as colorful as the country, including a rich history of traplines; mechanicking; cattraining across the eastern Brooks Range on the DEW line program; his first love, placer mining; and anything else required to make ends meet. (As an example of the hardiness of the early pioneers, he and his future wife Roberta recalled 70-mile hikes from Chicken to Eagle on the Yukon to attend Saturday night dances.) When the gold pretty well played out in Dahl Creek during the 1960s, Al switched to mining, sawing, and shipping out jade boulders found in the creek. The most recent jade miner on the claims is Ivan Stewart, a prominent Anchorage retailer who often takes gem and rock collectors to the creek. He operates out of the Dahl Creek cabin which I owned for a while.

Although far from being the most complex, my first Arctic mobilization had its moments. After several days of plowing deep snow, we finally broke through to the Ruby Creek tent camp site in blizzard conditions. Unfortunately the bulldozer quit, and we faced the 12-mile walk back to Dahl Creek along a trail blown full of granular snow. This wouldn't have been disturbing except Al was in the fever stage of an influenza attack while I was emerging from the same. Snowshoes being of no use since the snow sifted through the webbing, we waded and coughed our way out. At Dahl Creek, we remembered that the only grub left consisted of a tin of tea cached by an oldtimer several decades before.

By now Al was bedridden, so I took off for Kobuk during a lull in the blizzard, intending to follow the Cat trail. About two miles out, the blizzard struck again with ferocity. Whatever trail there was disappeared. Being confused, I burrowed into a drift. Not knowing if the ensuing warmth was real or illusion, I got up and pressed on toward Kobuk, some two miles distant. In time, I came to a flat, white expanse of what looked like the Kobuk River, my dilemma being whether to go up or down stream. By this time, I was pretty well beaten down and hardly up to pressing on in either direction. I walked out into the flat, hoping to find a dog sled trail. The wind let up briefly, and I found myself standing on the oxbow lake at the edge of Kobuk village.

My second appearance at the Bernhardts was hardly more auspicious than the first, although a change of clothes did give me the appearance of belonging. Once again, I was treated to Kobuk hospitality, this time laced with a good jolt of bourbon. With more history from Harry Brown and a meal under my belt, I left as the weather broke, and returned to Dahl Creek with a packboard of grub and a welcome letter to Al from Roberta advising him of her pending arrival, which meant superb cooking was on the way.

Assisted by nips of spirits some kind neighbor had cached in the pack at Kobuk, Al was sufficiently improved the next morning for us to walk back to Ruby Creek, get the Cat going, and start reopening the road. Within two or three days our preparatory job was done. Since the mobilization was still days off, we puttered around and cut up a frozen caribou given us by Leonard Douglas of Shungnak. Leonard often helped Al with mechanicking. Roberta showed up on schedule, and the meals took a dramatic turn for the better.

A few days later assorted geologists, cooks, drillers, laborers, and other staff landed at Dahl Creek or walked up from Shungnak and Kobuk, piled onto the go-devils (small freight sleds), and traveled to Ruby Creek to dig out the tents, move in, and get a hot meal. Andy Anderson, to us the gray eagle of the north, commenced

Geologists examine the rugged Bond Creek porphyry copper deposit in the Wrangell Mountains in 1970. (Joe Ruzicka, courtesy of Riz Bigelow)

Clint Degenhart stands in front of one of several copper discoveries he and the author made in the 1960s in the Chandalar region, 200 miles north of Fairbanks. (Riz Bigelow)

with another of his seasons of flying supplies, people, and samples from and to the Bettles staging area 130 miles to the east. The fixed wing support adventures of Andy would in themselves make true tall tales. During one period he supplied the entire 60-man camp and drilling operations with a single Cessna 180 as well as handling his other extensive bush business. My guess is he flew more hours in many days and weeks than he could be prevailed upon to remember.

The typical role of a newly hired assistant geologist (in this case, me) was distinctly labor-oriented in the 1950s, with technical responsibilities being gradually added on. As the rock bottom wage earner at camp, the assistant geologist obviously would start at the bottom of the labor heap, and stay there until season's end, with the carrot being a chance at re-hire and advancement to a technical position. It is a system which encourages diligence, particularly considering the tight job situation in 1959. The Ruby Creek project was no different.

My first mandatory Ruby Creek assignments included tent frame construction, rough plumbing, wiring and mechanicking, core handling, rock sampling, surveying, and substituting as a drill helper when one of the crew was sick. The work schedule for assistant geologists was 9 to 10 hours a day or more, 13 days on and one day off. In the evenings, I was able to map local outcrops, work on geologic sections and maps, and help the senior geologist log core samples.

In early August, my prospects took a sudden turn for the better when the senior core logger decided for his own good reasons to transfer to the Lower 48. Having previously been told that core logging provides the best experience there is, I volunteered to fill the gap until another permanent geologist could be transferred north. Corporate philosophy was that core logging is the most critical aspect of any drilling project, particularly in complex geologic environments such as Ruby Creek.

Core logging introduced me to a world unseen in Arctic climates, namely an ancient reef washed by a tropical sea. In several respects, the Ruby Creek reef complex I commenced to study is similar to modern-day reefs, such as the Bahamas, Florida Keys, South Pacific island atolls, and the Great Barrier Reef off the Australian coast. Obviously, either the Brooks Range region has suffered considerable climatic change since that ancient reef-building era, or the range isn't where it used to be. Current concepts hold that the ancient rock formations rafted thousands of miles northward into the Arctic from hospitable tropic regions millions of years ago. The greatest reefs in the world were built during the Devonian period, which occurred about 350 to 400 million years ago, and the Cosmos Hills complex, including Ruby Creek, is one of these reefs.

My detailed studies of more than 100,000 feet of drill core extracted from the Ruby Creek reef led to recognition of a clear transition from limestone sand deposited on the open ocean shelf or platform bottom to a steep reef front built in shallow water. The front was flanked on the open water side by a jumbled breccia zone formed from debris ripped off the reef front by violent wave action, probably abetted by voracious fish who bit off chunks of reef to get at organisms hiding inside. The reef-building corals, algae, and other creatures and the sea waged a constant battle with one another, the organisms building and the sea tearing apart. Fine-grained debris from the battered reef front was washed inward to be deposited in protected water or lagoons behind the reef front barrier, forming mud flats similar to those found in the protected waters of modern-day reef fronts. The reef front formed a sinuous, narrow buttress which separated the open sea sediment on one side from protected water sediment on the other.

The richest copper mineralization at Ruby Creek occurs within the reef front breccia and the reef front itself, with lower grades in the layered rocks deposited on the lagoon or protected water side of the reef. I found small nodules of hardened petroleum material (anthraxolite) in the reef, some of it enclosing bright copper minerals. But oil, which may have been present in ancient times, has long since been driven away.

From 1960 to 1962, I continued logging core; calculating reserves; working out the reef structure; and, with Lutz, plotting drilling strategy. It proved difficult to hit drill targets in the deeper portions of the deposit because the drill bits wandered away in one or more directions as the hole was drilled. In some cases, the bottom of the drill holes, rather than being directly under the collars, would be hundreds of feet distant, and some wound around like corkscrews. Special surveying equipment was lowered down the holes to determine the location at various depths. The wandering habit of drill holes obviously complicated attempts to correlate rocks and mineralization from one part of the deposit to another. Out of frustration, I finally worked with computer experts, who programmed the data so that a computer-controlled plotter could draw geologic and mineral maps across the drilled area at any depth I wanted. This provided the necessary technique for tracing the sinuous pattern of high-grade copper-bearing trends.

By 1961, the project had grown substantially in the face of positive drilling results. Chadwick's preliminary calculation of Ruby Creek reserves showed about 70 million tons of 1.2% copper, with minor silver locally. The 70 million tons included imprecisely known, very high-grade zones of up to 20% or more copper. The most spectacular intercept is a zone more than 60 feet thick of nearly 25% copper. Zinc, lead, cobalt, silver, and trace uranium also occur in the deposit. Five drill rigs were running around the clock in 1961, and sufficient geophysical, construction, surveying, and other activities were under way to induce Lutz to promote me to assistant project manager. There was sufficient work to keep both of us going 12 or more hours per day.

By the end of 1962, Lutz had sufficient confidence to propose that I phase him out as manager for 1963, that he might experience some new country, such as opening a Bear Creek office in Tennessee. He left the project in sound condition, thereby minimizing problems involved in my expanding responsibilities. Dick Walters, a young geology student, was soon assisting me with the core logging. Walters gained additional experience on other 1960s Ambler district exploration programs. In 1973, he and another of the 1960s Bear Creek students, Tom Andrews, would return to the Ambler district to conduct the successful Sunshine Mining Company exploration program. Anaconda would subsequently buy in with Sunshine and become operator.

The fluctuating Ruby Creek crew gave the appearance of a mini-United Nations with people from as far as India and South America, and as close as Kobuk. As the mid-1960s approached, local Eskimos increasingly phased out migrant staff. Besides being mechanically adept, the local people exhibited the resourcefulness and self-reliance of a people accustomed to making the most of limited resources. A simple example involved making screwdrivers out of nails and spikes. Drillers, drill helpers, geophysicists and equipment operators, carpenters, surveyors, mechanics, assay technicians,

The Ruby Creek (Bornite) copper deposit, in the Cosmos Hills, is an ancient coral reef complex, discovered in the 1940s by Rhiny Berg. The photo at left shows the 1,100-foot shaft (on the hill in the background) which was collared in the mid-1960s. In the foreground is an exploration drill rig, winterized for temperatures to -70°F. The photo below shows the Bornite camp. The name was changed from Ruby Creek in 1965 by Charlie Penny, to honor the peacock-blue copper mineral found there.
(Left, Joe Ruzicka, courtesy of Riz Bigelow; below, Kit Marrs; reprinted from *ALASKA GEOGRAPHIC®*)

and other trades increasingly took on local flavor.

The winter months were quiet ones until 1964, with Homer Cleveland, and sometimes his family, maintaining and guarding the plant and stores. A local Shungnak resident, Homer was able to cope with any winter problems, whether caused by unseasonal thaws or temperatures well below -50°F, and during the field season he handled various responsibilities as equipment operator, logistician, warehouseman, etc.

Kennecott Arrives

The annual winter tranquility was ended by Kennecott's decision to move in its mining division plant in 1964 to explore the Ruby Creek deposit from underground. Concurrently, as the Bear Creek division project geologist, my instructions were to assist in the transition, to conceive and propose a minerals exploration program designed to augment the Ruby Creek deposit, and to continue with exploration drilling at prospects near the Ruby Creek deposit, most notably at Pardner Hill. The wheels were finally in motion for me to embark upon adventures in the Brooks Range itself.

Never before had anything of the magnitude contemplated by Kennecott been done by a private company in the Brooks Range. The mobilization plan envisioned completing arrangements and purchases in the Lower 48 in a two- or three-month period, and assembling the entire plant, including shaft, hoist, and underground equipment, at the Seattle dock before the first ship of the spring season left for Kotzebue when the sea ice broke up. Everything would be disgorged 15 miles offshore onto shallow B&R barges for shipment to the Kotzebue dock, there to be stored until the ice cleared from the mouth of the Kobuk River. As soon as the ice moved out, the tug-powered river barges, some piloted by Eskimo captains, would move the freight upriver to the Kobuk landing, which had been constructed to handle the stores on board.

The complex B&R barging operations were capably managed by Ray Heinrichs, who some years later would move from Kotzebue to Girdwood where he and his wife would open the Kobuk Valley Jade Company. Once the river freight was off-loaded at Kobuk landing by early July, the two D-8s and trucks included in the shipment were to haul the bulky freight 15 miles north to Ruby Creek along the new gravel road.

Immediately upon arrival, construction of the mine plant and permanent housing for between 100 and 200 staff was to start, with everything but the mining equipment to be under cover before freezeup. A planned 1,000-foot vertical shaft was to be collared in September. The purpose of the shaft was to open up one of the several Ruby Creek high-grade copper bodies for sampling, and to eliminate the need of hitting elusive, high-grade zones with wandering surface drill holes collared 1,000 feet above.

Opinions on meeting the schedule

Al Stout and his Cat open the road from the Dahl Creek airstrip to the Ruby Creek camp in the spring of 1962. (Riz Bigelow)

varied from total confidence by the Kennecott engineering planners to dismal pessimism by the Bear Creek exploration staff. The Eskimo position was summed up by one spokesman: "Maybe you'll get up the river, and maybe you won't." This was the most realistic assessment offered.

Everything went according to plan until it came time to barge the equipment up the Kobuk. The loaded barges were ready, but the ice refused to leave the mouth of the river. When it did, the interior was locked in the worst drought in years. The tugs and barges ground to a halt, faced by shallows a short person could cross with dry knees. Even the sheefish on their annual spawning run schooled up in deeper pools waiting for rain. To make matters worse the normally predictable August monsoon failed to materialize. Barges were unloaded at improvised storage yards along the river, and went back for more loads. In this hopscotch fashion, the armada worked its way upstream several tens of miles each time the river rose, finally to grind to a permanent halt at Onion Portage, still 40 miles west of the Kobuk landing.

By this time, Charlie Penny, a Canadian mine manager with extensive northern experience, had taken over the mine manager's job for Kennecott; and with Ozzie Dundas, his old mine superintendent, was improvising a way to

keep the crew out of the cold during the approaching winter months. Penny went to Charlie Lee and other local Eskimo elders for expert counsel in August, 1964, and a logging scheme was worked out.

The local inland Eskimos, who are extraordinary woodsmen, believed there were plenty of logs at Ruby Creek and along the Mauneluk tributary to the Kobuk, miles upstream from Kobuk village. The assigment was to complete construction of the biggest log cabin in northwestern Alaska in a hurry. It worked, and by early winter the crew was moved into comfortable, if crowded, quarters.

Al Stout was called upon to mastermind the cattraining of the stranded freight from Onion Portage to Ruby Creek after freezeup. Before winter's end, the mobilization was completed with minimal fuss. By the following September (1965), or one year later, there were more than

— 103

Two geologists study their map during a recent reconnaissance in the Brooks Range. The lack of accurate maps did not deter extensive exploration in the 1950s and 1960s, although progress was occasionally delayed when geologists became lost. (Mark McDermott)

100 workers at Ruby Creek, the shaft was collared, and the Canadian shaft-sinking crew was on site. In the meantime, my crew was drilling what Lutz and I thought might be another coralline reef front at the nearby Pardner Hill prospect. We encountered high-grade copper mineralization in the first hole, and reef breccia mineralization soon after.

Into the Brooks Range

While the drilling was progressing, I broke away to briefly examine the Omar copper occurrence 100 miles to the west, 40 miles north of Kiana in the Squirrel River drainage. The Omar prospect was discovered in 1962 by Russ Babcock, at the time a young Bear Creek geologist. Babcock left after completing the reconnaissance and later went on to supervise Kennecott programs in such places as New Zealand and the Pacific Northwest. He finally moved to Alaska to head up Bear Creek's new Anchorage office in 1981.

I was soon joined at Omar by Doug Cook, the Bear Creek northwest district manager, a geologist who exhibited a propensity for finding mineralization others missed. Discovery of several new copper occurrences over a 7,000-foot distance led to staking the Omar area. This was followed by staking at the Frost prospect, five miles to the east. Frost is so-named because the mineralization occurs in the cold bottom of a steep canyon so deep the sun refuses to melt the ice in some years. I named one of the new Omar shows (outcroppings) the Blind Spot, because the deposit occurred where the geochemistry showed no indication of copper. The talus below the outcrop is so high-grade a blind person could invariably collect samples containing 5% to 10% copper. The name "Spot" was prophetic, because in 1966 one of my geologists, Bob Nusbaum, mined out the entire high-grade pod with a pick and shovel.

Normally, we did not have cooks at small temporary camps, but took turns cooking. Once, one of the Eskimo crew members volunteered to do all the cooking since he planned to make it a career, and no one objected (at that time). The first morning he cooked up a pancake. That is, he filled a deep frying pan to the brim with batter made from a box of flour and turned up the heat. Before long the material rose up, flooded over the side and down into the oil burners, putting the stove out for the remainder of the morning. Cornflakes were served for breakfast. That night, the two workers who came in on the first helicopter flight ate all the fried chicken our erstwhile cook had prepared on his second attempt. For the next two, he opened a can of already cooked chicken, and fried the poor bird all over again. When he arrived back at the camp, Doug Cook, who relished seafood, looked at the shriveled entities in the pan and exclaimed "Good! Oysters!" I don't recall what he finally ate for supper, but I do recall promoting the cook back to a field position by unanimous request.

In 1965 I was joined by a new assistant geologist who was working on a masters degree at Washington State University. Joe Ruzicka was one of a small corps of geologists destined to participate in many of our exciting Alaska projects from that time to the present, including supervision of projects in various other regions of Alaska. He would become a vice president of WGM in 1978.

Another event leading to recognition of world-class mineral deposits in the Brooks Range occurred in 1965 with discovery of the Arctic deposit. The season started off mundanely enough, with continuation of drilling at Pardner Hill and Ruby Creek, and detailed examination of the Omar and Frost properties, some 150 miles to the west. Charlie Penny and Ozzie Dundas were busy constructing the plant at Bornite. Charlie had changed the place name to Bornite to put an end to misrouting of freight and cheechakos to other Ruby Creeks and Bear Creeks in Alaska, and to honor the high-grade, peacock-colored copper mineral of that name.

While on a shuttle visit to Omar, I evaluated the old western Brooks Range geochemical data collected during the 1961 and 1962 reconnaissance. By taking certain liberties with the data, I happily discerned what seemed to be a subtle copper-in-stream-silt geochemical anomaly which extended from the limit of data coverage in the east near Walker Lake, westward along the south flank of the Brooks Range for more than 150 miles.

After Doug Cook made some supportive remarks, his boss, Paul Bailly, president of Bear Creek and later of Occidental Minerals, and Harry Burgess, vice president of all Kennecott exploration, gave approval to test my concept during what was left of the 1965 field season. It was late July when Joe Ruzicka and I launched the modest exploration program which was to culminate in discovery of the first known world-class mineralization in the western Brooks Range.

Between being lost, helicopter breakdowns, laryngitis, and real or imagined bear scares we successfully tested the new geochemical interpretation in the Omar area, finding several mineral shows. Thus reassured, we headed for the Bornite area.

Being temporarily unsure of our position in those days was commonplace. Not only did we lack maps, but the fog and clouds were ubiquitous. Essentially, we were wandering around a foreign region devoid of any signs of human occupancy past or present, with old, high-elevation, oblique photos, some of which were cloud covered, as our guide. Many of the canyons also wandered around the countryside. What we did have as a reliable guide was the helicopter compass, and on one foolish day we thought even it had deserted us.

Returning from Omar to Bornite, we decided to fly north from Omar over the divide and into the Noatak valley, eastward up the Noatak, then 90 miles south along the Ambler canyon to Bornite.

Ruzicka was navigating with the photo mosaic, and the pilot was compassman. The helicopter side racks were heavily loaded with five-gallon cans of avgas for refueling, sleeping bags, packs, and field tools. Bouncing along the Omar Creek bar to gain flying speed, we were soon in the air, northbound for the Noatak divide.

It wasn't long before we were in a quandary. Joe was ostensibly pointing us eastward toward various landmarks he identified on the mosaic. Unfortunately, the compass said we were going south, or back in the direction from whence we had come. We landed on a flat-topped ridge at 4,000 feet elevation, and Joe talked us into seeing the landmarks the way he did. We rattled the compass, but it would not agree. Tentatively assuming some disturbance or malfunction had upset the compass, and perhaps to demonstrate confidence in the navigator, we flew along the broad east-west trending valley. We soon spotted features ahead which looked remarkably like those in the Kobuk valley, which was supposed to be paralleling our course far to the south. Suddenly we burst out into the perplexing valley to find ourselves on line with the Great Kobuk Sand Dunes, with the Kiana Hills on our right, and the Jade Mountains and Cosmos Hills to our left. The compass was right. We had flown north up the Omar, made a sharp U-turn south, and thence southward along the Salmon River to the Kobuk. Ruzicka is normally a reliable direction finder, but obviously not infallible.

The next morning we started exploration of selective areas north of Ruby Creek. We followed up a piece of copper-bearing talus by a creek along the newly recognized anomalous copper belt. It was late August, the budget was gone, and with an early fall snowstorm blowing around our ears, we realized it was the end of the trail. Either we found a good showing now, or our Brooks Range reconnaissance days were over. A traverse up a steep and slippery slope led to an outcrop with a localized skimpy coating of green copper carbonate (malachite). Examination led us to conclude that this was not a Ruby Creek-type copper-bearing coral reef, but some sort of blanket-type copper-zinc mineralization in schist, a strongly sheared or foliated rock derived from non-carbonate (limestone) sedimentary and/or volcanic rocks.

World-Class Arctic

Arctic was the name Joe and I gave to the lode claims staked at the end of the 1965 field season. The discovery of mineralization at Arctic demonstrated the viability of the geochemical concept. I was confident we would now be allowed to return in 1966 to make additional discoveries, a belief fortified by Doug Cook, who came up to see what we had, and what we had missed. With that comfortable assessment, we took a few pictures in the snow and departed. From the staking of the great Arctic high-grade deposit to the present, the previously written off and ignored south slope of the Brooks Range would be the object of intense exploration, discovery, and claim-staking.

In 1966, the first drill hole was collared at Omar. As far as I know, this was the first core hole ever drilled in western Brooks Range mountain terrains, exclusive of the Cosmos Hills and a few accessible valley bottoms. Finding and examining mineralization in the remote Brooks Range was one thing in the 1960s; drilling was quite another. The drills and camp were staged at the long Kiana airstrip, from whence they were slung 40 miles north by our underpowered but reliable G-model wooden-bladed helicopter. We found considerable difficulty mobilizing equipment with the old helicopter, which could barely pick up 450 pounds.

Drilling results confirmed the presence of copper mineralization, and also very cold and deep permafrost. After various additives were mixed in to prevent the drill rods from freezing, Ralph Hull, the drill foreman, prevailed upon me to have the helicopter sling loads of wet and dry spruce wood from a valley bottom forest to the site. He arranged several barrels of water in a circle, and built a roaring fire between them. By giving the drill hole a shot of boiling water periodically, the frost was soon driven away from the hole, and no further problems were encountered to frozen depths of nearly 1,000 feet.

As usual for the 1960s, fog, rain, and wind plagued our efforts nearly continuously in 1966. One either flew around the fog, or sat and waited for the air to clear. There would have been little

Carrol Gray of Selawik stakes a claim in the
De Long Mountains in October, 1977.
(Greg Fernette)

A geologist takes a compass bearing from a claim post in the Brooks Range. (Mark McDermott)

to show for the effort at season's end had the crew not been prepared to work through the worst of weather. While carrying on this manner, Ruzicka and I discovered very impressive outcrops of copper sulfide mineralization at Dead Creek, named because the copper and zinc geochemistry at the creek mouth below the outcrops was very low.

After naming Dead Creek, we had a serious strategy conversation about nomenclature. Briefly, it occurred to us that decision makers far away might not understand how agreeable the mountains in the Arctic are, particularly if hit with names commonly applied by field workers, such as Arctic, Dead Creek, Rolling Pin Creek, Drowned Man Creek, Miserable Creek, Meat Mountain, Coldfoot, and the like. Consequently, we named subsequent discoveries along the narrow geochemically anomalous belt with more agreeable names, such as Picnic Creek, Steptoe Butte, Sunshine Creek, Hot, Red, and Horse creeks. Since Horse Creek is even farther north than other Ambler district discoveries, there have been no horses there, at least in this interglacial age. Still, the name made an unusually inhospitable basin seem somehow friendlier. Joe even suggested renaming Death Valley to Alpine Meadows for a psychological lift, as I recall.

Oil Shale

I normally made it a habit to visit some new region toward the end of each year. At the end of the 1966 season, Ruzicka and I decided to examine the North Slope oil shales which had been described by Irv Tailleur and Harry Tourtelotte in U.S. Geological Survey Open File reports. Prior to heading north, we arranged by radio with Don Ferguson, adopted son of the colorful Archie Ferguson of bush pilot and barging fame, to fly a cache of three or four barrels of avgas to some airstrip he knew about on the Kiligwa River near Liberator Lake. He said we just had to fly along the river until coming to the strip with the barrels.

We scuttled down the Bornite airstrip in our helicopter loaded with canned gas, K-rations, the lightest and coldest sleeping bags in camp, a tarp, rock picks, sample bags, and a sketchy map, and headed for the Liberator Lake area in the withdrawn petroleum reserve. According to our calculations, we could make the estimated 140 miles with a 10% reserve of fuel.

The intervening country consists of wild, mostly unexplored, tundra-covered basins, meandering rivers, and bare, rubble-littered mountains, seemingly devoid of animal life. By the time we reached the Kiligwa, fuel was low, radio contact long since gone, and the search for the airstrip under way. We found barrels and cans, literally thousands of them, along river bars, around the shore of Liberator Lake, and scattered across the tundra — the debris of Naval oil exploration of NPR #4 in the late 1940s and early 1950s. After several futile landings to check for full barrels, and with little fuel in the tank, we met with success.

We spent a restless night under the tarp and awoke to find new snow and a brisk north breeze. Quickly we set out to find exposures of thin, complexly sheared black oil shale along cutbanks, and on barren knobs poking through an endless sea of rolling tundra. Caribou on the move toward the Kobuk curiously examined the helicopter and us, much the same as they visit our many other camps and drill sites farther south during the spring and fall months.

The shale we examined was loaded with oil. Merely holding a lighter beneath it was sufficient to induce the oil to bubble out. Later, a piece of northern Alaska shale ignited in a hotel room had to be flushed down the toilet to put it out. Analyses showed the best shale to contain from 120 to more than 140 gallons of oil per ton, or several times the oil content in the average Green River shales of Colorado, which are now being appraised at a cost of billions of dollars. Not only does the North Slope oil bubble out readily, but the shale containing it is at least locally flammable, and the resultant ash contains significant metals. The shale oil is high quality light oil. We thought that somewhere along the hundreds of miles of scattered oil shale occurrences, economic deposits must exist. Many told us we were crazy, including some geologists in the private and public sectors who earlier had expressed similar sentiments about our chances along the south slope of the Brooks Range before the Arctic discovery.

The major physical problem we envisioned was to find a sufficient thickness at mineable depth and over a large enough area to constitute an economic deposit. Considering the almost impossibly high grade of some outcrops, we judged a thickness of about five feet at plus 100 gallons per ton in a flat-lying situation to be the minimum necessary for a mineable deposit. Obviously, the grade cutoff could be substantially lowered where thicknesses to 20 feet or more could be found. However, to date, in spite of regional mapping by government and industry geologists, no thick, flat-lying beds have been located. In addition, our euphoria over the high-grade oil shale was dampened somewhat by the fact that most of the oil shale occurrences were on the NPR #4, which had been withdrawn from public entry in 1923.

By 1967, I had drills operating at Omar, the Ambler district prospects, and the Cosmos Hills. Helicopter-supported crews were examining various new claim groups staked in the Ambler mineral district, many of them destined to be dropped in years to come as Bear Creek pulled in its horns. A large tent camp built at Dead Creek served as our exploration base of operations for the new Ambler district. I was beginning to edge into new territory, such as the Purcell Mountains, 40 miles south of Kobuk, and I extended my first probe into the northern Seward Peninsula. At the request of Charlie Penny, I also briefly investigated reported coal occurrences near Kiana.

A geologist examines a turquoise malachite (copper carbonate) outcrop in the Alaska Range.
(Mark McDermott)

Walkie-talkies (hand-held FM radios) were finally becoming available in limited numbers in the late 1960s. This was a considerable breakthrough, and pretty much eliminated hand and mirror signals. Our helicopter fleet also was being upgraded by phasing in the newer Bell G-4 and J2A models, and most notably the Hiller 12E, which could be coerced into picking up 900 pounds versus the 450 pounds with the old G and G-2 model choppers.

Drilling at Ambler

The first deposit drilled in the Ambler district was Dead Creek, chosen on the basis of the spectacular massive sulfide outcrops discovered there the year before. However, the results were disappointing, and we once again faced the prospect of having the program aborted. Noting that my budget was dipping dangerously low, and desperate for a drilling success in the new geologic environment, a drill rig was slung by helicopter to the Arctic prospect earlier than originally planned, specifically to the steep east face of Arctic Ridge. A prefab outhouse was also slung over from Dead Creek, which turned out to be an exciting maneuver since the outhouse flew as high as the helicopter's main rotor blade. The wind blew in the seat hole and lifted the structure upward. From this time on, bulky buildings were assembled on

Members of NANA, Inc., visit a drill rig at Sunshine Creek, in the Ambler district.
(Russ Babcock)

site. Truman Cleveland, a good carpenter and jack-of-all-trades, and Clint Degenhart, were sent over to the prospective Arctic camp site to receive and put up the camp.

The first drill hole behind the outcrop passes through several feet of massive copper-zinc-lead-silver mineralization. I had been instructed to drill holes 150 feet apart along the supposed edge of the deposit, but flush with success, I skipped a hole and moved out 300 feet, only to hit more massive sulfides. After two or three similar stepouts along the ridge behind the outcrop, and with winter winds in the air, I stepped 700 feet across the main ridge of the mountain, at right angles to the line of previous holes, and drilled again. The result was thicker ore. Recognizing the point of diminishing returns, I buttoned up the formal program for 1967 to take a busman's holiday. I now had a considerable number of interesting prospects, and at least a few million tons of indicated ore, and pretty much considered the world to be my oyster.

At the end of 1967, after sending the crews home, I took off for the Chandalar country about 200 miles to the east with Clint Degenhart. Degenhart was subsequently to supervise a variety of Alaska programs, on one of which the much publicized Red Dog discovery was made. As usual the weather was unpredictable, it being early September. We made several discoveries, staked mineralization in the beautiful Dall sheep country to the east of the present-day trans-Alaska pipeline corridor, and named

After a long day of work, geologists often spend the evening analyzing the data they have gathered. These men are working at their camp at Squaw Creek, in the Tanana district.
(Greg Fernette)

— *111*

the trend the Chandalar copper belt. Despite a strong urge to stay on and make additional discoveries, we were forced out by deteriorating weather and dangerous flying conditions. In the Chandalar, we ran into competition in AlVenCo, headed up by Clyde Wetherell, a former associate who was responsible for numerous discoveries in Alaska, Montana, and Idaho.

In 1968, we drilled out the Arctic deposit, examined earlier discoveries, and sought out new ones. I now had an imposing crew, and staggering options at my call, such as all conceivable types of geophysics, geochemistry, specialty geologists, drills, and most importantly, experienced Alaska exploration geologists.

The most significant 1968 development was proving up Arctic as a world-class deposit. My plan was to drill the property out along a modified 400-foot grid. Approximately 22 holes indicated reserves of between 20 and 30 million tons at 4.0% to 5.5% copper, 6.0% to 7.5% zinc, 1 to 2 ounces per ton silver, 1% lead, and minor gold values, the higher grades applying to the lower tonnage.

Winding Down in the Ambler District

In 1968 the Kennecott Mining Division suspended the underground appraisal at Ruby Creek. The shaft had been sunk close to the 1,100-foot level, well below the high-grade copper mineralization, and hit an underlying aquifer which discharged 15,000 gallons per minute into the shaft. Ozzie Dundas was in the cage on the way

down when he noticed the pumps on the upper level were discharging strange-looking material. He looked down to see the water rising upward to meet the downward hurtling cage and pulled the signal cord. The hoistman at the surface reversed the movement and brought the cage back up as fast as it had been going down. But for Dundas' quick reflex, honed during a lifetime of mining, he and the others in the cage would have been crushed into another world. The hole was plugged, and the underground drilling continued. A massive zone of high-grade ore was mined, but shortly Kennecott suspended the operation.

The successes at Arctic and other of our Ambler district discoveries were not enough to forestall consolidation and reduction of effort in what seemed to management to be an inhospitable operating climate, albeit a region of unequalled exploration opportunity. The Bornite operation reverted to more surface drilling, and the scale of effort was reduced at the Brooks Range properties. Numerous unstaked anomalies, discoveries, and claims staked during the golden 60s were left for others to pursue.

With the ambitious Brooks Range exploration programs drying up, my fortunes shifted toward southern Alaska. By 1970, we were operating out of trailer camps and lodges in eastcentral and southcentral Alaska, with fly camps established in areas too distant for economic helicopter commuting, but even those enterprises were severely interrupted

in the early 1970s as consolidation continued. I was also lucky enough to explore in the beautiful Prince William Sound and Alaska Peninsula regions during these final years with Bear Creek, with a break to attend the Harvard Business School under Kennecott sponsorship in 1971.

Changing Hats

A major personal change marked 1972. After a gratifying 14 years with one company, it suddenly occurred to me that unless I took a new tack I very well might never be in on the excitement of northern discovery again. I left Bear Creek with many misgivings in 1972 to start WGM Inc., an Alaska-based consulting company.

My most notable experience during the first few months with WGM involved a private investigator-type assignment commissioned by a major mining company. The company had received a tip that someone was sniping ore from a high-grade outcrop perched on a steep ridge 2,000 feet above a valley bottom near one of my old stomping grounds in the Wrangell Mountains. The plan was to helicopter to the outcropping ledge and investigate for evidence of pilfering.

The most memorable part of the venture proved to be getting there. Because of whiteout conditions, the helicopter had to land in the valley bottom. An adventurous state patrolman and I were forced to hike up the steep slope through waist-deep, wet snow. While I was clothed in reasonably adequate apparel, the patrolman was wearing clothes more fit for chasing down traffic violators. I had the added advantage of knowing from past experience that, by just putting one foot in front of the other, sooner or later we would reach the top of the hill, no matter how disturbing and lengthy the traverse looks from the startup point. After breaking trail and falling over buried ledges for an interminable period, I dragged myself up onto the trail at the mineralized ledge, peering over to watch my partner.

His words when he drew himself up to the ledge were, "I hope they get the chair!" At this time the weather broke, and the helicopter flew up to settle by an old mine building a few hundred feet away. We completed the geologic sleuthing, and subsequently found a substantial stockpile of high-graded, or stolen, ore packaged for shipment to a smelter. After mulling over the caper once the case was concluded, I decided finding ore, not high-graders of ore, is what appeals to me.

High-Grade at Greens Creek

Discovery of the first known major Alaska volcanogenic deposit at Arctic led me to the logical conclusion that there might be others in the state. A likely target seemed to be certain volcanic terranes along the Alaska Panhandle, where I had

---

A geologist finds himself in a precarious position while staking a claim in the Brooks Range.
(Mark McDermott)

A B&R barge lighters freight to the Kotzebue dock from a ship 15 miles offshore. (Riz Bigelow)

last been more than 15 years earlier. The program I had in mind would probably be successful, the only problem being to convince others. To my surprise, I found numerous companies attracted to the proposal. A four-company joint venture (see the *Greens Creek Project,* page 118) was formed to support the Pan Sound project.

The plan was to make one or more west-to-east exploration traverses across the north-south structural grain of the Panhandle, the first to be from Chichagof Island in the west, thence across Admiralty Island and the narrow strip of mainland to the Canadian border. Once finding a favorable belt, the plan was to follow it north and south, the same plan which had led to the earlier Brooks Range successes.

Since reconnaissances of the area had been completed by several major companies from the late 1950s to the 1970s, the plan required doing it more carefully to avoid coming up with the same results as prior workers. This meant the geologists would have to be landed above timberline, from which they would have to crawl, fall, slide, run, and clamber down drainages from top to bottom. Since there are no pickup points in most basins, once the geologist starts down, he is on his own until he reaches the coast or lower flats. Fortunately, by this time good radios were on the scene, and we had a compact turbine helicopter.

The serene beauty of the Alaska Panhandle as seen from passing tour ships and aircraft is a deceptive mask, as anyone who has worked the steeply inclined and treacherous rain forest terrain will verify. In many areas the only way to go is down, since the thick bushes and trees grow out horizontally or downward to form a near-impenetrable barrier from below. As in the Brooks Range, the most fragile element proved to be man, with the bears, deer, eagles, crows, rocks, trees, water, and devil's club being very much at home there.

Follow-up of selected metal anomalies, favorable rock debris, and geology soon led us to the discovery of the high-grade zinc, lead, copper, silver, and gold-bearing massive sulfides at Greens Creek on Admiralty Island. The best known claim group staked on the program was recorded as the Big Sore, a description which fits the iron-oxide-bearing ooze that marks the hillside discovery. Tom Andrews, who had previously made significant discoveries in the Ambler district, discovered Big Sore. I was cooling my heels on an adjacent ridgetop waiting for the helicopter to take me to another anomaly when Andrews called me down to examine the newly discovered occurrence. Tom said he named it the Big Sore in my honor.

Exploration 70s Style

Passage of the 1971 Alaska Native Claims Settlement Act (ANCSA) changed the course of Alaska mineral development, perhaps forever. Some of the state was closed to public entry in 1972, with only limited entry permitted in other areas. Some portions of the first 80 million acres of d-2 lands taken for proposed parks cut across major mineral trends. Prospectors working on contiguous enclaves of land found themselves hemmed in by a bewildering array of classifications, stipulations, and regulations; and some prospectors saw areas in which they had been acquiring data gobbled up, with no compensation offered for lost years and opportunities. Many of the prospective miners who began to appear in the hinterland in significant numbers about 1970 took their losses and beat a hasty retreat.

The post-ANCSA period has been a busy one for me. Vigorous competition enhanced the excitement in the small enclaves left open to the public, such as the Ambler mineral district, the De Long Mountains, and portions of southeastern Alaska. As other consultants did, I accepted government work in withdrawn areas, since the government replaced private industry as the financial investor. The result of one of these programs was the discovery of Red Dog, described on page 88.

But my most gratifying experiences of the 1970s involved the opportunity to assist Native corporations in taking inventory of large acreages of their Native selections to prioritize them and locate promising mineral deposits.

In 1972, Murray Watts introduced me to the Doyon leadership, including John Sackett and Tim Wallis. Sackett is now a state legislator and Wallis is president of Doyon. Watts was one of the pioneers who opened the Canadian north and Arctic Islands to mining. Doyon people very early recognized the necessity of prioritizing withdrawn lands before finalizing their land selections, knowing full well that what they finally selected would be what they would have forever. This, however, was only one of their problems. Widely scattered communities had to get together to appoint directors and officers, and wide-ranging corporate

goals and objectives had to be established within financial limits. Doyon also had to fight off all kinds of promoters with various schemes for spending their money for them.

After considering alternatives, in late 1974 Doyon invited Jack McOuat and me to line up companies to negotiate a minerals agreement involving a staggering acreage of approximately 22,000 square miles of selected lands. The problem was enhanced because the acreage was split into more than 20 separate blocks scattered across one-quarter of the state in the Yukon and Kuskokwim river basins. McOuat, another longtime Canadian Arctic minerals explorer, subsequently coordinated agreement negotiations.

We got lucky. Two companies for whom I was managing major programs in the interior and western parts of Alaska — General Crude Oil (GCO) and Union Carbide — opted to join in the minerals agreement. Charles Herbert, one of the true pioneers of northern mining and former state Commissioner of Natural Resources, was introducing Sohio/BP to local hard-rock minerals potential, and BP opted to participate. McIntyre Mines, a prominent Canadian mining company, also opted in after a chance introduction to Robert Fulton by Herbert. Fulton was responsible for proving up the major Brady Glacier nickel deposit in southeastern Alaska. The federal government retroactively put a stop to this one by including the deposit in Glacier Bay National Park and Preserve.

Top: In 1968, only a small camp marked Arctic, a world-class copper-zinc-lead-silver deposit discovered by the author and Joe Ruzicka in 1965.
Above: A bulldozer and drill rig work the Arctic deposit in 1968. The 1965 discovery of Arctic led to intense exploration and claim staking on the previously ignored south slope of the Brooks Range. (Both photos by Riz Bigelow)

Snow covers buildings of Independence Mine at Hatcher Pass, 13 miles northwest of Palmer. More than 100,000 tons of gold ore and more than 125,000 ounces of gold were extracted from the mine before it ceased operation three decades ago. Spurred by the renewed interest in gold production of the last few years, workers were scheduled to reopen the mine for production in July, 1982. (John and Margaret Ibbotson)

In due course, the Doyon negotiations culminated in a workable agreement, and in 1975 the program was on. I was fortunate in having a cadre of experienced geologists in the company to head the exploration crews. Joe Ruzicka managed the helicopter-supported regional appraisals scattered across interior Alaska. Numerous occurrences and anomalies were discovered, and a number of site-specific examinations were initiated. Most importantly, Doyon acquired valuable inventory data for more than 600 townships.

The Alaska Asbestos Project, one of the major ongoing mineral developments in the state, and the Doyon and Ahtna Inc. agreement provided additional opportunities for my company to participate in evaluation of mineral potential on Native lands. Reserves at the Alaska Asbestos deposit are now reported to exceed 50 million tons. The Ahtna agreement provided me with the chance to return to one of the world's most spectacular environments, the mountains surrounding the Copper River Basin in southcentral Alaska. Key figure in the negotiations was Herb Smeltzer, who continues to direct mineral affairs for Ahtna. Numerous other regional mineral exploration programs filled my days.

The U.S. Bureau of Mines press release in August, 1975, on our discovery of the Red Dog massive sulfides led to another adventure, the discovery of Lik. I was in the Ambler district with our Brooks Range client companies, GCO and New Jersey Zinc (NJZ), when a copy of the press release came to us. With other companies, we beat a hasty advance to the open lands adjacent to Red Dog in September. Other companies, including Cominco, were there. But weather finally forced us out of our hastily constructed tent camp in a copse of willows, and, with the competition, we retreated for the winter.

By 1976, the competitors for lands in the western Brooks Range near Red Dog had boiled down to Cominco and our clients, GCO and NJZ. Both groups got a piece of the action. Gaylord Cleveland, the senior geologist in charge of our field program, quickly discovered and staked what turned out to be a major massive zinc-lead-silver deposit, recording the claims as the Lik group, after Wulik River, the nearest stream. Cominco, led by Stewart Jackson, also staked part of the Lik trend. By the end of 1977, between 10,000 and 15,000 claims had been staked by the two agressive competitors. Various local and national newspapers picked up on the new strike.

In early 1978 we mobilized construction materials, drills, a bulldozer, and other equipment to a lake about 40 miles from Lik, and cattrained the freight to camp. The winter haul was masterminded by Rick Fredericksen and Jerald Harmon. Fredericksen supervised the critical 1978 Lik drilling project, and Harmon subsequently would reappear in 1982 to assist Cominco on its winter mobilization. Lik was the first major mobilization of a permanent metals mining exploration camp in the far western Brooks Range. The drilling program in 1978 totalled 45,000 feet. With indicated reserves published at 20 to more than 30 million tons of 12% combined zinc and lead, plus 1 to 2 ounces per ton silver, Lik quickly moved into the upper rank of Alaska lode deposits.

Meanwhile, the competition was not letting any grass grow under their feet. Ably led by Jerry Booth and Roy McMichaels, Alaska competitors I first ran into years before in Prince William Sound, Cominco was busily drilling, staking, and exploring. As noted before, they were also agressively figuring out how to get a piece of the nearby Red Dog deposit.

Memories Revisited

Major changes have marked Alaska mining history during the 30 years since I took my first mining job on the gold dredges. One by one the great dredges were shut down; by the end of the 1950s not one remained in operation in the Fairbanks district, with a few hanging on elsewhere for another decade before they too were shut down.

By the best of luck, I was destined to lead the first successful regional non-gold minerals exploration programs in the Brooks Range, culminating in discovery of the world-class Arctic deposit, and its neighbors in the Ambler mineral district. In subsequent years, good fortune enabled me to personally explore in virtually all of the great Alaska mineral provinces. The active discoveries resulting from these programs are almost too many to keep straight. I have been fortunate in being able to participate in many projects where the discoveries were made by others.

Most of all I am satisfied with meeting so many people who chose to live and work in the Alaska hinterland. I was here early enough to absorb the stories of the really oldtimers, to learn from Natives, prospectors, guides, and trappers about the ways and spirit of the Arctic, and to fly with members of the original cast of fixed wing and helicopter pilots. I look forward to the 1980s with full confidence that other Red Dog, Lik, Arctic, Alaska Asbestos, and Greens Creek deposits are still out there waiting for prospectors with an idea, miners' luck and perseverance.

This vein of native cinnabar, the principal ore of mercury, was found in the Kilbuck Mountains, east of Bethel. A dozen mercury mines have operated intermittently since World War I in southeastern Alaska. Mercury prices have been climbing in recent years due to increased demand, causing renewed interest in production in the district. (Third Eye Photography)

Greens Creek Project

By Doug Smith

Flying north over Chatham Strait and looking east up Greens Creek near Hawk Point on Admiralty Island, a small clearing may be seen on the hillside. This is the exploration for the Greens Creek Project, which is about 18 miles southwest of Juneau.

The joint venture that discovered the deposit (see *Prospecting Alaska,* page 88) was formed in early 1973 by Noranda Exploration, Marietta Resources International, Exalas Resources Corporation, and Texas Gas Exploration. Its success led to the formation, in 1978, of the Greens Creek Joint Venture for the continued development of the project. Bristol Bay Native Corporation, which owns land on Hawk Inlet near the mouth of Greens Creek, has joined with the other four companies in the venture. Thus far, development of the project has included claim-staking, metallurgical test work, geophysical surveying, excavation of a 4,200-foot adit (a tunnel with one

Editor's note: *Doug Smith is former public relations coordinator for Noranda Mining Inc., managing company for the Greens Creek Project.*

opening), 48,000 feet of diamond core drilling, and environmental studies.

In 1981 field workers conducted seismic surveys and shallow diamond drilling to further evaluate proposed tailings disposal sites and excavated a cross-cut tunnel from the existing adit to the mineral deposit. Ore samples were obtained and sent to a laboratory for detailed metallurgical testing.

So far, helicopters have supported all exploration and pre-development activity at Greens Creek. Minor surface disturbance has been limited to the preparation of drill sites and the clearing of a campsite and waste rock disposal area. During 1981, Noranda Exploration's management role was transferred to Noranda Mining Inc., as the project moved through conceptual engineering toward actual mining. Noranda Mining Inc., with headquarters in Salt Lake City, Utah, is the United States subsidiary of the parent company, Noranda Mines Limited, of Canada.

Initial clues of mineral values were found in stream sediments at the mouth of Greens Creek. Upstream exploration located the source of mineralization and the outcrop of the ore zone known as the

Big Sore because of the reddish-stained, natural ground seepage where little vegetation grows. Initial surface drilling at Big Sore indicated several horizons containing variable-grade silver, zinc, lead, copper, and gold ore. Continued drilling has now delineated a narrow, steeply dipping ore zone extending horizontally at least 3,500 feet. Diamond drill core intercepts have indicated geologic reserves above the 1,100-foot elevation, estimated at three million tons containing 0.5% copper, 2.5% lead, 7% to 10% zinc, 10 plus ounces of silver per ton, and gold at 0.1 ounce per ton. Geologists have not yet determined the final limits of the orebody.

The steeply dipping, narrow zone requires an underground mining method called cut and fill. Ore is removed, and waste rock, some tailings, and cement replaces the volume of mined-out ore. Production will be about 800 tons of ore per day, and full production is not expected before 1986 at the earliest.

Clue to the Greens Creek mineral find was the Big Sore, a reddish-stained scar on a hillside where little vegetation grew. (Doug Smith)

The Mining Process

By Greg Fernette

Mining is the process of extracting a valuable mineral from the earth so that we can make use of the mineral. The value of the mineral lies in its usefulness or in the fact that it contains something useful. The rock containing the valuable mineral is referred to as ore, a term which carries both economic and geologic meanings. A mineral deposit is not an ore deposit unless the minerals can be extracted at a profit.

The total mining operation consists of several stages of which mining is the first step. After mining, the ore must be processed to extract the valuable mineral and then smelted to extract the valuable commodity from the mineral.

Ore deposits are described in terms of their quality (grade), and size (tonnage). The grade is expressed as the percentage of valuable commodity contained in the ore. For example, the grade of a copper deposit might be 2% copper. Gold and silver are expressed as a ratio of ounces of precious metals per ton of ore. The tonnage is the total weight of the ore. Small deposits may contain a few hundred thousand tons of ore whereas large ones typically contain hundreds of millions of tons.

The inventory of ore in a mineral deposit is known as its reserves. Ore reserves are classified according to the degree of certainty with which the grade and tonnage are known. In the United States and Canada three categories of ore reserves are commonly used: proven, probable, and possible. Proven reserves are those which have been measured and sampled in enough detail so that the grade and tonnage is known with a high degree of certainty. This generally means with less than 10% possible error. Probable reserves are those where the dimensions and grade of the ore are known from more widely spaced sampling and by geological extrapolation. The degree of certainty acceptable for probable reserves is generally 70% to 80%. Possible reserves are estimates based mainly on geological extrapolation. Proven and probable reserves have been measured within defined limits and have a value. The total ore reserves of a mineral deposit are often expressed as the sum of the proven and probable reserves. Possible reserves have no real value but are an expression of the potential of a deposit.

Ore reserves must be further defined when it comes to mining. Two factors are important; the percent of extraction and dilution. No matter how carefully a mine is run, not all of the ore can be extracted. The percentage of ore that can be mined, i.e., the mineable reserves, depends on the geologic and engineering characteristics of the orebody and the mining method. The mining method is chosen to give the highest extraction possible within geologic and engineering constraints. In some deposits as little as 60% of the total ore can be mined. This factor must be taken into account in

Piles of gravel tailings, arranged in rows, stretch out behind this dredge, operated several decades ago by the U.S. Smelting, Refining and Mining Company at Fox, north of Fairbanks. With a dragline and buckets, the dredge worked its way forward, the gold falling into riffles inside and the tailings spewing off the belt in back.
(Steve McCutcheon; reprinted from *ALASKA*® magazine)

Glossary

Crosscut: A working that crosses the ore.

Drift: A working that parallels the ore.

Grizzly: A metal grate which prevents large pieces of rock or ore from entering the chute or ore pass.

Raise: A working excavated from below upward.

Skip: The car attached to a cable in a shaft that hoists the ore; the car that hoists workers is generally called a cage.

Working: Any opening or excavation in a mine made to exploit the ore, particularly the area where the ore is actually being mined.

planning the mining operation. Dilution occurs when unmineralized rock gets mixed in with the ore during mining. Some dilution occurs in all mining operations, and a 10% dilution is commonly planned for. Dilutions of 20% to 30% can happen in some types of deposits.

We can illustrate the effect of extraction and dilution on a hypothetical deposit with reserves of 1,000,000 tons of ore with a grade of 1% copper. At 90% extraction the reserves would be 900,000 tons at 1% copper. Dilution of 10% increases the tonnage to 1,000,000 tons but reduces the grade to 0.9% copper. Poor extraction tends to decrease the total reserves. Dilution increases the tonnage but lowers the grade since barren rock is being added to the ore.

Ore reserves, degrees of certainty in reserve estimates, extraction, and dilution affect the economic aspects of mining. A mine is basically a factory. It pays its operating costs, returns its initial investment, and generates a profit through the sale of its products. The inventory or raw material of the mine is ore. Ore reserves form the basis of the decision to spend the money to put the mine in operation. The reserves must be known with a high degree of certainty so the potential profitability of the mine can be assessed. The objective of mining is to extract the maximum amount of ore, with minimum dilution, in the cheapest and safest manner so as to realize a profit from selling the products of the operation.

With the above as background we can describe mining methods, mineral processing, and to a lesser extent metal smelting. Throughout the discussion we will emphasize metal or hardrock mining. There are two general types of mining: surface or open-pit, and underground. Each approach uses different methods and equipment.

Surface Mining

Metalliferous deposits which occur near the surface are mined by open-pit methods. Other types of deposits such as sand, gravel, coal, and iron ore are mined by quarrying and strip mining. Open-pit mining has many advantages over underground mining, chiefly lower cost, ease of mechanization, and greater safety. Open-pit mines range in size from small "dog holes" to excavations of one-half cubic mile or more. Because of the lower cost and higher productivity of open-pit mining, many large, low-grade deposits are mined in this way.

Prior to the start of an open-pit mine, soil and barren rock must be removed to expose the orebody. This process is known as pre-production stripping. In some deposits little stripping is needed whereas in others stripping may take several years. Open-pit mines are developed in a series of benches arranged either in a spiral or as levels with connecting ramps. Bench widths vary from 25 feet to more than 100 feet, and height ranges from 15 to about 70 feet. The width and height of the benches is determined by the rock strength and the size of the equipment being used. Smaller and narrower benches are needed in deposits with weak rock or where small equipment is necessary. Wide benches are needed to accommodate large equipment. Bench height and width are also related to slope stability. The working slope of a pit can be as low as 20° because of the necessity of maintaining benches as work space and preventing slope failure. As a deposit is mined out, the pit slope becomes steeper until the final slope is reached. This is the ultimate limit of mining and may be as steep as 70°. The ultimate pit limit is determined by a combination of slope stability and economics.

A major consideration in open-pit mining is the amount of barren rock which must be mined to allow mining of the ore. This is known as the stripping ratio. The stripping ratio ultimately determines whether open-pit mining is economical. The stripping ratio is related to the shape of the orebody, its depth, the final pit slope, and the grade of the ore.

Stripping ratios of 1.5-2:1, meaning 1.5 to 2 tons of barren rock must be moved for each ton of ore, are common; some mines can tolerate stripping ratios as high as 4:1. Since it costs the same to mine a ton of waste as a ton of ore, the effect of a high stripping ratio is to raise the operating cost of the mine. The ultimate pit limit is established by working out the break-even stripping ratio, i.e., the point at which the stripping cost exceeds the return from mining the ore.

Open-pit mining follows a drill-blast-load-haul cycle. First, holes are drilled in the rock for placement of explosives. Blast holes are typically 6 to 12 inches in diameter and drilled 15 to 30 feet apart in a grid pattern. The hole spacing is worked out to provide optimum breakage of the rock. The holes are then loaded with explosives and blasted. Several areas may be blasted at one time, and the mine is cleared of all personnel prior to the blast. The broken rock is loaded by power shovels or at smaller mines in front-end loaders. Large power shovels may have buckets capable of holding 20 to 25 cubic yards. The ore is hauled out of the mine in trucks, rail cars or in some cases, by conveyors. Most newer mines use trucks. Off-road mine trucks capable of carrying up to 200 tons are now in use.

The size of open-pit mines varies. In general, the more ore that is mined, the lower the operating cost per ton. Consequently, many open-pit mines are very large and may produce more than 100,000 tons of ore and waste each day. The Bingham Canyon mine in Utah is one of the largest mines in the world and produces 200,000 tons of ore and waste each day. The Quartz Hill molybdenum deposit near Ketchikan will be mined by open-pit methods at about 40,000 tons per day.

Underground Mining

Deposits which cannot be economically mined using surface methods must be mined from underground.

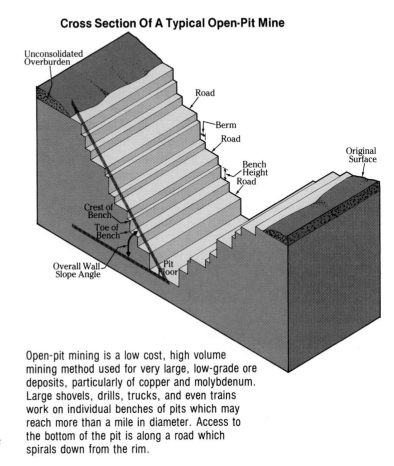

Cross Section Of A Typical Open-Pit Mine

Unconsolidated Overburden
Road
Berm
Road
Bench Height
Road
Original Surface
Crest of Bench
Toe of Bench
Overall Wall Slope Angle
Pit Floor

Open-pit mining is a low cost, high volume mining method used for very large, low-grade ore deposits, particularly of copper and molybdenum. Large shovels, drills, trucks, and even trains work on individual benches of pits which may reach more than a mile in diameter. Access to the bottom of the pit is along a road which spirals down from the rim.

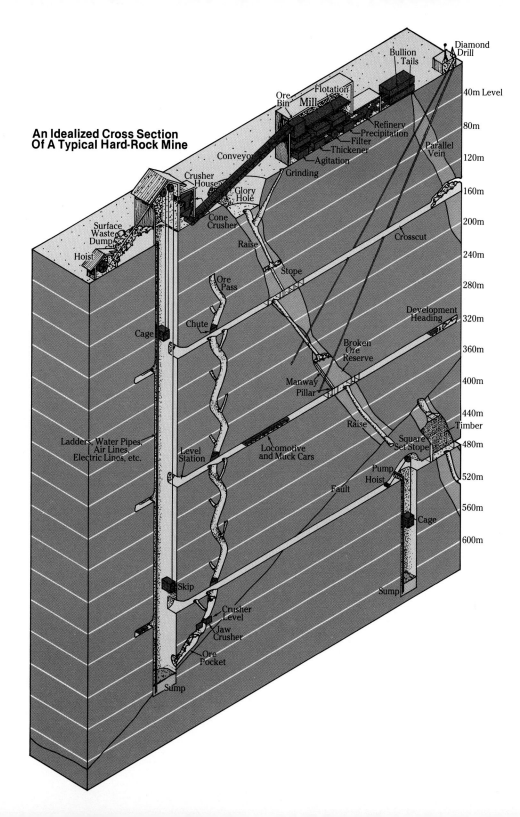

An Idealized Cross Section Of A Typical Hard-Rock Mine

In underground mining, openings are made in the ground to mine the orebody. There are two general types of openings or headings. The first are development headings. These are made to provide access to the ore, space in which to work, and passages for ventilation. The second are broadly known as stopes, which are the openings created when ore is removed. For this reason many underground mining methods are referred to as stoping. The mining method used on a particular deposit will vary depending on a number of factors; chiefly the depth of the orebody, its width and shape, the strength of the ore and enclosing rocks, the planned rate of mining, and safety of operation.

Underground mining methods can be grouped into three broad types: those where artificial ground support is needed; those using natural or no ground support; and the caving methods.

Underground mining proceeds in a drill-blast-muck-haul cycle similar to open-pit mining but using equipment designed to operate in confined spaces. Blast holes are drilled into the ore for explosives placement. The holes are drilled in rings or fans rather than grids as in open-pit mining. The holes are then loaded with explosives and blasted. Blasting is generally done at the end of each shift when all personnel are out of the mine. The broken ore, muck in mining jargon, is then mucked out and hauled to the surface by hoist, truck or conveyor.

Where rock strength is low and artificial ground support is required, four mining methods are most commonly used: square-set stoping, shrinkage stoping, cut and fill, and longwall mining.

Square-set stoping is used to mine steeply dipping deposits with weak ore and weak walls. Timber squares are formed to replace the mined ore and support the surrounding rock. Timbered and mined-out areas are then backfilled with tailings. This method is expensive and labor intensive. In the past it was used in many mines; however, today it is mainly an auxiliary method used in combination with other mining methods.

Shrinkage stoping is used to mine steeply dipping deposits with moderately strong wallrocks and ore. Mining progresses upward, and the blasted ore is left in the stope to support the wallrock. The broken ore is also used as the working platform. When ore is blasted, it increases in volume by about half. This swell factor is drawn off from the stope bottom as mining goes on. When all of the ore is blasted, the stope is then drawn off or shrunk. This method is generally used only on smaller deposits where more mechanized approaches are not possible. Its chief disadvantages are dilution from the walls and low selectivity. Shinkage stoping was a very common mining approach in the past.

Larger, steeply dipping deposits with strong ore but weak walls can be mined from bottom to top in a series of horizontal slices by the cut and fill method. Each slice is removed after blasting and replaced by fill material leaving enough room to mine the next slice. The ore must be strong enough to support itself. The walls are supported by the fill. This method lends itself to mechanization since modern rubber-tired mining equipment works well on top of the fill.

Narrow, shallow dipping or horizontal mineral deposits with weak ore and a weak back are mined by the longwall method. In this method the deposit is removed continuously all along the working face. Artificial props, such as timbers or in some mines hydraulic legs, hold up the back until mining is completed. The roof is then allowed to cave. This approach is often used in coal mining and is generally highly mechanized. It is most suitable to mining narrow, seamlike deposits.

Deposits with strong walls are mined by two principal methods: open stoping and room-and-pillar.

Open stoping covers a variety of techniques where little or no support is needed for the wallrock or the ore. Open stopes 100 feet wide and 200 feet high are common. Pillars of ore or cribs of timber are used for support if needed. The ore is drilled and blasted from development levels and extracted from draw points at the bottom of the stope. Open stoping can be mechanized easily and gives high extraction. It is also one of the cheapest underground mining methods.

The room-and-pillar method is used to

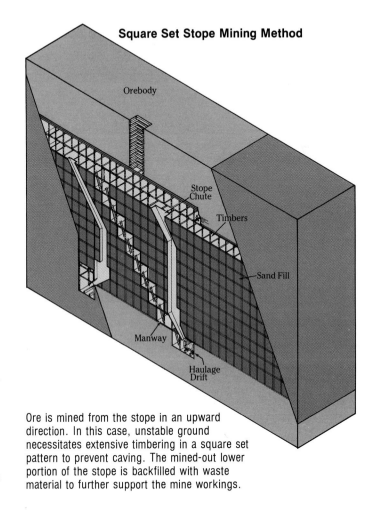

Square Set Stope Mining Method

Orebody

Stope Chute

Timbers

Sand Fill

Manway

Haulage Drift

Ore is mined from the stope in an upward direction. In this case, unstable ground necessitates extensive timbering in a square set pattern to prevent caving. The mined-out lower portion of the stope is backfilled with waste material to further support the mine workings.

— 125

Block Caving Mining Method

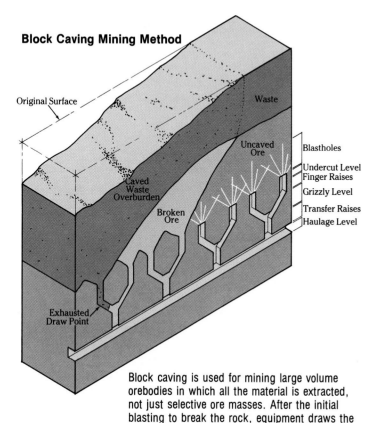

Block caving is used for mining large volume orebodies in which all the material is extracted, not just selective ore masses. After the initial blasting to break the rock, equipment draws the broken material from the lowest level. As the ore is drawn out, additional material caves into the void, eliminating the need for further drilling and blasting.

mine gently dipping, shallow, tabular deposits with strong walls and ore. A grid of rooms is excavated in the ore leaving uniform-sized pillars to support the back. This method, common in the United States, is flexible, relatively low cost, and is easily mechanized. Generally 30% to 40% of the ore must be left in the pillars. If the pillars can be recovered, extractions of up to 90% can be obtained.

Caving methods use gravity to break the ore and so are cheaper than other underground mining methods. Caving must be used in deposits with weak ore and weak walls because strong ore will not cave. As near-surface mineral deposits are mined out and mining costs go up, the caving methods are becoming more and more important. There are two principal cave mining methods: block caving and sublevel caving.

Block caving is most effective with large deposits of weak, highly fractured ore. The ore is undercut, and caving is induced by blasting. The ore then continues to cave under its own weight, and is extracted from regularly spaced draw points as it caves. The undercutting and much of the development must be done prior to mining so the development cost is high. On the other hand, the mining cost is low and high extraction can be obtained. The Alaska-Juneau Mine used a modified block caving method to mine 10,000 tons per day of low-grade gold ore.

Sublevel caving is a smaller scale caving method used to mine orebodies with weak ore and walls where greater selectivity is

Sublevel Caving

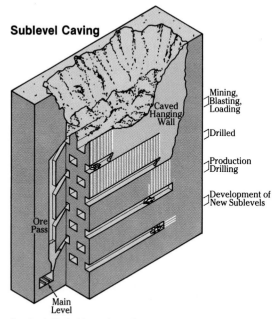

Ore is drilled, blasted, and removed from each sublevel in a downward-progressing sequence.

needed. The ore is blasted from development tunnels and allowed to cave. Sublevel caving differs from block caving in that the ore is caved one level at a time. The overlying rock caves with the ore. Up to 85% to 90% extraction can be achieved, but dilution is often high. Sublevel caving is a more economical method of mining in weak rock than methods using ground support.

Underground mines are developed in different ways. Development openings are generally made in the rock around the ore since openings in the ore are destroyed by mining or prevent ore from being mined.

Access is a prime consideration in development. Shafts and declines are used for access to orebodies below the surface. A vertical shaft is driven down to the orebody; ore, men, and equipment are moved in and out of the mine by hoists. A decline is an inclined tunnel which allows access by trucks or conveyors.

In a case where the orebody is inside a mountain, an adit, a horizontal tunnel, can be driven to the ore. In general, near-surface deposits are developed by adits and declines, and deeper deposits by shafts. Many underground mines have more than one means of access.

An underground mine is developed in a series of levels. Drifts are driven parallel to the trend of the ore, and crosscuts are excavated across and into the ore.

Passages are made: ore passes for ore to be moved through; tunnels for water drainage; sumps to collect water; passages for ventilation and for men to move between levels in the mine. Before a given block of ore can be mined, the development must be done. In underground mine development, openings are being prepared in various parts of the deposit while other parts are being mined. Development and mining must be planned so that as ore blocks are mined out, development of new ore is completed and mining can continue uninterrupted.

Mineral Processing

Most raw ores, except some coal and industrial minerals, are not directly marketable. Therefore, some kind of processing is necessary. In metallic ores the process is two-fold; first, concentrating to upgrade the ore and second, smelting to extract the metal. Concentration takes place at the mine and is considered part of the entire mining operation. Typically, a mine produces an ore concentrate which is sold to the smelter. Smelting and metal refining are complex topics; what follows is a simplified description of the copper smelting process.

Concentration, also known as extractive metallurgy, consists of four stages: crushing and grinding; classification; separation; and filtering and drying. The concentration plant is known as the mill, and the particular concentration process in use at a mine follows a plan known as the flowsheet. The objective of concentration is to separate the valuable minerals from the host rock. This is an important aspect of mining as some otherwise economically viable mineral deposits are not being mined because the ores cannot be concentrated.

Ore minerals occur as fine particles in the host rock, so the first step in mineral processing is breaking the ore into small particles; fragments of broken ore will range up to several feet in diameter. The first stage is crushing to break the ore down to fragments less than one inch in diameter. The next step is grinding, where the ore is fed into equipment known as ball or rod mills and ground to a fine powder. The size to which the ore is ground is related to the particle size of the ore minerals and the optimum extraction of ore minerals from the rock. This is determined in laboratory testing during the design of the mill. Many ores must be ground to micron size (one micron equals .001 millimeter) to allow separation of the ore minerals.

After crushing, the ore is classified according to particle size so that only particles within the correct size range go on to the next steps. The particle size range required for optimum extraction is often very narrow so close control must be maintained. Coarse ores are classified by screening, but fine ores are classified using hydrocyclones. The ground ore, mixed with water, is pumped through a feed tube in the side of a conical vessel, and the suspension is whirled around the cone. Centrifugal force moves the larger particles outward toward the wall of the cone, where they settle downward toward the apex. The coarse material is discharged and fed back into the mills for additional grinding. The fine material overflows from the top of the cyclone, is collected, and goes on to the next step.

The heart of extractive metallurgy is separation. The crushing, grinding, and classification stages prepare the ore for this stage. There are many methods of mineral separation; the method used is determined by the nature of the ore. Several methods may be required for a single ore. The three most common methods of separation are gravity, flotation, and hydrometallurgy.

Many ore minerals, such as gold, tin and tungsten, have a higher density than their associated minerals and can be

Workers inspect a turn-of-the-century churn drill while moving it to the Transportation Museum in Palmer. Denali Mining Company donated the steam-powered drill which was found on the company's property in the Valdez Creek mining district about 50 miles east of Cantwell. The Keystone drill is a self-propelled, steam-powered, churn drill that weighs about 12,000 pounds fully outfitted. This drill was made in Beaver Falls, Pennsylvania, sometime before 1915. A few of these drills were brought to Alaska before World War I for large-scale gold mining operations. George Sias sent the drill to Alaska in January, 1915, for a Valdez Creek mining company of which he was president. In 1907 he had purchased claims on upper Valdez Creek tributaries and in 1910 formed an association, the George W. Sias Syndicate of Boston, which pooled the assets of several northeastern capitalists owning Alaska mining interests. In 1913 the Boston claims, Dan Kain's claims on Lucky Gulch and lower Valdez Creek, Tammany Beach, and all other claims belonging to Pete Monahan, the original discoverer, and his partners were merged.

Called the Valdez Creek Placer Mines Co., this organization represented the first large injection of investor capital into the Valdez Creek mining district, a small but rich placer mining district, and into the upper Susitna region. The company was able to begin large-scale mining operations on Valdez Creek for the first time since discovery of gold there in 1903. In 1915 they brought in the Keystone drill to test the deeply buried Tammany Channel. In the next few years the company's claims were tested with the Keystone drill to determine where deeply buried gold-bearing gravels might lie. After this the drill was abandoned, probably because moving it would have been too difficult and expensive. (BLM)

separated using gravity techniques. The sluice box used in placer mining is a good example of gravity separation. Ore mixed with water flows down a trough over a series of riffles where the heavies are trapped. Another commonly used gravity technique is jigging, where ore and water are fed onto a pulsating screen. The lighter particles are brought to the top by the vibration and carried off by the overflow. The heavier particles collect on the screen and are drawn off through a gate. Shaking tables — large, inclined tables divided by numerous small, longitudinal riffles — are used to treat fine-grained ores which cannot be treated in jigs. The table is vibrated in a horizontal cycle with a slow forward motion and a rapid backward motion. Heavy particles move along the riffles and are washed off near the end of the table; lighter particles move down the table with little horizontal movement and are washed off near the back of the table.

A gravity method that is widely used to treat mineral sands and in extracting traces of tin and tungsten from some metallic ores is the Humphrey Spiral. It consists of a spiral trough with a collecting pipe in the center. Ore and water are fed into the spiral and washed around it. Lighter particles are carried to the outer edges of the trough, while heavier particles stay near the center and are collected in the pipe. A similar principle is used in wheel-type separators which are used for final processing of placer gold ores. The ore and water are fed onto the face of a tilted, dishlike wheel. As the wheel turns, the heavy and light fractions of the ore are separated by centrifugal force.

One of the most important techniques of mineral separation is flotation, a process used to separate components of complex sulfide ores and to separate sulfide minerals from host rock. Flotation is a selective process and can be used to separate minerals with only slight differences in physical properties, such as copper, lead, and zinc sulfides. In the flotation process air is bubbled through a suspension of finely ground ore and water, known as pulp. The particles adhere to the bubbles and are carried to the top of the flotation tank, where they are scraped off as froth.

The technique depends on the surface tension or wettability of mineral particles. Bubbles will adhere to particles with low wettability and cause the particles to float. Particles that are easily wettable will not adhere to bubbles and hence will sink.

Flotation sounds simple, but is chemically complex. The surface properties of ore and gangue (matrix or valueless) minerals vary within very narrow limits, and it is necessary to chemically treat the ore to insure that the proper particles float or sink. Organic reagents known as collectors, such as oils, organic acids, and organic bases, are used to increase the wettability of mineral particles so they will float. Other reagents known as conditioners are used to closely control the acidity of the pulp. Chemicals called activators render a mineral more amenable to flotation; depressors prevent minerals from floating. In addition, frothing agents such as pine oil must be added to the pulp to promote bubble formation. The pulp is run through flotation tanks up to a dozen times to separate as much of the ore as possible. Some ores require several different flotation processes.

Many ores are not amenable to physical techniques of separation such as gravity and flotation and must be treated chemically by processes known as hydrometallurgy. Hydrometallurgy is low cost and can be used to recover metal from very low-grade ores. There are three principal processes: cyanidation, leaching, and solvent extraction.

Cyanidation is used to treat gold and silver ores and to recover gold and silver from other ores. Gold and silver combine readily with cyanide to form soluble cyanide compounds. The precious metals can be dissolved from ore by treating the ore with cyanide solution. The gold and silver are then recovered by adding powdered zinc to the solution which combines cyanide and precipitates out the precious metals. Flotation concentrates are often cyanided to recover their gold and silver content. Low-grade gold and silver ores are piled into heaps and sprinkled with cyanide solution for several days to recover the metals.

Important in the treatment of some copper ores, leaching processes are used to treat oxide ores by methods known as

— 129

heap, dump, or vat leaching. Sulfuric acid produced from air pollution control systems is commonly used as a leaching agent. The acid solution dissolves the copper to produce copper sulfate solution. The copper is recovered by adding scrap iron (usually tin cans) to the solution which plates out the copper on the cans. In heap leaching the ore is piled into heaps on paved beds. Acid solution is sprinkled over the heaps, allowed to percolate through the piles, and recovered at the bottom. Dump leaching is a similar process but is done on low-grade waste or mill tailings as a final recovery step. Vat leaching is the treatment of ores in vats and is used on higher-grade oxide ores.

Solvent extraction is similar to leaching, but different solutions are used. Sulfide ores may be treated by solvent extraction techniques. Leaching and solvent extraction are also used to treat uranium ores.

Hydrometallurgy is used to recover ores in place by in-situ leaching or solution mining, whereby solutions are injected into the ore in the ground, allowed to react for a period of time, and then pumped out. If the ore is naturally porous, as in some uranium deposits, little

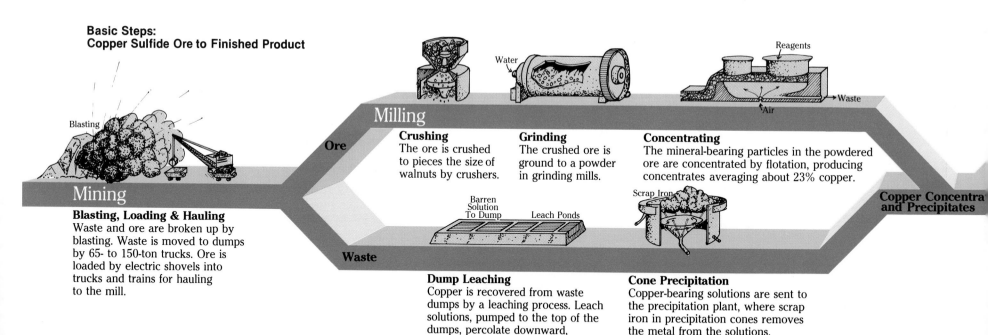

Basic Steps:
Copper Sulfide Ore to Finished Product

Blasting

Mining

Milling

Ore

Blasting, Loading & Hauling
Waste and ore are broken up by blasting. Waste is moved to dumps by 65- to 150-ton trucks. Ore is loaded by electric shovels into trucks and trains for hauling to the mill.

Water

Reagents

Waste

Air

Crushing
The ore is crushed to pieces the size of walnuts by crushers.

Grinding
The crushed ore is ground to a powder in grinding mills.

Concentrating
The mineral-bearing particles in the powdered ore are concentrated by flotation, producing concentrates averaging about 23% copper.

Scrap Iron

Barren Solution To Dump   Leach Ponds

Waste

Dump Leaching
Copper is recovered from waste dumps by a leaching process. Leach solutions, pumped to the top of the dumps, percolate downward, dissolving the soluble copper.

Cone Precipitation
Copper-bearing solutions are sent to the precipitation plant, where scrap iron in precipitation cones removes the metal from the solutions.

Copper Concentra
and Precipitates

preparation is needed. Other ores must be broken first. Solution mining eliminates many of the steps in conventional mining operations and, where applicable, can be done at low cost. Considerable research is now being done to develop solution mining technology.

The final stages of mineral processing are filtering and drying to recover water and reagents and to reduce the weight of the concentrate. The pulp from the mill is pumped into shallow, circular thickening tanks where the solids are allowed to settle. Water is recovered from the top of the tank. The thickened concentrate, which still contains considerable water and reagents, is next pumped to filter tanks where it is collected on the outside of drum-shaped filters by vacuum suction. As the drums rotate, water is sprayed onto the outside of the drum to dissolve any remaining reagents. The water is then sucked through the walls of the drum. As the drums rotate, the concentrate dries and is allowed to fall off. The final concentrate will contain only 1% to 2% water.

The reasons for using the complex processes can be better understood through an example. One of the common

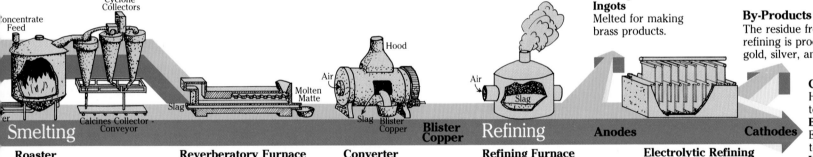

Casting
Ingots
Melted for making brass products.

By-Products
The residue from electrolytic refining is processed to recover gold, silver, and selenium.

Smelting

Roaster
Copper concentrates and precipitates may be roasted in a reactor to remove sulfur and to preheat.

Reverberatory Furnace
Raw or roasted concentrates and precipitates are smelted and a matte, containing 35% to 45% copper, is produced.

Converter
The matte is converted into blister copper with a purity of about 99%.

Blister Copper

Refining

Refining Furnace
Blister copper is further purified in an anode furnace to produce anode copper or a refining furnace to produce fire-refined copper.

Anodes

Electrolytic Refining
Copper anodes are electrolytically refined to produce high purity copper cathodes which are sold or melted and cast into various shapes.

Cathodes

Cake
Hot rolled and coil rolled to produce strip and sheet.
Billet
Extruded or pierced and drawn to produce tubing and pipe.
Wirebar
Hot rolled to rod and drawn to produce wire products.
Rod
Drawn to produce wire products.

A large earth mover at work and settling ponds full of muddy water proclaim an active placer mine along the Steese Highway north of Fairbanks. The Steese leads through what was once an important and rich gold mining area. With the rise in the price of gold in recent years, mining has been resumed, and a drive along this road will provide a lesson in placer mining methods. (Virginia McKinney, staff)

ore types is a massive sulfide ore composed mostly of pyrite (iron sulfide) with chalcopyrite (copper-iron sulfide) and sphalerite (zinc sulfide) with traces of gold and silver. This is similar to the mineralogy of the Arctic and Greens Creek deposits in Alaska. The problem is to separate the valuable minerals: chalcopyrite, sphalerite, gold, and silver, from the useless pyrite and other minerals. Additionally, the chalcopyrite and

sphalerite must be separated from each other, because the copper and zinc minerals require different smelting techniques. A copper smelter charges a penalty for zinc, and likewise a zinc refinery will not pay full value for copper.

After mining, the ore is crushed and ground to the proper size. Mineral particles coarser than 250 microns or finer than 10 microns will not float. The finely ground ore (pulp) is mixed with water; a conditioner to control the acidity of the pulp; and cyanide, a depressant, to prevent flotation of sphalerite and pyrite. The pulp is then fed through a series of flotation tanks and the chalcopyrite-bearing froth is collected.

After as many as eight flotation cycles, the pulp is again placed in conditioning tanks. The cyanide is removed and

replaced by copper sulfate, an activator and a collector. The copper ions replace the zinc on the surface of the sphalerite grains and attract the collector in the pulp so that the sphalerite becomes floatable. The pulp is again run through a series of flotation cells. The remaining pulp is now composed mainly of pyrite. If free gold and silver are present, the pulp is again treated with cyanide solution. The cyanide collects the gold and silver which are then precipitated out of the solution by adding powdered zinc.

If the process started with ore containing 2% copper, 5% zinc, 0.1 ounce of gold per ton, and 1 ounce of silver per ton, after milling there would be a copper concentrate containing 25% copper, a zinc concentrate containing 50% zinc, and gold and silver bullion. The concentrates would contain about 85% to 90% of the original copper, 75% to 80% of the original zinc, and 85% of the gold and silver. Some of the gold and silver would be in the copper and zinc concentrates. Of the metal contained in the ore, 10% to 15% of the copper, 20% to 25% of the zinc, and 15% of the gold and silver would not be removed and would be lost in the tailings.

The concentrate is the final product of the mine. Concentrate is sold to a smelter or metal refinery which, in turn, produces metal from the concentrate. Smelters are complex, expensive plants and are only built when there are guaranteed long-term sources of concentrates. Most American smelters were built more than 20 years ago, and newer mines must bear the cost of shipping concentrates to the smelter. The process of producing copper from mining through smelting is illustrated in the diagram on pages 130-131.

A prospector pans for gold in a creek with the aid of a small sluice. Although sluices vary greatly in size, from ones such as this to the much larger and longer varieties attached to dredges, all sluices work on the same principle: water is directed through the trough and over blocks or slats of wood attached to the bottom, called riffles, which catch and collect any particles of gold. (Ron Wendt)

Placer Deposits of Nome

By W.R. Kastelic

The first white men who had knowledge of placer gold in northwestern Alaska were members of a Western Union Telegraph Company expedition who, in 1865, were engaged in construction of a telegraph line from the United States to eastern Asia.

The first successful placer mining in the region resulted from the discovery of gold in the Council district in the spring of 1898. That summer a group of enterprising prospectors searched for gold along the Bering Sea coast. In July they became stormbound near the present site of Nome while en route to the Sinuk River, several miles west. They found some gold in panning the bars of the Snake River, but they continued their journey to the Sinuk and returned to Golovnin Bay from where they had started. One member of the party, John J. Brynteson, was more encouraged by the Snake River panning than the

---

Editor's note: *W.R. Kastelic has been involved with exploration and mining activities in Alaska since 1957.*

others and returned the following month to the area with two companions, Jafet Lindeberg and Erik C. Lindblom. The trio began prospecting and on September 20, 1898, found rich placers on Anvil Creek. They located claims on this creek and also prospected and located claims on Snow Gulch, Glacier, Rock, and Dry creeks. These streams have since proven to be the greatest producers in the region.

By the end of September, it was too late in the year to do much mining, but the news of their discovery brought an immediate influx of men from the Council district, increasing the population of Nome to nearly 3,000 by 1899.

Early in the summer of 1899, it was discovered that the sands of the beaches around Nome were rich in gold. The beach was free to anyone who had the means to dig up and wash the sand. It was soon lined with men, each one at work on his little patch of ground. By the end of the summer the richest spots on the beach were practically exhausted.

News of the successes of 1899 set in motion the great rush to the Nome area

that took place in 1900. During that summer more than 20,000 persons were landed on the Nome beach. A solid row of tents stretched for five miles along the beach, and the waterfront was piled high with freight of all kinds.

Beach mining could no longer support the population — Anvil, Dexter, and Glacier creeks were the big producers, but there was no ground left on them for latecomers. Thousands of men left Nome in the fall of 1900, discouraged and disgusted.

During 1900, about half of the production of the district was from the

---

Members of the staff of Lomen and Company (Gudbrand Lomen is in the center and his son Carl is at the extreme right) pose with a fortune in gold bullion in Nome in 1919. The Lomen family engaged in many businesses in Nome during the first part of the 20th century, including the Lomen Commercial Company, a drugstore, photographic business, and reindeer herding. After moving to Nome in 1900, Gudbrand Lomen served that city at various times as mayor, U.S. Attorney, and Federal Judge for the district.
(Lomen Collection, University of Alaska Archives)

The great rush to Nome took place in 1900, following several rich placer discoveries in the area. During the summer of that year, more than 20,000 people were landed on the Nome beach. A solid row of tents stretched for five miles along the beach, and the waterfront was piled high with freight of all kinds.
(Powell Collection, University of Alaska Archives; reprinted from *ALASKA SPORTSMAN*®)

properties of the original discoverers, Brynteson, Lindeberg, and Lindblom.

The most important event of the next four years was the discovery of the Second Beach in 1902. The creeks continued to be the big producers until 1904, although they never again reached the peak attained in 1900. By the end of 1903 the richest producer of the district, Anvil Creek, was almost exhausted.

The years between 1900 and 1904 marked a period of expansion in methods and consolidation of ownership. The partnership of Brynteson, Lindeberg, and Lindblom was incorporated as the Pioneer Mining Company in 1902. The pumping plant of the Wild Goose Company, on the Snake River, was built in 1901 and started supplying water to the gravel of the Dexter area. With completion of the Miocene Ditch, in 1903, to provide water at a high pressure to the placer areas, hydraulic elevators were introduced and used extensively in the mining operations from then on.

In the fall of 1904, rich placer deposits were found beneath the tundra of the coastal plain near Little Creek. This led to the discovery of the famous Third Beach, from which more gold was eventually extracted than from the combined production of the other beaches.

This discovery also focused attention on the possibilities of additional beach deposits beneath the coastal plain. Intensive prospecting resulted in the discovery of the Intermediate and Monroeville beaches in 1906, the

Submarine Beach in 1907, and several other concentrations beneath the tundra surface.

Submarine Beach was the last important discovery to be made in the Nome area. During the following years, extensions of the known deposits were proven, and more economical methods of mining were developed. Ground sluicing, followed by hydraulic elevating, were the first big steps toward less costly mining.

Attempts at dredging the thawed portions of the deposits were made as early as 1903. The first attempts were unsuccessful. Better conceived efforts were started about 1911, and during the following few years there were as many as eight dredges operating at one time on the Nome coastal plain. Most of these were very small dredges, and their digging was largely confined to thawed ground. Frozen ground had to be thawed with steam, involving so much expense that its dredging was impractical. Successful large-scale dredging could not be done until a more economical method of thawing the ground was developed.

The invention and perfection of the thawing process were historically important steps for they made available for dredge recovery millions of dollars in gold, previously locked in the frozen gravel of many parts of Alaska.

Mining Methods

The mining life of the Nome district has been extended far beyond its early expectations through the combination of

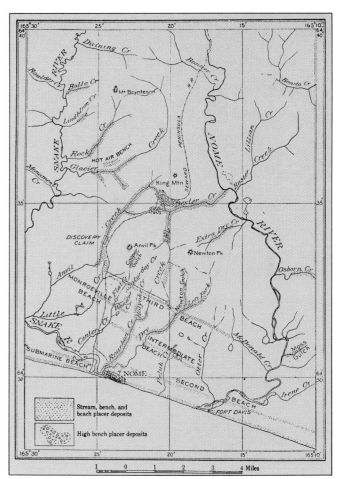

This 1913 map shows the distribution of placers in the vicinity of Nome. (U.S.G.S. Bulletin #533)

— 137

Early in the summer of 1899 gold was discovered on the beaches of Nome. The sands were free to anyone who had the means to dig them up, and the beach was soon lined with men. These miners are at work with ''long toms,'' set up on the water's edge so there was always water available for washing down the sluices.
(Alaska Historical Library; reprinted from ALASKA® magazine)

timely new discoveries, man's ingenuity in developing lower cost methods of handling the deposits, and by an increase in the price of gold.

Following exhaustion of the rich creek bed deposits, production in the Nome area has come almost exclusively from the marine deposits of the coastal plain. These deposits were worked by sinking shafts and following gold deposits horizontally — an expensive method that meant only high-grade ground would pay the cost of

extraction. When water was delivered to the area at sufficient pressure so that it could be used effectively, open cut hydraulic operations on the shallower deposit superseded underground mining.

The ground that could be handled successfully by hydraulic methods was nearing exhaustion when the cold water thawing method of ground preparation was developed. Millions of yards of low-grade ground that could be handled by no other means were now available for dredging. Nome was given another long-term reprieve.

Dredging

Most of the muck and gravel deposits in Alaska are solidly frozen from surface to bedrock. Areas which are covered by moss and/or a layer of decayed vegetation will generally remain permanently frozen. The vegetation provides an insulating blanket which effectively prevents the deposits from thawing during the short summer season. Certain creek areas, where the placer deposits are relatively thin (8 to 15 feet), are known to thaw naturally once the insulating cover is removed and the gravels are exposed to the sunlight for a period of a year or more. For deep dredging in permafrost, artificial thawing is required.

The thawing process is accomplished by introducing ambient temperature water at relatively low pressure into the ground through pipes extending to bedrock. As the water percolates upward to the

surface, the frozen ground absorbs some of the heat contained in the water and the thawing process begins. The approximate time required for ground preparation is two years, after which dredging may begin. To enable dredging operations in Alaska to continue for the maximum of what is a short operating season (usually 180 to 250 days a year), the dredges are equipped to provide steam heat to critical areas. Surface frost is thawed directly ahead of the dredge so that the equipment can begin operating as early in the season as possible.

Once the ground is prepared, the material being dredged is brought to the surface by buckets which discharge into a dump hopper, from which the gravel passes to a trommel screen. Slotted perforations are included in part of the last screen section to catch occasional nuggets. Gravel washing is done by nozzles on a spray pipe extending the full length of the screen. Material too large to pass through the screen is conveyed to waste piles; the smaller screened particles pass to the gold recovery system. This may be either sluices, in which the gravel is passed over a series of riffles which catch the heavier material, or jigs, vibrating screens which separate the ore from the gravel.

The rush to Nome was the result of only one of many gold discoveries in Alaska around the turn of the century. Beach and stream placers in the area eventually produced 3.6 million ounces of gold, first by panning and later by dredging.

In 1975 rising gold prices prompted the reactivation of Alaska Gold Company's dredges at Nome. The operations had been shut down in 1962 because economic production had become impossible in the face of rising costs and fixed gold prices. Alaska Gold Company currently operates two dredges during the mining season — #5 (left), built in 1941; and #6, built in 1956, using parts salvaged from dredge #3 which had capsized three years earlier. Total employment during the past several seasons has peaked around 160. Dredges #1 and #2 (below), both wooden hull boats built in 1922, have been retired but are still standing. Dredge #4 only operated for two seasons before the owner at the time, Hammon Consolidated Goldfields, sold it and #4 was moved to the Candle area. (Left, Mark McDermott; below, Mark J. Rauzon)

Marine Mining

By Cleland Conwell

Marine mining is defined as "a commercial recovery of minerals other than oil and gas from the surface of or below the seabed by operations connected only indirectly with land, i.e. by ships or pipelines."

In Alaska, offshore placer mining operated prior to 1940 near Golovnin Bay. When the ice was thick enough to support a clamshell scoop and truck, holes were cut through the ice. Sand and gravels were brought from the ocean floor with the clamshell, loaded into trucks, and transported to the shore for sluicing during the summer.

By the mid-1970s, the only Alaska

Editor's note: *Cleland Conwell, a mining engineer and mine inspector formerly with the Alaska Department of Natural Resources and now retired, contributed much of this information on marine placer prospects in Alaska.*

offshore mine operating in the state was on Castle Islands near Petersburg. Alaska Barite Company began mining this small outcrop of barite about 1963. By 1967 the company was working offshore where they drilled and blasted the ore under water. The broken material was then recovered by a clamshell scoop and loaded onto a barge. The barge was pulled close to shore; the rock pulled ashore with a dragline, crushed, and stockpiled. The barite was then loaded directly onto an ocean vessel. About 100,000 tons of barite were mined each year until 1980 when Chromalloy, the principal operator at that time, closed the mine.

In 1981 Cook Inlet Exploration and Development, Inc. announced discovery of workable deposits of gold and other materials in the tidelands and submerged lands between Point Woronzof and Point Campbell near Anchorage. The company hopes to extract three to five pounds of heavy mineral concentrate for every 3,000

pounds of gravel dredged from the Cook Inlet bottom. Plans call for further testing to take place in summer, 1982, with commercial production to begin in summer, 1983. Operators also hope to market sand and gravel, a by-product of their dredging, in the Anchorage area.

Alaska had approximately 23,000 acres under lease for marine mining as of March, 1982. At that time an additional 140,000 or so acres were held on offshore prospecting permits.

This high altitude aerial photo, taken at low tide, shows the beach terrain from Point Woronzof (top) to Point Campbell (bottom), near Anchorage. Cook Inlet Exploration and Development, Inc., has discovered placer deposits of gold and other minerals in the area's tidelands and submerged lands. Further testing is to take place during the summer of 1982; dredging is scheduled to begin in summer, 1983. (BLM)

N

Cook Inlet

Point
Woronzof

Earthquake
Park

Point
Campbell

Anchorage
International Airport

Gold Panning Techniques

Story and photos by Leah Madonna

Unlike other forms of outdoor recreation, panning for gold is one of the least expensive in which to participate. Unlike many sports, panning for gold can easily be mastered by anyone, regardless of age, sex, or physical strength.

First let's discuss the equipment. Gold pans are available in sizes from a 10-inch to a 16-inch. The pans may be steel or plastic. Pans may be smooth inside or have one or more rows of riffles. Riffles are raised ridges which help retain the gold and other heavy minerals when panning off the lighter sands. The best pan is a matter of personal preference.

A small shovel and a container, such as a small glass vial with a screw cap to keep the gold, are the only additional tools needed. Some panners include a pair of

Editor's note: *This step-by-step guide to gold panning is excerpted from* Alaskan Prospectors & Miner's News, *Summer Quarter, 1981. Leah Madonna is editor of the newsletter, and the material is reprinted here by permission.*

tweezers to pick out the small nuggets or flakes, but there are other techniques available. A magnet is carried by some to extract the magnetic particles of black sand sometimes found with the gold.

The techniques of panning for gold are simple. Upon selecting a promising prospect area, look for likely spots or natural obstacles which might slow or retard the movement of heavy material passing through during spring flooding, such as natural depressions, under large boulders, in potholes of bedrock, and similar barriers.

When shoveling into this material, work the shovel down several inches into the more compact material. Place this material

into the pan, including the large rocks, roots, and other debris. Do not cast any of this material from the pan at this stage.

Move the pan to the stream, selecting a spot where the current is not too swift. Grasp the pan firmly in both hands, totally submerse the pan and contents under

water. Vigorously rotate the pan in a semicircular motion. Hold the pan level without any tilt or angle. The motion is similar to that of turning a steering wheel rapidly from side to side. At this point the lighter silt and sand particles are washing over the top of the pan and into the stream. Larger rocks, finer gravel, and heavy concentrate remain in the pan.

While holding the pan in a level position under water, use one hand to break up any clay or grass clumps. This material should be thoroughly broken apart so that any gold trapped in the clays,

against roots, or clinging to larger rocks has been washed free. Large rocks, roots, and grasses may be cast from the pan once this is accomplished.

Holding the pan horizontal, place it beneath the surface of the water and again rotate vigorously, forcing specific gravity concentrate and gold to precipitate to the bottom of the pan while simultaneously

working the lighter material to the top. Any large rocks may be removed from the pan at this time.

After thoroughly washing and removing the larger rock material, you are ready to wash the lightweight material from the pan. Hold the pan firmly with a slight angle so that a fan is formed, as shown below.

The tip of the pan should remain beneath the water throughout the washing and concentrating of the minerals. The pan tip is then rocked forward and backward, dipping slightly to one side to allow fresh water to enter, and then to the other side to allow water to flow from the pan. This rocking and dipping method allows the lighter sands and gravels to be lifted by the water's action and to flow from the pan into the stream.

Approximately every dozen back-and-forth rocking motions should be followed by rotating the pan to the horizontal position and agitating it beneath the water's surface. This reconcentrates the heavy minerals and allows the lighter materials to work up to the surface where they can more easily be removed by the panning action. Tip the pan forward with

the gentle agitation to produce the fan shape as shown here. You are now ready

to resume the panning action. This procedure is continued until the equivalent of a couple of tablespoons of material is left in the pan.

In the first stages of panning, while there is much gravel still in the pan, it is reasonable to increase the speed of the rocking and dipping process. As long as the pan is held at the same angle and the steps are followed, the gold will continue to be concentrated at the lowest level in the pan. At times you will need to pull more of the medium-sized rocks from the pan by hand as some will not flow over

the lip with the light sands at the gentle angle used.

When the material left in the pan appears to be approximately one cup or

less, slow down the panning and watch the material being washed over the lip more carefully. When a dark red or black band of sand appears on the edge of the sand remaining in the pan, you have reached the heavy mineral concentrates. Red garnet, magnetite, and hematite are common. These are the heaviest materials left in the pan with the exception of gold which usually lies beneath these sands.

Work down the material remaining in

the pan only use more caution. When the mineral concentrate is reduced to one or two tablespoons, you are ready to examine the contents for gold. With the pan containing about one-half cup of water and the concentrate, hold the pan level and begin rotating it, gently forcing the water to swirl in a circular motion. This will force the lighter concentrate to move along the path with the water, leaving the gold concentrated in a sparkling trail behind it.

To extract the small flakes of gold, lick your finger, and place it against the gold, and then dip your finger into a container of water. The gold will drop into the container upon contact with the water.

Coal Resources of Alaska

By Robert B. Sanders

Although Alaska's Natives and some of its early explorers may have utilized coal and oil shales as fuels, the first written record of coal interests in the state is that of Capt. Nathaniel Portlock, who discovered and used coal at Port Graham, on the Kenai Peninsula, in 1786. The first serious attempt at commercial utilization of Alaska coal began in 1855 when the Russian American Company began mining coal at Port Graham for export to California. Although the export market never developed, the mine produced coal for local and maritime markets until 1865. Later in the 19th century, it became standard practice for whaling ships and U.S. revenue cutters to take on coal from beds near Cape Sabine on the Arctic coast. Riverboats plying the Yukon, Kuskokwim, and other rivers also obtained small

Editor's note: *Robert B. Sanders, a former mining manager for the State of Alaska and member of the University of Alaska faculty, is currently employed as a geologist in private industry.*

quantities of coal for local use, and at least 16 mines operated along the Yukon during the 1890s. These were all abandoned by 1910, as river traffic decreased, and what little traffic remained had converted to oil fuel.

The need for large amounts of heat for domestic use and to thaw frozen ground for placer gold mining was met with coal wherever it was available, and at least 100 small mines operated around the turn of the century. The operators' rights to the coal were apparently *pedis possessio* (by actual possession), but nevertheless coal interests were bartered well before the general mining laws of the United States were extended to the Territory of Alaska in 1900.

In addition to the mines along the Yukon and other navigable rivers, around the turn of the century mines were located at Admiralty Island, Herendeen Bay, Chignik, Cape Lisburne, Kachemak Bay, Unga Island, Nyac, and Chicago Creek. The last, near Candle on the Seward Peninsula, entered an 80-foot lignite seam in 1903 and produced almost continuously

into the 1940s, despite early attempts by the federal government to halt the mine's unlicensed exploitation of the coal.

The mineral laws of the United States were extended to the Territory of Alaska by the Act of June 6, 1900, making it possible for prospectors to claim coal as a locatable mineral. Many coal entries were made under this act in the Bering River and Matanuska Valley coal fields by prospectors apparently unaware that this law permitted location only on surveyed land, of which there was none in these areas.

The Alaska Coal Act of April 28, 1904, allowed location without the precedent government survey and most of the earlier claims were relocated under this authority. However, because of the accusations of fraudulent claims by "dummy entrymen"

Evan Jones, sometimes known as the father of the Alaska coal industry, examines a coal seam near Homer about 1946. Jones was instrumental in development of the mines at Jonesville and Houston. (Steve McCutcheon)

This 1860 view shows the Russian coal mine site and village at Port Graham, on the Kenai Peninsula. The Russian American Company began mining coal at Port Graham in 1855 for exportation to California. The entrance to the mine is visible at water level, near the center of the picture.
(Collection of Western Americana, Beinecke Rare Book and Manuscript Library, Yale University; reprinted from *The ALASKA JOURNAL®*)

on behalf of East Coast monopolies, all of the claims became suspect. Spurred by a biased Washington press and *Collier's Weekly* magazine, the matter of Alaska coal claims became a national sensation and ammunition in the growing ideological feud between Gifford Pinchot, chief of the Bureau of Forestry and champion of preservationism, and R.A. Ballinger, commissioner of the General Land Office and later secretary of the interior. In response to the controversy, on November 17, 1906, President Theodore Roosevelt withdrew all Alaska public lands from entry under the coal claims laws. Although initially done under questionable authority, Congress validated the withdrawal in the Act of May 28, 1908. Enmeshed in the Pinchot-Ballinger controversy, legal processing of the coal claims stagnated, leaving the claimants in the unenviable position of

having to do annual assessment work, but being unable to remove or sell their coal. Under these conditions, most of the claims were abandoned, with only two of the 900 claims going to patent.

At that time, domestic production supplied only 2% of the territorial coal consumption, the remainder being imported from British Columbia, Australia, Japan, or Washington State at an average consumer's price of $15 per ton. In addition to the many claimants and investors who were financially ruined, consumers who had to buy expensive imported (and import-taxed) coal, while local coal could have been had for $3 per ton, were understandably unhapppy. Pinchot was burned in effigy in Katalla, then a town of several thousand which hoped to serve as a railhead for Bering River coal. In Cordova the people shoveled tons of the expensive imported coal into Prince William Sound as a "Coal Party Protest."

During the congressional investigation which followed, it was found that some of the General Land Office staff had been on a clandestine Bureau of Forestry payroll, allegedly hired to disrupt and delay the land office patenting operations while leaking information to Pinchot with which to embarass Ballinger. Several hundred people lost large sums of money when caught in the middle of these dirty politics, and work ceased on the several coal railroads that had begun in the Bering River area.

Between 1880 and 1915, the total

reported coal production of the Territory of Alaska was 70,000 short tons valued at approximately $450,000. This was mainly the production of the Wharf Mine at Port Graham, which produced 1,000 to 3,000 tons of sub-bituminous coal per year at a price calculated to have been $3 to $6 per ton, but also includes several thousand tons of coal produced from the McDonald property on Bering Lake in 1907. Not included in these figures are the pirated output of the illegal Chicago Creek Mine on the Seward Peninsula and the mines at Herendeen Bay, Chignik Bay, and Unga Island, and other mines operated with the local and native economy.

In 1914, President Wilson authorized construction of the Alaska Railroad, choosing a route which closely passed the Matanuska, Little Susitna, Broad Pass, and Healy coal fields. That same year, the federal government, now having a vested interest in coal development, enacted the Alaska Coal Leasing Act under which mines were developed in what was to become McKinley National Park and the Nenana, Matanuska Valley, and Bering River coal fields. Also in 1914, the U.S. Navy undertook extensive testing of Matanuska and Bering River coal, concluding that the former was suitable, but the latter unsuitable, for naval use. This proved the end of the lingering dreams of Katalla and Bering River entrepreneurs.

The building of the Alaska Railroad to the Matanuska coal field in 1916 and to the Nenana coal field in 1918 created the market and transportation necessary for large scale mine development. Between 1916 and 1940, coal production increased fairly steadily to 174,000 tons per year. Primary production was of bituminous coal from the Wishbone Hill district of the Matanuska coal field and of sub-bituminous coal from the Healy Creek and Suntrana areas of the Nenana coal field.

The tremendous military buildup in the Anchorage and Fairbanks areas during and after World War II created market and profit incentive for further exploration and development, and additional mines were opened at Healy, Nenana, Jarvis Creek, Broad Pass, Costello Creek, and in the Little Susitna and Wishbone Hill areas of the Matanuska Valley. The price of coal jumped about 50%. Similarly, lack of fuel forced Wainwright and Barrow to open coal mines. Most of these wartime ventures were short-lived, but overall production rose rapidly through the postwar years to 861,000 tons in 1953. The military market grew so rapidly that the switch from coal to diesel fuel by the Alaska Railroad in the early 1950s did not adversely affect the Alaska coal industry. In fact, production continued to increase in the face of this transition, peaking to about 925,000 tons per year in 1966 and 1967. The 1968 congressional decision to convert the Anchorage military bases to gas power generation signaled the doom of the last Matanuska Valley mine, the Evan Jones, and displaced about 100 workers.

The only mine surviving the pandemic transition to gas and oil was the Usibelli Coal Mine at Healy in the Nenana field. This stripping operation produces approximately 800,000 tons per year of sub-bituminous coal from three 17- to 20-foot-thick beds, primarily for public utility and military markets in the Fairbanks area. The price varies greatly between contracts, depending on the contract specifications for values added by sizing, transportation, loading, etc., but averages approximately $1.25 per million Btu (British thermal units), compared with number two fuel oil at $8.78 per million Btu at the local bulk price of $1.15 per gallon.

Land Status

Under its mandate to designate mineral lands, the federal government officially classified approximately 33 million acres in Alaska as prospectively valuable for coal. This represents about 9% of the state. The majority of these coal lands were selected by the State of Alaska under the Statehood Act or by the Alaska Native corporations formed under the Alaska Native Claims Settlement Act (ANCSA). However, much coal land remains under federal title in the National Petroleum Reserve-Alaska (NPR-A), and in many of Alaska's national wildlife refuges, Chugach National Forest, the newly created Denali National Park and Preserve, Kobuk Valley National Park, and Yukon-Charley Rivers National Preserve. Additional coal may exist in areas transected by waterways

— 149

protected as wild and scenic rivers. The extent to which most of these federally controlled coal fields can be prospected and developed is not clear as the regulations pertaining to the new units created under the Alaska National Interest Lands Conservation Act (ANILCA) of 1980 have not yet been finalized as of August 1, 1982. All or parts of the Broad Pass, North Slope, Circle-Eagle, Kobuk, Lisburne, Lower Yukon, Etolin Strait, Bering River, Kenai, and Nenana coal areas or fields are involved in this temporarily unsettled status.

The State of Alaska has title to most of the Cook Inlet (Susitna Basin) coal region, including the Beluga, Yentna, Little Susitna, and Kenai coal fields; the Matanuska field; the central portion of the Nenana coal belt (Healy coal field); and portions of the North Slope, Herendeen Bay (on the Alaska Peninsula), and Robinson Mountain (on the Gulf of Alaska west of Icy Bay) fields. State selections pending include additional lands in the foregoing areas, as well as in the poorly studied Seward Peninsula coal areas and among the abandoned coal sites that occur along the Yukon and Koyukuk rivers. Some of the state selections conflict with units created under ANILCA and will presumably be denied.

Acquisition of coal rights from the State of Alaska follows procedures based on those of the old federal system of the Mineral Leasing Act of 1920, with lands classified for competitive or non-competitive leasing and with a system of

coal prospecting permits which may be converted to lease upon the proof of discovery of a commercial coal deposit. As of July 1, 1982, there were 53 state coal leases (involving nearly 150,000 acres); and seven coal prospecting permits under application for conversion to coal leases (totaling more than 16,000 acres). Since October, 1975, however, no new coal leases or coal prospecting permits have been issued by the Department of Natural Resources, except through these discovery-based conversion to lease provisions of a coal prospecting permit. This freeze was apparently an outgrowth of the Kachemak oil lease sale court decision regarding the need for greater public notice prior to lease issuance and the administration's disenchantment over royalty provisions. New statutes have corrected the original problem and new lease royalty regulations were adopted in 1982. Issuance of coal leases is scheduled for early 1983.

Several of the 13 Native corporations established under ANCSA acquired coal lands. The most significant holdings are: Cook Inlet Region, Inc.'s interests in the Cook Inlet-Susitna coal region, especially in the Beluga coal field; Doyon Limited's interests in the Nenana coal belt, especially in the Farewell area and in the Eagle-Circle area; Arctic Slope Regional Corporation's interest in the North Slope coal field; Chugach Natives, Inc.'s interests in the Bering River coal field; and The Aleut Corporation's and Bristol Bay Native Corporation's interests in the Herendeen Bay-Chignik coal field.

In 1920 the U.S. Navy built a mining town at Chickaloon, but it had to be abandoned shortly after when it was discovered that the coal in the area could not be mined economically. This undated photo shows the mining operation, with the powerhouse at the extreme left and dormitory at the center of the photo.

Acquisition of coal or exploration rights on these privately administered lands would be through private negotiation, with the state and federal governments not involved except with surface mining controls, safety, and taxation.

The Surface Mining Control and Reclamation Act of 1977 affects all significant coal mining, both surface and underground, regardless of land title. The state is attempting to assume jurisdiction (primacy) over surface mining and a surface coal mining statute closely following the federal law has been passed. Regulations and performance standards are being prepared, and a decision on primacy is hoped for in early 1983. Until this is resolved, the working conditions and constraints under the act will remain unknown. However, it may be safely stated that all phases of mining, including exploration and the very availability of mining lands, will be severely impacted.

Resources

Early attempts to estimate Alaska's coal resources, such as those by Alfred Brooks (1901 and 1909) and George Gates (1946),

In 1913 the Naval Coal Commission sent an expedition to the Bering River coal field to collect samples. From top to bottom, members of the expedition pose on a paddlewheel riverboat used for pulling barges of coal on the Bering River; members of the expedition and local crew members sit for a group shot at their camp; and miners stack bags of samples at the mouth of the No. 4 mine on Trout Creek.
(All photos courtesy of Robert B. Sanders)

152 —

were based on such incomplete and unreliable data that they gave only a general idea of the importance of the resource. The great interest in coal during and after World War II resulted in several excellent studies on coal resources by the U.S. Bureau of Mines and the U.S. Geological Survey, compiled into statewide estimates by Farrel Barnes in 1960 and 1976. More recent data has been inexplicably ignored in various Department of Interior resource estimates of the d-2 lands, with Barnes' now grossly outdated statistics continuing to be quoted. Worse, many qualitative and quantitative statements now known to be false have been blindly repeated, perpetuating the errors through repetition.

The total resource data given here are statistically ludicrous in that they are the sum of data expressed to the nearest billion tons and nearest thousand tons. Considering significant figures, the total Alaska onshore coal resource is estimated to be 216 billion to 4,216 billion tons, of which 141 billion tons are identified resources. An additional 1,430 billion tons are believed to lie beneath Cook Inlet (to 10,000 feet), raising the upper total limit to 5,646 billion tons.

Numbers in parentheses refer to locations shown on the map at right.

North Slope

The area north of the Brooks Range may constitute the world's largest coal province. It is also one of the least known and least probable for large scale

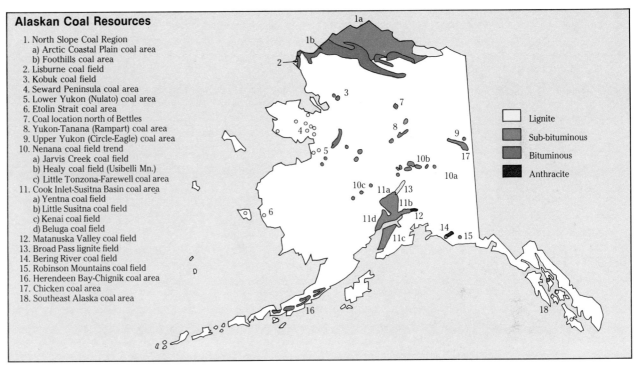

Alaskan Coal Resources

1. North Slope Coal Region
   a) Arctic Coastal Plain coal area
   b) Foothills coal area
2. Lisburne coal field
3. Kobuk coal field
4. Seward Peninsula coal area
5. Lower Yukon (Nulato) coal area
6. Etolin Strait coal area
7. Coal location north of Bettles
8. Yukon-Tanana (Rampart) coal area
9. Upper Yukon (Circle-Eagle) coal area
10. Nenana coal field trend
    a) Jarvis Creek coal field
    b) Healy coal field (Usibelli Mn.)
    c) Little Tonzona-Farewell coal area
11. Cook Inlet-Susitna Basin coal area
    a) Yentna coal field
    b) Little Susitna coal field
    c) Kenai coal field
    d) Beluga coal field
12. Matanuska Valley coal field
13. Broad Pass lignite field
14. Bering River coal field
15. Robinson Mountains coal field
16. Herendeen Bay-Chignik coal area
17. Chicken coal area
18. Southeast Alaska coal area

Lignite
Sub-bituminous
Bituminous
Anthracite

Classification of Coals by Rank

Class[1]	Group[1]	Heat Value Range,[2] in Btu per pound
Anthracite	Meta-anthracite	—[3]
	Anthracite	—
	Semianthracite	—
Bituminous	Low volatile bituminous coal	—
	Medium volatile bituminous coal	—
	High volatile A bituminous coal	14,000
	High volatile B bituminous coal	13,000 to 14,000
	High volatile C bituminous coal	11,500 to 13,000
Sub-bituminous	Sub-bituminous A coal	10,500 to 11,500
	Sub-bituminous B coal	9,500 to 10,500
	Sub-bituminous C coal	8,300 to 9,500
Lignitic	Lignite A	6,300 to 8,300
	Lignite B	to 6,300

[1] Coals are listed in descending order of quality, i.e., anthracite, while more difficult to burn, will give off more heat than lignite.
[2] The amount of heat given off during burning is measured in Btu, or British thermal units. One Btu is defined as heat required to raise the temperature of one pound of water 1 °F. The higher the Btu rating, the greater the amount of heat the coal will provide.
[3] Above 14,500 Btu, heat value stabilizes and is no longer a good criterion for classification. Harder, more compact anthracite and low and medium volatile bituminous coals are more difficult to ignite and are generally not acceptable for home use.

— 153

utilization. In the west central Arctic (1a), including NPR-A, coal occurs in the 1,000- to 15,000-foot-thick Corwin formation. Of the approximately 150 coal beds, 28 are described as thick.

On the Arctic coastal plain (1a), thick, wet tundra vegetation generally restricts coal outcrops to stream cuts. This coal is generally of sub-bituminous A rank, with low ash and sulfur content, and occurs in simple, broad, open folds.

To the east of NPR-A there are few coal outcrops, with most data coming from seismic shot holes and oil well logs. This coal is generally less mature and of lesser rank (sub-bituminous C and lignite) than is the coal to the west.

As one approaches the Brooks Range foothills (1b) to the south, coal is found in progressively tighter and less symmetric folds, and its rank increases to high volatile bituminous B.

Significant locations include the Corwin Bluffs, where 80 beds of up to nine feet in thickness have been described; the Cape Beaufort area, where 12- to 17-foot-thick beds occur; and on the Kukpowruk River, where a 20-foot-thick bed of high volatile bituminous coking coal (coal which, when heated in the absence of air, swells to form the hard, bubbly mass of carbon known as coke) is found. The last area has

Usibelli Coal Mine's walking dragline, the Ace in the Hole, is shown here working in Poker Pit. The dragline is capable of moving about 1,000 cubic yards of overburden an hour.
(Jill Shepherd)

Thick seams of coal are exposed in Usibelli Mine's east vitro pit. The mine produces about 800,000 tons of sub-bituminous coal annually from a series of three 20-foot-thick beds.
(Robert B. Sanders)

Coal is exposed along the bank of the Kukpowruk River, on the western Arctic slope, where a 20-foot-thick bed of high volatile bituminous coking coal is found. (Gil Mull)

been opened and extensively studied since 1954 by Morgan Coal Company, Union Carbide Corporation, and Kaiser Engineers.

Although the presence of coal appears widespread in the Nanushuk and Colville groups near the eastern edge of NPR-A, points of actual observation are few and far between. This makes correlation and resource estimation difficult. A recent estimate, by Ross Schaff, state geologist, in 1980, places the total resource of the North Slope at between 402 and 4,000 billion tons of hypothetical resources, plus 60 to 146 billion tons of identified resource, or, between 462 and 4,146 billion tons of coal.

Problems with access and transportation, plus the lack of a large local market, make it unlikely that large scale development of the North Slope coal fields will occur in the near future. Use for village needs, however, is considered overdue in light of high local energy costs and the proximity of the coal. The most likely large scale exploitation of the resource may be as liquid or gaseous pipeline feedstock through *in situ* conversion, but this would be many years in the future.

Along the coast of the Lisburne Peninsula (2), where the Brooks Range meets the sea, low volatile bituminous coal is found in the Kapaloak formation of the Lisburne Group. The area has been severely deformed, and the coal beds are described as crushed, broken, and without persistence.

Alaska Interior

The interior of Alaska (the area between the Alaska and Brooks ranges) contains several areas where coal-bearing rocks occur. Although Alaska's best known field lies in this part of the state, no determination of the extent and distribution of coal, or even the delineation of coal-bearing basins, has been made for much of the area. Exploration costs in these areas would be high, but the potential for large volumes of coal is also high. Transportation may be the critical factor for development.

Nenana Coal Fields: A series of individual coal-bearing basins up to 30 miles wide extends in a discontinuous belt for at least 150 miles along the north side of the Alaska Range. Although several of the basins bear individual coal field names, such as Jarvis Creek, Teklanika, Hood River, Healy, Lignite, Suntrana, and Tatlanika, they are sufficiently similar that they can be considered under a single title. The coal in these basins is generally sub-bituminous C or B, with a low sulfur content, and varying between 8,500 and 9,500 Btu. Throughout most of the area, the overlying sandstone is not excessively hard, making stripping operations favorable.

The easternmost coal field identified in this area is the Jarvis Creek coal field

Coal is loaded onto a truck at one of the strip mining operations at the Usibelli Mine at Healy, the only currently active coal mine in Alaska. (Steve McCutcheon)

156 —

A coal seam is exposed in a cutbank of clay near Ninilchik, on the Kenai Peninsula.
(Chlaus Lotscher)

(10a), near Big Delta on the Richardson Highway. There are reported to be 30 coal beds greater than one and one-half feet thick, and one seam eight to ten feet thick. The coal ranges from 7,800 to 8,300 Btu, typical for Nenana coal, but contains 1.0% to 1.3% sulfur, which is uncommonly high. This field has been explored under a federal coal prospecting permit, and an application for conversion to lease is pending.

The Healy, Lignite, and Suntrana coal fields lie in the central portion of the Nenana belt, along the Alaska Railroad and the Parks Highway (10b). Several properties in this area were developed with the construction of the Alaska Railroad in 1918 and many operated during and shortly after World War II. Sub-bituminous C coal occurs here.

The Usibelli Mine (10b), the only currently active mine in the state, produces about 800,000 tons of coal annually from a series of three 20-foot-thick beds. Reserves of at least 250 million tons are estimated on Usibelli's state and federal leases. The coal is sub-bituminous C, averaging about 7,800 Btu, with 27% moisture and 0.2% sulfur, which is considered typical of the Nenana coals.

The western end of the string of Nenana coal basins was originally thought to be the thin and dirty sub-bituminous beds observed in the Kantishna Hills. Recently, however, several related coal outcrops have been discovered about 100 miles further west in the Farewell-Little Tonzona area (10c). The U.S. Geological Survey reports seven beds thicker than 30 inches. The coal of the thickest (110-foot) bed is similar to that at Jarvis Creek in quality, being richer in sulfur than the Nenana coals at Healy. Other coals in the area are of elevated rank and marginally bituminous. Speculative resources of 1.5 billion tons could be present.

The coal resources of the Nenana coal fields are believed to be about seven billion tons identified and ten billion tons undiscovered (i.e., speculative and hypothetical), for a total reserve of

Other Occurrences in the Interior Region: Borderline sub-bituminous to bituminous coal is found in two-foot-thick beds in several locations along a 120-mile stretch of the Kobuk River, in particular between Kiana and Shungnak (3). The extent and distribution are unknown.

About 36 miles northeast of Bettles, on the middle fork of the Koyukuk River (7), a bed of bituminous coal and extensive additional float (loose pieces of coal) have been reported. Again, the extent and distribution are unknown.

Along the lower parts of the Yukon River (5), in the Kaltag to Galena segment, bituminous coal in one- to three-foot beds are reported at several locations in the Kaltag formation. Several small mines were operated for the riverboat market at the turn of the century, including the Pickert Mine, near Nulato, where a seam of fair- to good-quality coking coal was reportedly worked. A bed of coal has also been reported in the vicinity of Anvik.

Coal and lignite have been reported from several sites along the lower Kuskokwim River, including a report of a six-foot bituminous coal bed, according to Barnes' 1967 data.

Along Etolin Strait, on Nunivak and Nelson islands (6), bituminous coals with high coking values are reported, but in beds less than two feet thick. North along the coast, around Unalakleet, coal was once mined from beds reported to be up to eight feet thick.

Several areas of lignite-bearing rocks occur in a complex of isolated basins on the Seward Peninsula (4). A steeply dipping, 80-foot bed of lignite at Chicago Creek on the Candle River was opened in 1908 and mined almost continually until after World War II. Farther upstream on the Candle, steeply dipping lignite beds were also mined. The state is studying these occurrences and may develop the coal for use in Kotzebue.

Near the confluence of the Yukon and Tanana rivers (8), thin bituminous coal was mined for the riverboat traffic at the turn of the century. Although the known coal beds are thin, impure and of limited horizontal continuity, the area has not been explored sufficiently, and should remain of interest for the potential local market. Several miles to the north, at the confluence of the Dall and Yukon rivers, a bed of sub-bituminous coal was described by the U.S. Geological Survey in 1973.

Thin, sub-bituminous coal seams are present in open folds along an 80-mile

A geologist studies the 50-foot-thick Capps Bed in the Beluga coal field, on the west side of Cook Inlet. (Cleland Conwell)

segment of the upper Yukon River near the Canadian border (9), between the towns of Eagle and Circle, both of which are served by road. At Washington Creek, five coal beds have been reported. Schaff estimates hypothetical resources of 100 million tons in this area. A pocket of bituminous coking coal was mined near the mouth of the Nation River. Most of the Circle-Eagle coal is now within Yukon-Charley Rivers National Preserve and is off limits, even to investigation.

About 50 miles south of the upper Yukon River coal area at Chicken (17), an outcrop of vertically dipping strata includes a sub-bituminous coal bed which was opened in the 1930s. The extent of the coal is unknown, but the potential area is limited to only a few square miles.

So little is known about these areas of outcrop that resource estimation, even on a speculative basis, is of dubious value. With the exception of Chicago Creek, no resources have been estimated as identified. The hypothetical resources of the middle and upper Yukon areas (8 and 9) have been estimated at 200 million tons, but this figure ignores the Kobuk, Koyukuk, Seward Peninsula, Unalakleet, lower Yukon, Etolin, Bettles, and other occurrences. The total resource from these areas is unknown.

Southcentral Alaska

Cook Inlet-Susitna Basin Coal Region: The sedimentary basin now partially occupied by Cook Inlet contains enormous coal resources. In dealing with the coal, this area has been traditionally divided into several coal fields: the Yentna coal field (11a), lying north of the Castle Mountain fault; the Little Susitna coal field (11b), extending into the Matanuska Valley; the Kenai coal field (11c), occupying the western part of the Kenai Peninsula; and the Beluga coal field (11d), lying to the west of Cook Inlet. Because of differences in stratigraphy, the adjacent Matanuska and Broad Pass coal fields (12 and 13) are not discussed as portions of the Cook Inlet-Susitna Basin coal region.

The thickest and highest ranked coal in the Cook Inlet-Susitna Basin coal region is in the Beluga area (11d), where at least eight seams of 8,000 Btu sub-bituminous coal occur in beds more than 20 feet thick. These include the Canyon Bed, the Drill Creek Bed, the Capps Bed, the Chuitna Bed, and the Beluga Bed, with indicated resources totaling 1,727 million tons. Additional beds are known, and information from local oil explorations indicates 42 significantly thick coal beds in the 7,450 feet of Tyonek strata penetrated. Although some of these thick coal beds have been traced for several miles along rivers, there is a lack of data away from the rivers, so Barnes' 1967 identified resource estimate of 2.25 billion tons is based on only a small part of the possible coaliferous area.

Based on more recent data, at least 750 million tons of coal has been identified as being economically extractable under present conditions from approximately 50,000 acres in the Capps and Chuitna areas. Resources for the entire Beluga area are unknown, but this area alone probably exceeds the 29-billion-ton resource estimate ascribed to both the Beluga and Yentna coal fields in 1975. Most of the Beluga coals range from 6,600 to 8,200 Btu, with 16% to 22% ash, 20% to 30% moisture, and 0.1% to 0.2% sulfur. Recently discovered beds beneath the Chuitna Bed are cleaner. Plans for the sale of bulk coal and conversion of the coal to methanol are being seriously considered at this time.

The coal sequence of the Beluga coal formation dips eastward under Cook Inlet as a syncline and extends in the subsurface of the Kenai Peninsula (11c). Estimates in 1975 placed 1.3 trillion tons of sub-bituminous coal to a depth of 10,000 feet under Cook Inlet, of which 53 million tons are in beds more than 20 feet thick. The prospects of recovery from beneath Cook Inlet and the Kenai Peninsula are intriguing.

In addition to these Tyonek formation coals, the younger Beluga and Sterling formations exposed on the Kenai Peninsula contain coal. The coals found near the surface on the Kenai Peninsula are less mature than are the Tyonek coals of the Beluga field, with greater ash and volatiles and less fixed carbon. The coal is

The Evan Jones Mine, the largest in the Wishbone Hill district, just northeast of Palmer, produced about six million tons of coal before closing in 1968. Here, coal is being loaded into railroad cars in 1963. (Steve McCutcheon)

of generally dull appearance, with considerable evidence of woody and bark tissues, and are of marginal lignitic to sub-bituminous rank. Most beds are two to three feet thick, but seven-foot beds are known, including one mined several times at Homer. Estimates in 1975 placed 24 billion tons of hypothetical coal resources on the Kenai Peninsula. The majority of the Kenai coal field is under state and native title, with intensive recreational, private, and municipal surface use, which will probably preclude surface mining. There may be potential for underground recovery, however.

The Tyonek formation coals of the Beluga field reappear north of the Castle Mountain fault and Mount Susitna intrusives in the Yentna coal field (11a). Around the western margin of the basin, moderately to steeply dipping coal seams have been reported, including 15-foot beds on Johnson Creek and the Nakochna River, a 25-foot bed near Mount Fairview, and a 55-foot bed on Sunflower Creek. These western margin coals are dirtier but drier than those of the Beluga coal field, with 5,400 to 9,450 Btu as received, with 6% to 40% ash, 20% moisture, and 1.7% sulfur. Identified resource has been reported as 500 million tons in five 10- to 45-foot-thick beds in the Nakochna area.

In the more central and eastern portion of the Yentna Basin, these coals are up to 8,000 feet deep, but surface exposures of younger, thinner (up to six feet deep) beds of dirty, low rank sub-bituminous coals have been utilized for years by placer miners of the Dutch and Peters hills. The hypothetical resource must be several billion tons. The Alaska Railroad and the Parks Highway follow the eastern margin of the Yentna Basin.

Coals of the Little Susitna coal field (11b) are similar to those of the adjacent eastern margin of the Yentna field: platy, dirty lignitic to sub-bituminous coals in thin beds. The only known commercial deposit, at Houston, was exhausted through surface and shallow underground mining, producing about 90,000 tons of sub-bituminous coal during the 1940s.

The total coal resource for the Cook Inlet-Susitna coal area (i.e., the Beluga, Kenai, Yentna, and Little Susitna coal fields and that beneath Cook Inlet) are believed to be approximately 1.5 trillion tons, of which 11 billion tons are identified resources. At least 750 million tons have been earmarked for immediate mining.

The Broad Pass Lignite Field and Nearby Locations: The Broad Pass lignite field (13) is an apparent northern extension of the Cook Inlet-Susitna Basin coal region following the Chulitna River. These are lignitic coals in five- to ten-foot horizontal beds believed to be younger than the coals in the Yentna Basin to the south. Although of low heat value, the field's location adjacent to the railroad makes this an interesting prospect.

West of Broad Pass, a small outlying area of sub-bituminous coal at Costello Creek was mined between 1940 and 1954. At Yanert, on the Alaska Railroad in Denali National Park and Preserve, a small amount of coal was mined shortly after World War I. At least two other mines operated in the park area, including one at Highway Pass where a bed was mined for use in the park buildings.

Matanuksa Coal Fields: To the east of the Little Susitna coal field are older and more mature coals of the Chickaloon formation (12). The rank of these coals has been increased due to pressure and heat of the mountain, building to progressively increased rank eastward up the Matanuska Valley, from high volatile bituminous at Wishbone Hill to anthracite on Anthracite Ridge.

In the Wishbone Hill district three series of coal beds occur in a large, steeply dipping faulted syncline. The coal beds are thin, and run 12,000 Btu with 11% ash and 0.3% to 0.5% sulfur. The most productive mines were on the gentler-dipping southside of the syncline.

The largest mine in the district, Evan Jones, produced six million tons of coal before closing in 1968. Eight beds were mined, including one (the #3 seam) 8 to

---

This tipple at the old Suntrana townsite is still being used for coal that must be sized for domestic use by Usibelli Coal Mine. A tipple is where raw coal is off-loaded into a crusher unit, sized, loaded onto rail cars, and shipped. Coal is also stockpiled here until needed. Unmined and burning or burnt seams (red seams) are visible in the hills around the site. Coal seams ignite by spontaneous combustion and smolder for years. Smoke seen coming from these seams, especially in cold weather, gave this area the name "the Burning Hills." (Polly Walter, staff)

12 feet thick. Underground mining operations ceased in 1952, leaving an estimated 100 million tons of identified resources. Also on the south side are Eska Mines, operated by the Alaska Railroad intermittently from 1919 through World War II as a contingency supply. Identified resources of 600,000 tons remain in the Eska property.

Coal beds on the steeper-dipping north side of the Wishbone Hill syncline were exploited by the Wishbone Hill, Buffalo, Baxter, and Premier mines. The coal beds are quite variable in both thickness and quality. A Bureau of Mines core-drilling program, operated from 1949 to 1958, indicated that the area is structurally complex, with numerous small faults offsetting the coal beds. Although a large resource of coal existed, estimated at 112 million tons by Barnes in 1967, the most readily exploitable six million tons have already been removed, the remainder being too deeply buried or in blocks too small to attract development at this time.

The Chickaloon coal district encompasses 12 square miles of Chickaloon formation outcrops exposed in a complexly folded and faulted syncline, intruded by igneous rocks. Low-volatile bituminous coal occurs in beds up to 14 feet thick. Although some samples have shown strong coking tendencies, the intense deformation and lack of coal bed uniformity, purity, and continuity have discouraged mining. In 1920 the U.S. Navy built a coal mining town at Chickaloon, but had to abandon it when it was later discovered that the coal could not be mined at a reasonable cost and was not generally satisfactory for naval use. Hypothetical resource has been estimated at 23 million tons in a small portion of the area.

The Anthracite Ridge district at the eastern end of the Matanuska Valley coal field contains thin and discontinuous seams of semi-anthracite and, locally, anthracite, in a complex of tight folds and faults. Although most of the coal exposures are beds measured in inches, beds to 10 and 16 feet thick have been reported. Based on a study of the 90 known outcrops and eight cores, several million tons of coal, mostly semi-anthracite, were estimated to be present in 1936.

Total resources for the Matanuska Valley coal field have been estimated at 248 to 274 million tons, including identified resources of 99 to 125 million tons. The total resource is probably closer to 500 million tons, with a little more than 100 million tons as identified resource.

Gulf of Alaska Tertiary Basin

The Bering River coal field (14) on the Gulf of Alaska is the state's most historically renowned coal field, being the site of the Alaska coal scandal — the Pinchot-Ballinger controversy — that shook the Roosevelt and Taft administrations. After 60 years of study by numerous geologists from the federal, private, and military sectors, the area remains problematic. Coal in this 120-square-mile area occurs in the Kushtaka formation, and ranges from low-volatile bituminous in the west to semi-anthracite in the east. Hypothetical resources to 3,000 feet are 3.6 billion tons, of which only 1,500 tons are classified as measured resources.

Coal in beds up to six feet thick have been reported from the Robinson Mountains (15), apparently in the Kultieth formation.

Alaska Peninsula

Chignik-Herendeen Bay: High volatile bituminous coal occurs in the Chignik formation at Herendeen Bay, in the Chignik area (16), and presumably in the hundred-mile area in between. The coal beds are generally one to two feet thick, but four- and six-foot beds have been reported in the Chignik area. Estimates in 1975 place hypothetical resources of 240 million and 2.9 million tons in the Chignik and Herendeen Bay areas, respectively, exclusive of the unexplored intervening area.

Unga Island: Beds of lignite occur on Unga Island and in the adjacent portions of the Alaska Peninsula. The only analytic data on this coal showed 26% ash, 25% moisture, and 0.5% sulfur, giving a rating of 8,100 Btu.

Southeastern Alaska

Coal occurs at several locations in the Alexander Archipelago (18). On Kuiu, Kupreanof, Zarembo, and Prince of Wales islands, thin beds of lignite occur. At

Kootznahoo Inlet on Admiralty Island are two- to three-foot-thick beds of impure, sulfurous bituminous coal. A small mine supplied Juneau with some of this coal prior to 1929.

Conclusion

The total coal resource in Alaska is estimated to be 216 billion to 4,216 billion tons, of which only 141 billion tons are classified as identified resources. An additional 1.3 trillion tons are believed to lie beneath Cook Inlet.

The major hurdle to be overcome in developing Alaska's coal resources is transportation. Surface transportation facilities for bulk products in Alaska are very poorly developed. The potential for developing these facilities is decreased by severe physiological barriers such as the Alaska and Brooks ranges, between which are hundreds of miles of wetlands. The icebound coast of the northern half of the state essentially precludes effective direct ocean access to the state's largest coal province. Although a great percentage of Alaska's coal resource is currently deemed unexploitable because of lack of transportation and specific land designations such as parks, the state has such an enormous coal resource distributed over such a large area that there remains an overwhelming number of development prospects. Also, because the state's geology is so poorly known, the potential for discovery of new coal fields exists.

New growth — a test mixture of grasses and legumes — covers scars left from mining coal at one of Usibelli Mine's reclamation areas. Owner Joe Usibelli pioneered the revegetation of mined land in 1971, before it was required by federal law. (Charles Boddy)

From Katalla to Kuparuk

The History of Oil in Alaska
By Mike Hershberger

The presence of oil and gas in Alaska was known to Europeans as early as 1853, when Russian colonists detected oil and gas seeps on the west shore of Cook Inlet near the Iniskin Peninsula.

A prospector, known only as Edelman, staked claims on these oil and gas seeps in 1892. This was the earliest known effort to develop petroleum reserves in the then-territory of Alaska. A description had been published in 1869 of "oil seeps near Katmai" on the Alaska Peninsula; and more oil seeps, this time in the Katalla and Yakataga areas on the Gulf of Alaska, were discovered about 1896.

The claims staked by Edelman were abandoned for unknown reasons, but in

Editor's note: *Former newspaper reporter and member of the Alaska House of Representatives, Mike Hershberger presently works as manager of public affairs for the Alaska Oil and Gas Association. The following is an excerpt of an article which originally appeared in* The Anchorage Times, *November 9, 1981.*

1896 claims were staked again on the Iniskin Peninsula and also in the Katalla and Yakataga districts. The actual drilling of oil wells was started in the Iniskin area of Cook Inlet where a wildcat well came in at Oil Bay in 1898. Reports of that early well indicate that an oil flow of 50 barrels a day was hit at 700 feet. Unfortunately, the drillers decided to probe deeper; and at 1,000 feet the drill entered a water strata which choked off what otherwise might have been Alaska's first oil production.

Earlier production might have occurred somewhere along the Arctic coast where Eskimos are reported to have taken advantage of natural oil seeps to fuel their stone lanterns. In at least one instance, a seep was set afire. The Roald Amundsen party, first to navigate the Northwest Passage, refers to the light from such a conflagration which was visible for many miles. We know today that the Teshukpuk Lake section of the Arctic coastal plain includes many known oil seeps.

The first actual oil production came in 1902 at Katalla. The Katalla strike

occurred at about the same time sourdoughs were scratching for pay dirt in the beach gravels near Nome, and a year after a giant well came in at Spindletop, in Texas.

Although early efforts to develop oil in Alaska were vastly overshadowed by the concurrent gold rush, these activities did constitute a serious, if unscientific, effort.

Drilling near known oil seeps, the oil hunters pounded their old cable tools into the ground in the Cook Inlet area, at Katalla, on the Alaska Peninsula, and even on the Seward Peninsula near Nome. Only Katalla produced oil commercially, when, in 1907, a little oil was sold for fuel to the nearby Copper River railway project. Some 500 people made up the community which grew as a result of hope fed by the discovery of oil.

The Chilkat Oil Refinery was built in

The trans-Alaska pipeline snakes its way from Pump Station #1 at Prudhoe Bay. The first oil flowed through the pipeline in June, 1977, and continues at a rate of 1.5 million barrels per day. (Steve McCutcheon)

Alaska was the site of much oil speculation around the turn of the century, with prospectors drilling near known oil seeps in the Cook Inlet area, on the Alaska Peninsula, near Nome on the Seward Peninsula, and at Katalla, on the south coast of Alaska, about 50 miles southeast of Cordova. The only commercial production during this period was recorded at Katalla in 1907, when a small amount of oil was sold for fuel to the nearby Copper River railway project. The town prospered, and several wells were producing by the time the photo at left was taken, about 1920. Katalla's main street, shown above in an undated photo, was lined with hotels, restaurants, and saloons. Estimates have placed the population of Katalla as high as 10,000 during the boom year of 1907, but the number gradually declined, particularly following the fire which destroyed the refinery in 1933.
(Left, U.S.G.S.; above, Ray Moss Collection, Alaska Historical Library)

1911 at Katalla Slough, and its products were sold in Cordova the same year that Kennecott Copper shipped its first load of minerals through the town. A score of shallow wells, all drilled with cable tools, eventually produced about 154,000 barrels of oil from the 60-acre Katalla field. That amount is almost equal to two days' present production from the Cook Inlet area. Oil production in Katalla came to a stop in 1933 when fire destroyed the refinery. A marginal operation during most of its life, the plant did not justify being rebuilt, and oil from Katalla was no more.

The year 1904 actually marked the end of the first oil age in Alaska. Some reasons for the demise included failure to obtain oil in any meaningful quantity, the high cost of exploration, the difficulty of obtaining title to oil lands under the placer mining laws then in effect, and the increasing supply of oil on the west coast of America because of rapid development of oil fields in California.

In 1910, the United States government withdrew lands from oil and gas leasing, a move that halted all exploration until the passage, in 1920, of the oil and gas leasing act. This act spurred renewed oil activity in Alaska.

A 200-foot communications tower rises above the central production facility at Kuparuk, about 30 miles west of Prudhoe Bay. Production began in December, 1981. The facility currently processes 80,000 barrels of crude oil a day for delivery to the trans-Alaska pipeline at Prudhoe Bay. (Courtesy of ARCO)

Most of this renewed interest centered on the known oil-bearing areas of southern Alaska, but some attention was diverted to other areas where indications of petroleum were not known, or, if reported, were not yet confirmed. Those areas included the Chignik district on the Alaska Peninsula, the Anchorage vicinity and other areas in the Cook Inlet-Susitna Valley area, and near Killisnoo on Admiralty Island in southeastern Alaska. Several wells were drilled in the Kanatak district on the Alaska Peninsula between 1923 and 1926, the first such exploration undertaken in Alaska by major oil companies. The first test well in the Yakataga district was drilled during 1926 and 1927. A well reportedly drilled to a shallow depth on the outskirts of Anchorage in 1920 is recorded in the name Oil Well Road. From 1926 to 1930 a test well was drilled near Chickaloon in the Matanuska Valley.

Between 1938 and 1940, two deep test wells, one on the Iniskin Peninsula and one in the Kanatak district, were drilled with rotary equipment. Failure of these two wells to produce oil in commercial quantities, plus the advent of World War II with its restrictions and withdrawal of land for leasing, put a temporary end to oil exploration.

Back in 1923, the government had reserved some 37,000 square miles in northern Alaska as Naval Petroleum Reserve #4. Petroleum exploration began in 1944 and was suspended in 1953. In the decade from 1945 to 1955, 37 test

Oil from a natural seep covers the water of Johnston Creek (also known as Johnson Creek), about 15 miles east of Cape Yakataga. The iridescent film of iron oxide is often mistaken for oil. Iron oxide film literally covers many swampy areas, tidal flats, pools, and sluggish streams. (Gil Mull; reprinted from ALASKA GEOGRAPHIC®)

— 171

Shortly after the discovery of the north Cook Inlet gas field, in 1962, a blowout occurred at the initial exploratory well. Fortunately, no one was injured, and the well was set on fire for safety reasons. Drilling was begun on a relief well, but the onset of winter delayed completion until the following spring. The discovery well burned for 13 months before it could be successfully shut off. (Steve McCutcheon)

wells and 45 core tests were drilled on 18 structures with minor success.

In 1957, Richfield Oil Corporation discovered oil at Swanson River on the Kenai Peninsula, thus beginning the modern petroleum industry that had emerged in Alaska.

By 1959, three wells were producing oil on the Kenai Peninsula. Investigations for oil were soon extended offshore, and additional oil and gas fields were brought into production. By the end of the 1960s, five fields in the Kenai-Cook Inlet area were producing oil, and nine fields were producing natural gas.

By 1968, the Swanson River oil field was yielding about 13 million barrels a year, and the offshore fields were just coming into production. The result was to increase the state's production of oil from 14 million barrels in 1966 to 66 million in 1968. By 1975, Alaska ranked seventh among oil-producing states.

And in 1968 came announcement of the discovery of oil at Prudhoe Bay, the largest oil field ever found in North America. In September, 1969, a lease sale of additional Prudhoe Bay tracts netted the state $900 million in bonus money (see *Alaska Mineral Revenues*, page 200). In relatively short order, the field was defined, development wells were sunk, and plans were laid for a pipeline to the port of Valdez. The first barrel of oil reached Valdez via the trans-Alaska pipeline in July, 1978.

Kuparuk, a new field which shipped its first oil in December, 1981, rounds out the history of oil in Alaska. Atlantic Richfield is doing the first phase of development at Kuparuk, about 30 miles west of Prudhoe Bay. In spring, 1982, Kuparuk was producing 80,000 barrels per day; plans call for production to reach 250,000 barrels per day by the late 1980s. Oil from Kuparuk moves eastward through a 26-mile pipe to Prudhoe Bay where it joins the trans-Alaska pipeline at Pump Station #1.

Potential Hydrocarbon-bearing Basins of Alaska and Offshore Continental Shelves

The shaded areas indicate basins with potential hydrocarbon formations. The potential for most of these basins, however, is very low.

The Base Operations Center, one of three SOHIO camps at Prudhoe Bay, is a miniature city. In addition to offices and accommodations for 476 workers, the base offers its residents an indoor swimming pool, basketball and volleyball courts, a complete dispensary, a 127-seat theater, and an indoor arboretum. Workers' shifts are arranged on a one-week-on, one-week-off basis. (Steve McCutcheon)

Oil flows for 786 miles through the trans-Alaska pipeline from Prudhoe Bay to the ice-free port of Valdez. Here it is stored and loaded onto tankers, bound for refineries in the lower 48 states. (Steve McCutcheon)

Geology of the Arctic Slope

Geologic Origin of the Arctic Slope and the Prudhoe Bay Oil Field
By Gil Mull

The Prudhoe Bay field formed as the result of a unique combination of separate geologic events which began about 375 million years ago.

The field is located at the north edge of a large east-west trending sedimentary basin flanking the north side of the Brooks Range. Resembling a misshapen trough, this feature, the Colville basin, has a gentle north flank and a very steep south flank near the front of the Brooks Range. Formed at the time the Brooks Range began to rise, near the beginning of the Cretaceous period, about 140 million years ago, the Colville basin received debris eroded from the Brooks Range. The debris was then swept northward by streams across a large delta to the shores of a marine seaway located where the Arctic Slope is today. As the sediments

Editor's note: *Gil Mull is a petroleum geologist, formerly with the U.S. Geological Survey and currently working for the state Division of Geological and Geophysical Surveys.*

accumulated through the 70 million years of the Cretaceous period, the Colville basin gradually filled and its shoreline shifted northeastward. In the deepest part of the basin, sediments four to five miles thick — consisting of shale, sandstone, conglomerate, and, in some areas, extensive coal beds — accumulated. The northern edge of the trough was buried by sediments that range from about one-half mile thick near Barrow to about one and one-half miles thick at Prudhoe Bay, and still thicker to the east. This northern edge of the buried trough, known as the Barrow arch, acted much like a sill separating the Colville basin from the much larger Arctic Ocean basin to the north. The Prudhoe Bay oil field lies squarely on the crest of this sill. However, important geologic events in the evolution of the Prudhoe Bay field occurred about 240 million years before the beginning of the Brooks Range and Colville trough.

During the late Devonian period, about 375 million years ago, an earlier mountain range formed across what is now northern Alaska. By early Mississippian time, about

360 million years ago, this large mountain range was reduced by erosion to a nearly flat plain with a few low hills at the edge of a large continent that lay to the north. A thin layer of conglomerate, sandstone, and shale covered the eroded roots of this old mountain chain. During the Mississippian and early Pennsylvanian periods, a duration of about 45 million years, northern Alaska was covered by a warm, shallow sea in which corals and other marine organisms flourished, and up to 2,000 feet of limestone and dolomite were deposited. These carbonate rocks are known as the Lisburne formation, and the underlying sandstones, conglomerates, and shales are known as the Kekiktuk and Kayak formations. The Lisburne shoreline lay generally along the trend of the present coastline, but with an important difference in that the land lay to the north.

The Colville River flows past Cretaceous rocks that dip toward the Arctic coastal plain near Umiat, more than 70 miles south of Harrison Bay on the North Slope.
(Gil Mull; reprinted from *ALASKA GEOGRAPHIC*®)

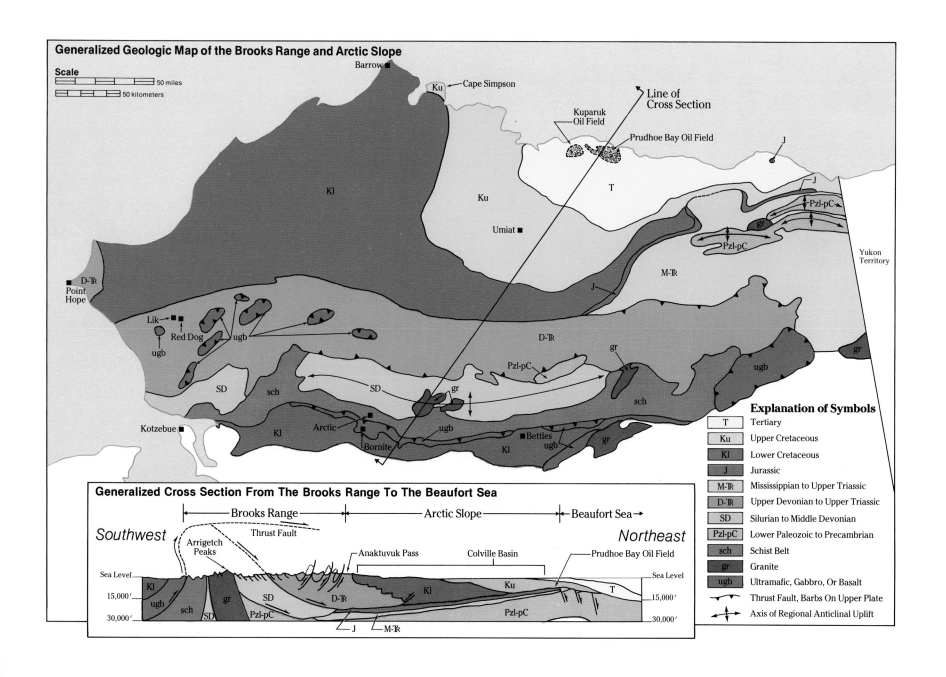

Generalized Geologic Map of the Brooks Range and Arctic Slope

Scale
50 miles
50 kilometers

Barrow

Cape Simpson
Ku

Line of
Cross Section

Kuparuk
Oil Field

Prudhoe Bay Oil Field

J

Kl

Ku

T

J

Pzl-pC
gr
Pzl-pC

Umiat

M-TR

Yukon
Territory

D-TR
Point
Hope

J

Lik
Red Dog
ugb

ugb

D-TR

gr

Pzl-pC
gr

ugb

SD

sch

SD

gr
Pzl-pC

ugb

sch

gr

Kotzebue

Kl

Arctic

ugb

Bettles
ugb

gr

Bornite

Kl

Explanation of Symbols

T	Tertiary
Ku	Upper Cretaceous
Kl	Lower Cretaceous
J	Jurassic
M-TR	Mississippian to Upper Triassic
D-TR	Upper Devonian to Upper Triassic
SD	Silurian to Middle Devonian
Pzl-pC	Lower Paleozoic to Precambrian
sch	Schist Belt
gr	Granite
ugb	Ultramafic, Gabbro, Or Basalt

Thrust Fault, Barbs On Upper Plate

Axis of Regional Anticlinal Uplift

Generalized Cross Section From The Brooks Range To The Beaufort Sea

Brooks Range — Arctic Slope — Beaufort Sea

Southwest   *Northeast*

Thrust Fault

Arrigetch
Peaks

Anaktuvuk Pass   Colville Basin

Prudhoe Bay Oil Field

Sea Level   Sea Level

Kl
ugb
sch
gr
SD
Pzl-pC
SD
D-TR
Kl
Ku
T

15,000′   15,000′

30,000′   30,000′

J   M-TR

Pzl-pC

During the late Pennsylvanian and part of the Permian peiod, about 270 to 310 million years ago, the shoreline moved southward as sea level dropped, probably as a result of the large amounts of water tied up in vast glaciers in the southern hemisphere. When the sea level rose again, thin sandstone and shale was deposited over the top of the dead carbonate banks until the Triassic period, about 250 million years ago, when a relatively gentle uplift of the land to the north occurred. From this uplift a series of sediment-loaded, braided streams spread a blanket of up to 400 feet of sand and gravel southward. These coarse grained sediments reached their maximum coarseness and thickness in the Prudhoe Bay area, and formed the Sadlerochit Formation, which was destined later to become the major reservoir horizon in the oil field.

From the late Triassic through the Jurassic periods, marine deposition prevailed in the Prudhoe Bay area. The main basin of deposition lay to the south, and nearly 4,000 feet of silt and mud which formed black shale was deposited on a gently sloping shelf south of the

---

This generalized cross section of the Prudhoe Bay area shows the stratigraphic relationships of major rock horizons. Rich, organic shale of the Cretaceous period unconformably overlies old rock horizons. Oil generated in the Cretaceous shale has migrated into old rock horizons wherever they are porous and adjacent to the unconformity.

Prudhoe Bay area. At Prudhoe Bay itself, however, probably less than 2,000 feet of shale was deposited over the Sadlerochit Formation.

Near the beginning of the Cretaceous period, about 140 million years ago, a profound geologic event affected what are now the Arctic regions of Alaska and Canada. There is abundant evidence that the Brooks Range began to form at that time as the result of a collision of two pieces of the earth's crust, or lithosphere. The compression from the collision resulted in the uplift of a large pile of the crust in much the same fashion as a snow plow or large bulldozer piling up material in front of its advancing blade. In the case of the Brooks Range, the blade of the plow appears to have been a piece of oceanic crust — crust typical of the type found under the oceans — that overrode the edge of a large fragment of continental crust. In the process, dense rocks known as ultramafic rocks, normally found at depths of more than five miles beneath the ocean floor, were thrust onto the top of relatively light sedimentary rocks and are preserved as remnants at a number of localities in the Brooks Range. The zone of convergence is known as a subduction zone. In most subduction zones, one plate of dense oceanic crust is overridden by another plate of oceanic crust, or by a plate of relatively light continental crust. But in the case of the Brooks Range, for reasons not clearly understood, the relatively light continental crust was apparently overridden by dense oceanic

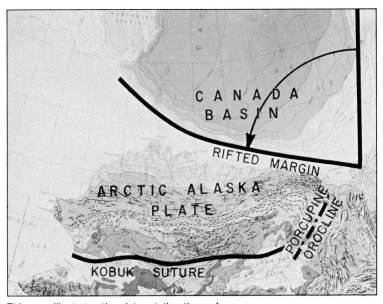

This map illustrates the plate rotation theory for the origin of northern Alaska. A number of earth scientists believe that the Brooks Range was formed when a piece of the continent rotated counterclockwise away from the Arctic Islands in Canada. The theory suggests that the mountains were formed by the snowplowlike effect of the continental crust colliding with another piece of the crust to the south. Simultaneously with the rotation, the southern Arctic Ocean basin north of Alaska was formed. (Gil Mull)

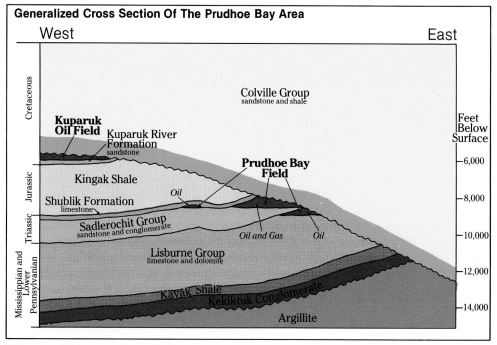

Generalized Cross Section Of The Prudhoe Bay Area

West   East

Cretaceous

Colville Group
sandstone and shale

Feet Below Surface

Kuparuk Oil Field   Kuparuk River Formation
sandstone

—6,000

Jurassic

Kingak Shale

Prudhoe Bay Field

Shublik Formation
limestone

Oil

—8,000

Triassic

Sadlerochit Group
sandstone and conglomerate

Oil and Gas   Oil

—10,000

Mississippian and Lower Pennsylvanian

Lisburne Group
limestone and dolomite

—12,000

Kayak Shale

Kekiktuk Conglomerate

—14,000

Argillite

This generalized cross section across the Brooks Range and Arctic Slope shows the style of folding and faulting of the major rock units of northern Alaska. In this generalized geologic map of the Brooks Range and Arctic Slope, the colors show approximate areas of exposure of distinctive rocks of various ages in northern Alaska.

crust; this is a special case of subduction known as obduction. In a subduction zone the leading edge of the downgoing slab of crust theoretically eventually reaches a depth at which the rocks become fluid and are reabsorbed into the crust or may rise back to the surface as granitic plutons or in volcanoes. Evidence in the Brooks Range suggests that in some areas more than 300 miles of continental crust has been consumed in the subduction zone at the south edge of the range.

But, remarkably, at the same time that extreme compression was apparently occurring in the Brooks Range, evidence from seismic data and from drilling suggests that near the coastline of the present Arctic Ocean, extensional faulting was occurring. The evidence suggests that here a piece of continental crust was being rifted or torn apart. Although the exact mechanics of the process are not clear, most modern geologists are convinced that, for example, in the geologic past North and South America were rifted or torn apart from Europe and Africa, and that the two pieces have subsequently drifted several thousand miles away from each other. This concept of continental drift or plate tectonic theory, as it is

Brown sandstones and conglomerates from the Sadlerochit Formation, the major reservoir of the Prudhoe Bay field, are tightly folded with the gray limestones of the Lisburne Formation in this photo of the Franklin Mountains west of Schrader Lake in the Brooks Range.
(Gil Mull; reprinted from *ALASKA GEOGRAPHIC®*)

Three types of rocks are exposed in the 30-mile-long Ignek Valley on the north flank of the Brooks Range. On the horizon, limestones from the Lisburne Formation appear gray; the brown outcrops are sandstones and conglomerates from the Sadlerochit Formation; the red weathering slopes come from oxidation of the rich, organic shales from the Cretaceous period. (Gil Mull)

Rock cores from the Prudhoe Bay discovery well demonstrate the effect of porosity in various rock types. At lower left is porous sandstone from the Sadlerochit Formation stained brown when it was invaded by oil. Top is a dolomite from the Lisburne Formation. Again, the brown area reflects staining from the invasion of oil; the lighter bands are areas of lower porosity where the oil was not able to penetrate. At lower right is a light colored unstained porous sandstone and conglomerate from the upper Sadlerochit Formation where it is within the gas cap of the Prudhoe Bay field. (Gil Mull)

known, has long been controversial, but a large mass of geologic and geophysical evidence has convinced most earth scientists.

The coast of northern Alaska appears to be analogous in origin to the Atlantic coasts of North America and Europe. A number of lines of evidence suggest that a relatively small fragment of a much larger continent was rifted away and drifted relatively southward to a collision zone with oceanic crust at the south side of the Brooks Range. This fragment has been named the Arctic Alaska plate. According to this theory, the Arctic Ocean basin did not exist prior to this episode of rifting.

Somewhat more controversial are the ideas of how and why this rifting occurred. However, there are lines of evidence suggesting that the Arctic Alaska plate was rotated counterclockwise 80° about a pivot point located near the Mackenzie River delta in Canada, and that the opposite side of the rift is the edge of the continental shelf offshore from the Arctic Islands of northern Canada. Unfortunately, critical bits of geophysical and geological evidence are inaccessible beneath the Arctic ice pack, but for the time being this seems to be a very workable hypothesis.

In the context of this hypothesis then, the Brooks Range was formed by the

compressional or bulldozer effect at a convergent plate margin. The Colville basin formed north of the Brooks Range, and during the Cretaceous and Tertiary time was the site of deposition of sediments eroded off the rising mountain range, and the Barrow arch or sill at the north edge of the Colville basin is the rifted edge of the old continent. At rifted margins, erosion attacks the edges of the continent and trims or planes off the jagged edges resulting from the rifting. Younger sediments are then deposited over the truncated edges of the older rocks; this relationship is known as an angular unconformity.

Exactly these relationships are present, buried beneath the younger sediments at Prudhoe Bay, and are also exposed in outcrops in the Arctic National Wildlife Refuge of the northeastern Brooks Range. At Prudhoe Bay, faults are present in which blocks to the north are downdropped toward the Arctic Ocean basin. One of these faults forms the northern edge of the main oil field; south of the fault zone the rocks dip gently southward toward the Colville basin. On the northeast, a major angular unconformity near the base of the Cretaceous age rocks dips gently toward the Arctic Ocean and truncates the fault zone and all of the pre-Cretaceous rock strata — including the porous sandstones and conglomerates of the Sadlerochit Formation. A large portion of the oil and gas reserves in the Prudhoe Bay field are located at the high point or intersection between the three major surfaces — the southward dipping Sadlerochit Formation, the fault zone on the north, and the northeastward dipping unconformity. At Prudhoe Bay the unconformity is critically important because the overlying Cretaceous rocks are relatively impermeable shales that form on the northeast the seal to the oil trap. But in addition, these overlying shales also have an extremely high content of organic matter that was deposited with the muds when they were laid down on top of the unconformity. Such shales with high organic content are excellent source beds for oil and gas, which are formed by the alteration of the organic material. At Prudhoe Bay the rock strata underlying the unconformity are generally poor hydrocarbon source beds. As a result of the various bits of evidence, many geologists believe that the source of the oil and gas in the Sadlerochit Formation, and the other lesser reservoir beds, is dominantly from the rich organic shales of Cretaceous age that overlie the Sadlerochit

at the unconformity. The unconformity and overlying shales act both as the seal to the trap and also as the source of the hydrocarbons.

Although the Sadlerochit Formation is by far the most important reservoir horizon in the Prudhoe Bay area, almost every rock horizon that has any porosity and is truncated by the unconformity contains oil. West of the main Prudhoe Bay field, the Kuparuk oil field, just coming into production, is also controlled by the Cretaceous unconformity.

Geological evidence then suggests that the Prudhoe Bay field would not have formed or be the giant size it is if:

1. The Sadlerochit Formation had not reached nearly its maximum thickness of coarse sandstone and conglomerate in this area;
2. The subsequent burial history of the Sadlerochit Formation had not left it with a relatively thin overlying layer of sediment. Much more rapid early burial of the Sadlerochit would have greatly reduced the porosity of the rocks, and therefore their capacity to contain large volumes of oil and gas;
3. The Colville basin had not formed to the south, resulting in the gentle southward dip or tilt of the rocks;
4. The rifted plate margin with its

associated faults had not cut across the area of thick, porous Sadlerochit sandstone and conglomerate;
5. The unconformity with rich organic shales had not truncated the Sadlerochit Formation;
6. The subsequent burial history of the Cretaceous shales, combined with the heat flow from the earth's crust, had not been sufficient to generate oil that could flow into the porous Sadlerochit Formation rocks buried beneath the unconformity.

The coincidence of all of these most favorable factors in the proper timing was critical to the formation of the giant accumulation. Absence of any one factor would probably have prevented the formation of any hydrocarbon accumulation at Prudhoe Bay. Any major reduction in the porosity of the Sadlerochit Formation or in the organic content of the overlying Cretaceous shale would have resulted in a much smaller field. The field resulted from a one-in-a-million chance of a fortuitous combination of geological attributes that took at least 360 million years to form. Similar combinations of favorable factors are not likely to occur elsewhere in northern Alaska or the off-shore Beaufort Sea, but smaller individual fields are likely to be present in the area.

History of Arctic Slope Oil Exploration

By Gil Mull

Discovery of the giant Prudhoe Bay oil field on the shore of the Beaufort Sea in 1968 focused worldwide attention on Alaska and thrust the state into a leadership role in United States oil and gas production.

The Arctic Slope of Alaska, that area of coastal plain and foothills north of the Brooks Range, and the adjacent Beaufort Sea continental shelf have become the center of intense oil and gas exploration that will continue for many years. Revenues from hydrocarbon production at Prudhoe Bay account for approximately 85% of Alaska's total unrestricted revenues, and in addition are building a permanent fund in which all Alaskans will share in the years to come. Impacts of this discovery, for better or worse, affect all Alaskans, and indeed have a marked effect on some of the United States'

Editor's note: *This article incorporates information provided by H.C. Jamison, C.H. Selman, Leo F. Fay, and G.H. Pessel, as well as the author's own files.*

domestic and international policies. Although great public attention surrounded construction of the trans-Alaska pipeline from Prudhoe Bay to Valdez, and monuments have been erected to immortalize the builders of the line, little attention has been paid to the history of exploration that led to the discovery of the Prudhoe Bay field.

The history of petroleum development in northern Alaska probably began sometime in the 19th century, when Eskimo travelers along the coast discovered natural oil seeps near Cape Simpson, 50 miles southeast of Barrow and 150 miles northwest of Prudhoe Bay, and at Angun (Ungoon) Point, 30 miles southeast of the village of Kaktovik on Barter Island. For many years, residents of the area traveled to these seeps to cut out blocks of oil-soaked tundra to take back to their homes for use as fuel. These deposits were unknown to the outside world until 1919 when pioneering geologist and explorer Ernest de K. Leffingwell mentioned their presence in his report on his classical scientific studies of the

Canning River region, more than 60 miles southeast of Prudhoe Bay. Leffingwell spent the years 1906 to 1914 mapping the geology of the area, and although he had not actually visited the seeps, he had heard reports of them and mentioned them in a general discussion of the economic potential of the area. As a result of this report, mineral claims were staked in the early 1920s in the area of the seeps at Cape Simpson.

In 1923, a large area surrounding the seeps at Cape Simpson and extending south to the crest of the Brooks Range was withdrawn from oil and gas or mineral leasing to become Naval Petroleum Reserve #4 (NPR-4). During this era, the Navy had become increasingly aware of its dependence upon oil to fuel its fleet and was concerned about future supplies. Leffingwell's report of oil seeps, combined

---

The Prudhoe Bay discovery well stands out in stark contrast to the emptiness of Prudhoe Bay in February, 1968, when this photo was taken. The ice pad which served as an airstrip is in the foreground. (Gil Mull)

with the geological data from the U.S. Geological Survey geologist F.C. Schrader, suggested to the Navy that this area might contain its future supplies of oil. In a pioneering exploration in 1901, Schrader had crossed the Brooks Range (not yet named) through Anaktuvuk Pass, traversed down the Anaktuvuk and Colville rivers to the coast and then west to Barrow and Cape Lisburne. Although Schrader neither saw nor heard about the oil seeps, his geological data suggested the presence of a major sedimentary basin. Leffingwell's report proved that the sediments in this basin in some places, at least, could contain hydrocarbons. And significantly, Leffingwell named the Sadlerochit Formation for a distinctive series of beds that are exposed in the Sadlerochit Mountains.

Following the establishment of NPR-4, a flurry of geological exploration brought U.S. Geological Survey geologists P.S. Smith, J.B. Mertie, Jr., Sidney Paige, James Gilluly, W.T. Foran, and others to other portions of the Brooks Range and Arctic Slope to further study the outlines of the geological framework of northern Alaska. Many of these little known and unheralded early geological explorations, beginning with Schrader and Leffingwell, were expeditions by dog team, foot, and

This aerial shows the Deadhorse airstrip which serves the Prudhoe Bay complex. In the distance is a drill rig and one of the feeder pipelines which carries oil to the main trans-Alaska pipeline. (Gil Mull)

boat with hardships that far exceeded in severity the trials of the builders of the pipeline more than 50 years later. Most of these men were out of contact with civilization for months, living off the land, and feeling their way across a terrain that, in an era prior to airplanes in Alaska, was still virtually unmapped. Some of the names that were left on features at the time — No Luck Lake, Disappointment Creek, Desperation Lake — reflect in a small way the rigors of their explorations.

During the 1930s and the early years of World War II, little attention was paid to northern Alaska. But during the war, the Navy again realized its need for dependable fuel supplies and embarked upon an aggressive program of oil exploration. Preliminary field parties were sent out in 1944, but by the time geophysical crews and drilling rigs were moved to this remote area, the war had ended. Exploration nevertheless continued until 1953. Surface geological mapping was carried out by the U.S.G.S. throughout the Brooks Range and Arctic Slope by boat, Weasel tracked vehicles, and foot traverses. This surface mapping, geophysical work, and drilling of a number of exploratory wells on NPR-4 added a large amount of technical data to the file of knowledge of the geology of northern Alaska. Many U.S. Geological Survey geologists still active in the profession began their careers in this second generation of exploratory efforts. But, in all of NPR-4, only a small, non-commercial oil field at Umiat and

Roughnecks handle drill string coming out of a hole at one of the Prudhoe Bay drill sites.
(Steve McCutcheon)

— 191

Oil seeps blacken the tundra at Cape Simpson, 150 miles northwest of Prudhoe Bay. In the 19th century Eskimo travelers found the seeps. In 1919, pioneer geologist Ernest de K. Leffingwell reported the seeps in his study of the Canning River region, thus becoming the first to spread knowledge of oil on the North Slope beyond the local Eskimo community. (Gil Mull)

small gas fields at Barrow and at Gubik, near Umiat, were discovered, along with other insignificant accumulations of hydrocarbons.

Following the cessation of Naval exploration in 1953, another lull in activities ensued until the Richfield Oil Corporation discovery of oil at Swanson River on the Kenai Peninsula in 1957 focused the attention of the oil industry on Alaska. This discovery of a giant field (more than 250 million barrels), the first in Alaska, proved beyond any doubt that Alaska had the potential for producing major quantities of oil and gas. By summer, 1958, oil industry geological field parties working out of tent camps had fanned out across most of Alaska, and in 1959 they began studying the Arctic Slope. This third generation of geologists had the advantage of transportation by helicopter, and were able to build on the foundation of the U.S. Geological Survey's framework. Interest in northern Alaska was stimulated also by the availability there for the first time of lands released for leasing by the Bureau of Land Management. These lands lay to the east and south of NPR-4, in the low, rolling, northern foothills of the Brooks Range, and covered a number of surface anticlines. Seismic exploration by industry geologists began in 1962. The following two years saw the beginning of industry drilling activity in the general Umiat area. Six shallow, exploratory holes were drilled on surface anticlines in the Umiat area; all were dry holes except for a small gas well at East Umiat.

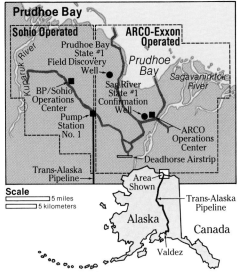

Sixteen owners have an interest in the entire Prudhoe Bay field, but these owners have agreed to develop the field as a unit. According to a unitization agreement which became effective April 1, 1977, two operators act on behalf of the owners. One of the operators, Sohio Alaska Petroleum Company — their Base Operations Center is shown at left — manages the western part of the field. ARCO Alaska, Inc. operates the eastern part. (The map above shows the division of field operations.) Development and maintenance costs, and the oil produced from the field, are shared by the owners according to a formula previously agreed upon by all the parties. (SOHIO)

A Bell G2 helicopter and Cessna 180 floatplane provide support for this early oil industry geological field camp at Cache One Lake, southeast of the junction of Ivishak and Sagavanirktok rivers. (Gil Mull)

During this same period two other significant events occurred. In 1960 the federal government established the Arctic National Wildlife Range (now the Arctic National Wildlife Refuge), covering the entire eastern end of the Arctic Slope and Brooks Range from the Canning River to the Alaska-Yukon border. The state, as part of its land entitlement under the Statehood Act, selected more than 1,800,000 acres of the Arctic coastal plain bordering the Beaufort Sea between NPR-4 and the wildlife range. This swampy lake-covered area contains no surface rock exposures but was recommended for selection by the state's only geologist, Tom Marshall, who recognized some general geological similarities of the Arctic Slope to petroleum-bearing areas in the Rocky Mountains of the western United States. Selection of the coastal plain area had an additional advantage because it eliminated potential future disputes between the state and federal governments over the definition of navigable streams in upland areas. If the surrounding lands were state lands, it thus became unnecessary to define the limit of navigability of streams flowing into the Arctic Ocean. The lands thus selected included Prudhoe Bay, an obscure geographic feature named more than 130 years earlier by Arctic explorer Sir John Franklin (for Capt. Algernon Percy, Baron of Prudhoe and later Fourth Duke of Northumberland) in the first penetration by white men along the Arctic coast west of the Mackenzie River in Canada.

[According to the author's research, the correct pronunciation of Prudhoe Bay is *Prud-ho,* rhyming with mud.]

In late 1964, the state received tentative approval for its land selections from the federal government, and in December held a competitive sale for leases in the area of the Colville River delta. British Petroleum and Sinclair Oil acquired a large block of land on which two wells were drilled in 1966 and 1967. In July, 1965, a second sale of Arctic Slope leases was held by the state, this time including lands in the Prudhoe Bay area. In this sale Richfield Oil (now part of Atlantic Richfield Company) and Humble Oil (now Exxon Company, U.S.A.) as partners, acquired more than 71,500 acres of land covering the crest of a subsurface geological structure adjacent to Prudhoe Bay. At that time the only information available was seismic data combined with geological predictions on the nature of the subsurface rock types projected from the outcrops in the Brooks Range 80 to 130 miles to the south and east. At the time, the nearest exploratory well was in NPR-4, 75 miles west of Prudhoe Bay. British Petroleum, with lower bids, acquired nearly 82,000 acres located lower down the flank of the structure.

Also during 1965, Richfield, recognizing the logistical problem of moving giant drilling rigs to remote areas of the Arctic, pioneered in the use of the Lockheed C130 Hercules cargo plane for hauling heavy equipment to the Arctic. Richfield arranged for Alaska Airlines to lease a

C130 for the first commercial use of what had previously been a military aircraft. The first equipment was flown in from Fairbanks in March, 1965, and in January, 1966, a snow-and-ice airstrip was built on the tundra at a location called Susie #1, about 80 miles east of Umiat. During a two-week period of operating nearly around the clock when the weather permitted, a massive airlift of more than 80 loads was flown from Fairbanks to the Susie ice strip. This airlift included the entire drilling rig broken into plane-sized components, drill pipe and supplies, plus modular units to make a camp for the drilling crew and support personnel. With Humble (Exxon) as a partner, Richfield drilled the exploratory well at Susie to a depth of 13,500 feet — the deepest well ever drilled on the slope. It was a dry hole.

Also in 1966, Richfield Oil was merged with the Atlantic Refining Company, and the new firm — named the Atlantic Richfield Company — inherited all of the operations and lands acquired by Richfield, including the land at Prudhoe Bay. Following the failure at Susie, the drill rig was moved overland 60 miles north to the drill site that had been prepared at Prudhoe Bay. This well, named Prudhoe Bay State #1, the second well to be drilled on the Arctic Slope by the company and its partner Humble (Exxon), was begun in April, 1967. It too had a snow-and-ice airstrip built across the tundra and on two small lakes so, with the coming of summer on the slope, the work

Light from a low-hanging sun glances off the trans-Alaska pipeline terminal as it winds past 5,600-foot Mount Wiehl (left) and 4,200-foot Sukakpak Mountain in the Dietrich River valley on the south slope of the Brooks Range. The first crude oil from the Arctic began its 800-mile journey from Prudhoe Bay to Valdez on June 20, 1977. (Steve McCutcheon; reprinted from *ALASKA GEOGRAPHIC®*)

was suspended until after freezeup in the fall.

In November, 1967, drilling resumed at Prudhoe Bay State #1. Hydrocarbon indications were soon seen and in December, at a depth of 8,202 feet, the sandstone and conglomerate horizon known as the Sadlerochit Formation was encountered. At Susie, in a deeper part of the sedimentary basin, this formation was not reached by the drill, but at Prudhoe Bay the formation was at a much shallower depth. Very strong indications of gas were seen in the drill cuttings from this formation. On December 26, 1967, a drill stem test of more than 200 feet of the Sadlerochit Formation was run, with an immediate strong flow of high pressure gas to the surface, the first production from the Prudhoe Bay reservoir. The test was an unqualified success and gave the first concrete indication of hydrocarbons at Prudhoe Bay. Accompanied by some minor press coverage in January, 1968, drilling continued until oil was encountered deeper in the hole. In March, 1968, another drill stem test recorded 1,152 barrels of oil per day, and the companies and the state of Alaska had the first clear indication of a major oil field

Oil tanker *Williamsburg* empties its seawater ballast at the Alyeska marine terminal, Valdez, prior to taking on oil. The two green storage tanks at the lower left hold nearly one day's flow of oil, the amount required to fill the tanker. Turnaround time at the scenic port is 24 hours. (Polly Walter, staff)

below the gas. Subsequent wells in the field have been tested at flow rates of 20,000 to 30,000 barrels of oil per day.

In April a second well, Sag River State #1, was begun seven miles to the southeast of the Prudhoe Bay discovery well. Here the Sadlerochit Formation was more than 300 feet deeper, and much of the more than 400 feet of sandstone and conglomerate was found to be oil-saturated. Atlantic Richfield and Exxon then retained DeGolyer and McNaughton, an internationally recognized petroleum consulting firm, to make an independent evaluation of the results of the first two wells. This firm electrified the world with its report that Prudhoe Bay "...could develop into a field with recoverable reserves of some 5 to 10 billion barrels of oil, which would rate it as one of the largest petroleum accumulations known to the world today." With this announcement the rush to the Arctic was on, and Alaska has not been the same since. Subsequent evaluations indicated that the field contained 9.6 billion barrels of recoverable oil and 26 trillion cubic feet of natural gas. This accumulation is almost twice the size of the next largest field in North America, the giant East Texas field, and contains almost one-third of the known oil reserves and 12% of the gas reserves in the United States. Since completion of the trans-Alaska pipeline to Valdez in 1977, the field has produced more than 2 billion barrels of oil and is currently producing at the rate of 1.5 million barrels per day. Its discovery was thus the result of the accumulation of geological knowledge of northern Alaska acquired by government geologists during nearly 70 years, combined with the exploratory expertise of industry geologists and geophysicists trained in the evaluation of data in oil and gas exploration.

Subsequent exploration along the Arctic coast and adjacent Beaufort Sea has revealed additional oil and gas accumulations, although none are apparently the size of Prudhoe Bay. West of the main Prudhoe Bay field, the Kuparuk oil field is just coming into production. This field contains about 1.3 billion barrels of recoverable oil from a shallower horizon than that of the Prudhoe Bay field, and is the 10th largest field ever discovered in the United States. When it comes into full production in the mid-1980s at a planned rate of 250,000 barrels per day, Kuparuk will be second only to Prudhoe Bay in daily production in the United States.

A confirmation well, called Sag River State #1, seven miles southeast of the discovery well, was drilled in April, 1968. Results of this and the discovery well prompted Atlantic Richfield and its partner, Humble (Exxon) to hire an independent petroleum consulting firm to evaluate the Prudhoe Bay field. The consultants reported that Prudhoe Bay might contain ''recoverable reserves of some 5 to 10 million barrels of oil, which would rate it as one of the largest petroleum accumulations known to the world today.''
(Gil Mull)

Alaska Mineral Revenues

By G. Michael Doogan

When the First Alaska Legislature convened at Juneau on January 26, 1959, it faced the task of supplying government to 225,000 residents spread over the state's 586,000 square miles.

"We had a thousand crying needs," recalls Ketchikan Representative Oral Freeman, a member of that body, "and we didn't have the money to take care of them all."

What the new state had was $18.5 million in unrestricted revenues; that is, revenues not dedicated to a specific purpose. Of that, $8 million (44%) came from the individual income tax.

This lack of funds ($18.5 million was about $82 per Alaska resident) had been at the bottom of much opposition to statehood, both in Alaska and Congress.

"We had a bunch of mossbacks in my area who wanted to make it two states

Editor's note: *G. Michael Doogan is a former newspapaperman and legislative aide who now works as a private fiscal consultant.*

and have the cutoff line at Yakutat," says Freeman. "Their argument was that Southeast produced most of the revenue (from its fisheries) but the rest of the state would spend most of it."

[The Territorial Budget for 1931-1932 shows that 73% of all General Fund revenues came from fisheries.]

Freeman's "mossbacks" had not been the only ones concerned about Alaska's finances. Congressional opponents to admitting Alaska to the Union had argued that the then-territory's miniscule economy would not provide enough money to pay for an adequate state government. Alaska, they claimed, would be a ward of the federal government for years to come.

The framers of the state constitution, who convened in 1955 at the University of Alaska at College, near Fairbanks, had been well aware of the problem of financing state government. As. E.L. "Bob" Bartlett, then Alaska's delegate to Congress, had pointed out in his address to the convention, Alaska's resource wealth was the cornerstone of any financial plan for the new state.

"The financial welfare of the future state and the well-being of its present and unborn citizens depend upon the wise administration and oversight of these (resource) developmental activities," Bartlett said. Further, he warned the convention delegates, "if the public domain of Alaska is frittered away without adequate safeguards, the State of Alaska will wend a precarious way along the road that leads eventually to financial insolvency."

Based upon both their concern with the state's solvency and their experience with industries that had taken much away from Alaska and left little behind, the delegates adopted Article VIII of the constitution, dealing with natural resources. Article VIII

An offshore rig conducts exploratory drilling on the Middle Ground Shoals oil field in Cook Inlet in September, 1962. Production from this field, which began in 1965, provided Alaska its own petroleum revenue, which accounted for 21% of total unrestricted revenues by FY 1972. By FY 1982, it is estimated that oil will generate 85% of those revenues. (Steve McCutcheon)

In FY 1960, Alaska received a total of $2,980.27 in petroleum revenues, all of which came from production on federal lands — the Swanson River field on the Kenai Peninsula. This 1960 photo shows the dril rig of a Standard-Richfield well.
(Steve McCutcheon)

charges the legislature (in Section 2) with providing "for the utilization, development, and conservation of all natural resources belonging to the state, including land and waters, for the maximum benefit of its people. Article VIII also grants (in Section 8) the authority to lease state land for mineral exploration and development. Thus Alaska, in addition to the taxing powers available to all states, secured "for the maximum benefit of its people" additional sources of revenue — bonuses, rents, and royalties — by the convention's decision to allow the state to lease rather than sell its mineral-bearing lands.

This was not done exclusively in the expectation of oil revenues, although many Alaskans were aware at that time that the North Slope — where then-Naval Petroleum Reserve #4 lay — held better than average prospects. Alaskans had faith that the land they would receive upon becoming a state, 104 million acres of it, would hold enough mineral wealth to insure the state's solvency. Perhaps gold, which had fueled Alaska's second boom (the boom cycle to date generally is considered to be furs, gold, fish, military spending, and oil) would make a comeback. Or the vast coal reserves would prove economically exportable. Whatever the expectation, oil proved to be the basket in which most of Alaska's eggs lay.

Unfortunately for the members of the First Alaska Legislature, none of those eggs hatched in time for their budget considerations. Their revenues for Fiscal year (FY) 1960 (Alaska's fiscal year runs from July 1 to June 30) contained $2,980.27 in petroleum revenues. Ironically, this revenue came from oil production on federal lands — the Swanson River field discovered in 1957. Provisions of the Mineral Leasing Act of 1920, confirmed in the Statehood Act, required the federal government to give the state 90% of its royalty share.

It was not until late 1965, when oil production on the state-leased Middle Ground Shoals field in Cook Inlet began, that the state started receiving its own petroleum revenue. By FY 1972, when three other state-leased Cook Inlet fields were in production, petroleum revenues accounted for 21% of the state's unrestricted revenues.

By FY 1972, the vast Prudhoe Bay field had been discovered (1967-1968) and leased (1969). The lease sale had brought more than $900 million in bonus bids to the state and raised the expectation that the field soon would be producing large sums of money on a regular basis for the state. But delays in the construction of the trans-Alaska pipeline, designed to deliver Prudhoe Bay oil to market, shattered that expectation.

Thus, in FY 1976 the state began collecting a reserves tax, a tax on oil still in the ground, to keep itself solvent. Reserves tax collections pushed petroleum revenues to 54% of unrestricted revenues that year and the one following. When oil began flowing through the pipeline in June, 1977, the reserves tax was repealed automatically. Other taxes and the state's royalty clicked in and petroleum revenues accounted for 55% of unrestricted revenues in FY 1978, 69% in FY 1979, and 86% in 1980. By FY 1981 that figure was 89%, and for the next two fiscal years the Alaska Department of Revenue estimates that figure at 85% to 89%.

The long and short of it is that today state revenues are oil revenues. (Not oil and gas, just oil. Natural gas revenues account for about 0.5% of petroleum revenues.) And Prudhoe Bay revenues are most of these. Estimates are that Prudhoe Bay production provides 93% to 95% of unrestricted oil and gas revenues.

Petroleum Revenues

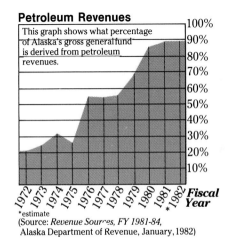

This graph shows what percentage of Alaska's gross general fund is derived from petroleum revenues.

*estimate
(Source: *Revenue Sources, FY 1981-84*, Alaska Department of Revenue, January, 1982)

Petroleum Revenue Sources

Petroleum revenues come from four types of taxes and three types of ownership rights.

Taxes, and their estimated FY 1983 revenue production (all estimated revenues are subject to change as world oil prices fluctuate), are:

Production (severance) tax, a sliding scale tax on the value of oil and gas at the wellhead, producing $1.1 billion. The normal production tax rate is 12.25% to 15%, but this decreases under the so-called economic limit factor as production from a well decreases;

Conversation tax, a levy of 1/8th of one cent per barrel on oil, the value of which is included in the production tax figure;

Corporate income tax, a percentage of the income derived by oil and gas companies from their Alaska operations, producing $258 million;

Property tax, a maximum levy of 20 mills (a mill is 1/10th of one cent per dollar of assessed value) on certain oil and gas exploration, production, and transportation properties, producing $149 million.

Ownership rights, and their estimated FY 1983 revenue production, are:

Bonuses, cash payments for the right to acquire a lease, for which there is no revenue estimate;

Rents, fees paid annually to maintain rights to lease, producing $5.5 million;

Royalties, a percentage of oil produced from a lease or its equivalent value in cash, producing $811 million.

In addition to these unrestricted revenues, petroleum production gives the state a significant amount of money for the Alaska Permanent Fund. The fund, the so-called savings account created in 1976 by a voter-approved constitutional amendment, receives a minimum of 25% of non-tax resource revenues. The permanent fund contribution is estimated to be $273 million in FY 1983.

The ownership income picture has begun to shift significantly. Currently producing fields (Cook Inlet, Prudhoe Bay) were leased under a cash bonus/fixed royalty system, meaning that the bidder offering the most up-front cash (the bonus) got the lease and was required to pay an annual rent and, on production, a fixed 12.5% of the oil produced or its cash equivalent. But some more recent leases were offered under a sliding-scale royalty (the royalty share rises as the value of production rises) or a net profits (the state receives a percentage of the profits produced by a lease) system. Under both of these systems, leases which produce large amounts of oil produce more revenue to the state than they would have

Taxes and royalties collected on coal production account for a very small percentage of Alaska's revenues. Here, coal is being loaded into Alaska Railroad cars at the Usibelli Mine near Healy. (Steve McCutcheon)

under the cash bonus/fixed royalty system. Both systems defer income and subject the state to higher risk while offering the chance of higher total revenues if the lease produces significant amounts of oil.

The federal government also reaps substantial revenue from petroleum production in Alaska. On its own leases, the federal government traditionally has used a cash bonus/fixed royalty system, with the royalty set at 16.66%. Recently, however, the federal government has used the sliding-scale royalty system on some leases. In addition, the federal government charges the oil companies both an income tax and a windfall profits tax on all United States production, including that in Alaska. The income tax, like any income tax, is a percentage of income, while a windfall profits tax is a percentage of profits on oil sold for more than a certain amount per barrel. Although there are no annual figures readily available for federal petroleum revenue from Alaska operations, a recent state study shows that the federal government will realize about 36.5% of the total profit derived from Prudhoe Bay, or some $404 billion. (That study shows the state receiving $327 billion, or about 29.5%, and the oil companies receiving $372 billion, or about 33.5%.)

Other types of mineral extraction contribute little to the state's coffers. The major identifiable source of such revenue is the Mining License Tax, a tax levied against mining operations with net income of $40,000 or more annually. The tax rate is 3% on operations in the $40,000 to $50,000 range, 5% on operations between $50,000 and $100,000, and 7% on operations of more than $100,000. In FY 1980, for example, the Mining License Tax produced 0.00002% of unrestricted state revenues ($56,005.23). In addition the state receives a sliding-scale royalty of between 5 cents and 35 cents a ton on coal production. No figures are available for the small amount of revenue this royalty produces. Likewise, there are no figures available for the amount derived from corporate income tax payments made by mining corporations. Since the state's individual income tax has been repealed, there is no individual income tax revenue from mining.

Although the state's system of dealing with non-petroleum mining currently is under review and may be substantially changed, at present the system is much less sophisticated than that used for oil and gas. Although the state has the authority to lease for minerals, it continues to use the traditional discovery, location, and filing method of awarding mineral leases. Except for the coal royalty, the state charges no royalty on other minerals although, again, it has the authority to do so. In lieu of lease rents, the state requires proof of annual lease improvements of not less than $200 annually (except for claims lacking access due to native land claims problems, where an "intent to hold" form must be filed).

Federal policy toward non-petroleum mining is, if anything, even less complicated than that of the state. The federal government charges no taxes against mining operations other than personal or corporate income taxes, receives no royalties, and requires a minimum of $100 in annual improvements per lease. Other than these differences, federal policy is the same as that of the state. It must be noted, however, that, like state policy, federal policy also is undergoing review and may be changed in the near future.

Until such reviews are completed and changes made, however, the federal and state governments will continue to draw most of their Alaska revenue from oil and gas operations. Unlike their colleagues in the First State Legislature, the members of the Twelfth State Legislature, dealing with FY 1983 revenues in the spring of 1982, are not facing a shortage of funds. Their task is to supply government to 400,000 people using $2.7 billion in unrestricted revenues (or about $6,750 per Alaska resident).

Mineral Industry Education in Alaska

By Dean Earl Beistline

Alaska's stimulating and colorful heritage, to a large degree, evolved from its abundant supply of mineral resources, the development of which established the current foundation for the state's affluent society and sound economy. Soon after the purchase of Alaska by the United States from Russia in 1867, an enthusiastic group of prospectors and miners pioneered the grueling quest, stretching along the coastline to the Interior, in search of the vast mineral riches hidden within the frontier land. This determination and persistence generated immense resource discoveries and consequent stampedes, causing the formation and eventual existence of extensive major mine development. Subsequently, this overnight industry boom created the need to establish a number of transportation routes that have become the heart of Alaska's

Editor's note: *Earl Beistline taught for more than 35 years at the University of Alaska, Fairbanks, where he is now dean emeritus of the School of Mineral Industry.*

present-day transportation system. In addition, a number of Alaska cities can trace their roots back to these various aspects of the mineral industry.

During this early period, the importance of the industry to the economic growth of the community and state was easily recognized; the mining industry thus became a matter of everyday knowledge for the community, from adolescence to adulthood.

A hiatus in the mining industry occurred within Alaska toward the beginning of World War II which resulted in a decline in knowledge and appreciation for the industry. Yet, in more recent years, increased activity in mineral exploration has proven the existence of large metallic mineral resources. In addition to this, a high degree of interest presently exists in Alaska's enormous coal resources, and the discovery of extensive oil and gas resources, accompanied by major production, has brought about a more appreciative Alaska public. Free market gold prices have stimulated a large number of family-sized placer gold

operations. This has, in turn, enhanced the public's knowledge of gold mining. In addition, the continued growth of the world's population, with the increasing per capita consumption of minerals, has created a demand for Alaska's vast mineral resource potential. As President Reagan has stated, one of our national objectives is to become self-sufficient in mineral products to meet our national requirements for society and defense purposes. Therefore, with the well

Dean Earl Beistline of the University of Alaska, Fairbanks, School of Mineral Industry leads a group of Dillingham High School students through the U.S. Army Cold Regions Research and Engineering Laboratory (CRREL) permafrost tunnel. The tunnel, located at Fox, 10 miles north of Fairbanks, is excavated through silt and gravel and into the local bedrock, exposing material that has been frozen more than 30,000 years. Visitors to the tunnel are required to wear hard hats because of rocks which occasionally fall from the roof, which is held together by frozen material, with no other means of support. To prevent thawing, the interior temperature of the tunnel is maintained at 22 °F by refrigeration. (Polly Walter, staff)

During a field trip to the Usibelli Mine at Healy, Professor Don Triplehorn of the University of Alaska, Fairbanks, left, discusses a volcanic ash deposit in the coal with one of his students.
(Michael Holman)

recognized fact that Alaska's tax income from its oil industry amounted to nearly 90% of the state's income in 1981, it may be assumed that Alaska's mineral supply will play a very important part in this national objective.

This bright outlook for Alaska's future in the mineral industry is indicative of the excellent, stimulating career opportunities that are and will continue to become available for Alaskans and others within this challenging field. A liberal definition of the mineral industry would include all facets of operations such as prospecting, exploration, development, production, recovery, and marketing, and generally pertain to metallic and nonmetallic minerals, including energy minerals such as oil, gas, coal, and uranium.

Current Offerings

Presently, there are a number of mineral industry educational programs offered in Alaska at various levels. Following is a review of many of these offerings as provided by administrators of the respective units or from published program information.

Overall, no formal requirements presently exist within Alaska's public school system that require courses to be offered in elementary grades with emphasis on earth sciences and the mining industry. Occasionally, subject matter dealing with rocks, minerals, and general geology has been discussed in class, however, the extent of such instruction is based upon an overall

interest and knowledge of the teacher, with a general science approach in each field. An occasional class field trip may expose students to some element of geology and earth sciences, but usually does not include other phases of mining operations or stress the importance of the industry to the economy and society.

Relatively few high schools offer courses in geology, earth science, and natural history. More formal courses directed toward the mineral industry would not only broaden a student's educational background, but would also enhance the importance of mineral resources to the American way of life.

University of Alaska

The University of Alaska has a number of programs in various fields pertaining to geoscience and mineral industry.

Alaska Petroleum Extension Program

The Alaska Petroleum Extension Program is an educational service coordinated through the University of Alaska, Community College, Rural Education and Extension (CCREE). The program is a cooperative effort among industry, university, community colleges, the Alaska Vocational Technical Center, and the Alaska Department of Education to prepare Alaskans for careers in the petroleum industry.

Community Colleges

Community colleges such as Ketchikan Community College, Kenai Community College, and Northwest Community College, in Nome, offer courses in physical geology. Anchorage Community College offers geology courses such as Elements of Geology, Physical Geology, Historical Geology, Geomorphology, and Introduction to Paleontology. Occasional workshops and/or seminars are also offered in response to specific community or industry needs.

In addition, community colleges of the University of Alaska, such as the Kenai Peninsula Community College and Tanana Valley Community College, offer technology programs leading to associate degrees in petroleum technology. The objectives of their programs may be summarized as:

Kenai Peninsula Community College

The Department of Petroleum Technology at Kenai Peninsula Community College offers majors in operations, process control instrumentation, industrial electronics, and petroleum engineering. All majors lead to an Associate in Applied Science Degree except petroleum engineering, which is a transfer degree.

Since its beginning in 1971, Kenai Peninsula Community college has trained more than 500 people for the petroleum industry. The immediate placement rate is presently 82.9%. Students considering Kenai Peninsula Community College should apply during the early spring to avoid heavy competition for classes.

Tanana Valley Community College

Tanana Valley Community College offers an Associate in Applied Science degree in petroleum technology. The two-year program is aimed at preparing students for work in the petroleum industry through a general introduction to geology, drilling, production, and refining.

College of Environmental Sciences, University of Alaska, Fairbanks

The Division of Geosciences offers a Bachelor of Science degree in geology, Master of Science, and Doctor of Philosophy degrees in geology and geophysics. At the undergraduate level, the Bachelor of Science in geology is offered with options in general geology, economic geology, petroleum geology, and geophysics. The program is designed to produce graduates who have a strong background in the basics of the profession, who are environmentally aware, and who have Alaska experience.

The Master of Science and Doctor of Philosophy degrees require optional thesis research. Thesis studies typically span the entire spectrum of geology and solid-earth geophysics.

School of Mineral Industry, University of Alaska, Fairbanks

The School of Mineral Industry, which has statewide responsibility for instruction, is composed of the Department of Mineral Engineering, Department of Petroleum Engineering, Mineral Industry Research Laboratory, and a mining extension program.

In the Department of Mineral Engineering three programs are offered:

Mining Engineering, Geological Engineering, and Mineral Preparation Engineering.

Mining Engineering places particular emphasis upon the exploration and development of mineral resources and the economic aspects of mining. Degree requirements include core courses in engineering and humanities, yet technical electives are offered for development in areas of exploration, mining, or mineral beneficiation.

Geological Engineering is a branch that deals with the application of geology. Geological engineers work closely with man's environment in the true sense of the word. Properties of earth materials, exploration activities, geophysical and geochemical prospecting, site investigations, and engineering geology are all phases of geological engineering.

Students in both Mining Engineering and Geological Engineering may initiate their programs in Anchorage and transfer to Fairbanks upon completion of their freshman and sophomore years. The programs lead to Bachelor of Science and Master of Science degrees.

Mineral Preparation Engineering teaches the specialized use of engineering and scientific principles to separate finely disseminated valuable minerals in the earth's crust from valueless material, including the handling of large quantities of material in an environmentally acceptable manner. A program leading to a Master of Science degree is offered.

The Department of Petroleum

Geology students from the University of Alaska, Fairbanks, study sections of Suntrana Canyon during a field trip to Usibelli Coal Mine.
(Thomas K. Bundtzen)

Engineering offers classes dealing with the various aspects of exploration, drilling, production, and transportation of petroleum fluids. In addition to the standard science and humanities courses that characterize all other professional engineering degrees, the program requires a large number of courses in geology and chemistry. The curriculum emphasizes reservoir engineering, while all courses present problems relating to drilling and production operations in the Arctic and offshore. At the University of Alaska, Fairbanks, degrees offered are a Bachelor of Science and Master of Science in Petroleum Engineering.

Usibelli Coal Research Laboratory and the Mining and Mineral Resources Research Institute of the Department of the Interior are parts of the Mineral Industry Research Laboratory (MIRL). The purpose of the laboratory is to conduct research in various areas of the mineral industry to supplement fundamental knowledge and aid in the further discovery, recovery, and utilization of Alaska's mineral resources. Present emphasis is placed on coal research, identification of Alaska's untapped mineral resource supply, and mineral recovery methods. To disseminate current information, research reports are published and conferences are held periodically on topics such as placer mining and coal mining. Numerous requests pertaining to the mining industry are received in person or by letter and are answered by personnel of MIRL.

Extension programs, two to five weeks in length, offered to various communities in Alaska include non-credit courses designed for special interest in rock and mineral identification, geology, mineral prospecting and exploration, and other phases of the mineral industry. Credit courses are available, through special arrangement, for those who desire to become more knowledgeable in geology and the mineral industry. In the 1981-1982 school year, sixteen courses were offered in 11 Alaska communities. Requests for course information may be made to the Dean, School of Mineral Industry, University of Alaska, Fairbanks, Alaska 99701.

Summer Session, University of Alaska, Fairbanks

During the summer sessions, a one-week course, The Alaska Workshop, is offered. This course includes an orientation to the mining industry in Alaska, supplemented with field trips utilizing the school's Silver Fox Mine and the Cold Regions Research and Engineering Laboratory (CRREL) permafrost tunnel.

A one-credit course in Alaska gold is also offered. The course includes the early history of Alaska mining and is at a level to allow elementary and secondary teachers to receive credit toward recertification.

Other Schools

Sheldon Jackson University

At present, Sheldon Jackson University in Sitka offers a geology course which is available for students who have an interest in geology and the mineral industry. Because of the potential for an increase in mining in southeastern Alaska, consideration is being given to offering courses that may be related to such activities.

Alaska Pacific University

Alaska Pacific University, in Anchorage, did not offer any courses in geology or earth science during the first semester of 1981-1982; however, personnel of the U.S. Geological Survey are occupying a building on campus and consideration is being given to offering faculty appointments to qualified individuals.

Scheduled for the second sememster of the 1981-1982 school year was a course in Historical Geology.

Alaska Vocational Technical Center

The Alaska Vocational Technical Center Oil Technology Department's Roughneck Development course is designed to train students as rotary drill helpers for the Alaska petroleum industry. Instruction covers welding, offshore and land-based drilling rigs, industrial tool identification and use, rigging, emergency medical training, basic operation of equipment, and the maintenance of pumps and gasoline engines.

Challenges in Mineral Industry Education

For the general public to become more knowledgeable about the mineral industry, and in preparation for the career-minded youth, a sound, comprehensive minerals education program is essential. Such a program should be initiated within the elementary grades to include specific courses in geology, earth sciences, mineral resources, and descriptions of Alaska mining operations. Hence, the more formal programs can then follow at high school and college levels, with professional and technological exposure offered in areas such as geology, mining engineering, geological engineering, petroleum engineering, mineral preparation engineering, and mining extension courses on various topics designed for the interested public. Workshops, seminars, conferences, and guest lectures are very much a part of such programs.

Alaska's arctic, sub-arctic, and temperate environments offer many professional career opportunities in the mineral industry. However, many of our young people and adults are unaware of such favorable circumstances. Therefore, it is suggested that a greater emphasis be placed on mineral industry instructional programs aimed at elementary and secondary school levels; and that increased professional and technological instruction be offered, supplemented by extension courses and public lectures.

Such instruction could be supplied by way of formal courses, special workshops, projects and/or guest lectures, as well as using television. Above all, subject matter should deal with reality and be taught at the student's appropriate level. An orientation course for the mineral industry could include topics such as:

Identification of Rocks and Minerals
General Geology
Mining Operation:
    Formation of Ore Deposits
    Prospecting
    Exploration
    Development
    Production
    Recovery
    Marketing
Oil and Gas Industry:
    Petroleum Geology
    Exploration
    Production
    Refining
    Marketing
Land Availability and Accessibility
Environmental Considerations
Economic Impact on: Community, State,
    Nation, World
Career Opportunities

School of Mineral Industry personnel from the University of Alaska, Fairbanks, 99701, are available for assistance in designing and implementing educational programs at various levels within the state's school programs.

Alaska Geographic® Back Issues

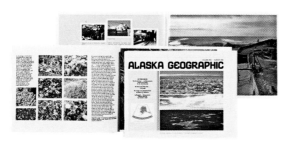

The North Slope, Vol. 1, No. 1. The charter issue of *ALASKA GEOGRAPHIC*® took a long, hard look at the North Slope and the then-new petroleum development at ''the top of the world.'' *Out of print.*

One Man's Wilderness, Vol. 1, No. 2. The story of a dream shared by many, fulfilled by few: a man goes into the bush, builds a cabin and shares his incredible wilderness experience. Color photos. 116 pages, $9.95

Admiralty . . . Island in Contention, Vol. 1, No. 3. An intimate and multifaceted view of Admiralty: its geological and historical past, its present-day geography, wildlife and sparse human population. Color photos. 78 pages, $5.00

Fisheries of the North Pacific: History, Species, Gear & Processes, Vol. 1, No. 4. The title says it all. This volume is out of print, but the book, from which it was excerpted, is available in a revised, expanded large-format volume. 424 pages. $24.95.

The Alaska-Yukon Wild Flowers Guide, Vol. 2, No. 1. First Northland flower book with both large, color photos and detailed drawings of every species described. Features 160 species, common and scientific names and growing height. Vertical-format book edition now available. 218 pages, $10.95.

Richard Harrington's Yukon, Vol. 2, No. 2. The Canadian province with the colorful past *and* present. *Out of print.*

Prince William Sound, Vol. 2, No. 3. This volume explored the people and resources of the Sound. *Out of print.*

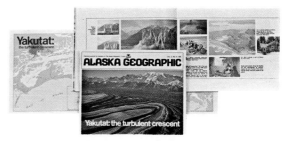

Yakutat: The Turbulent Crescent, Vol. 2, No. 4. History, geography, people — and the impact of the coming of the oil industry. *Out of print.*

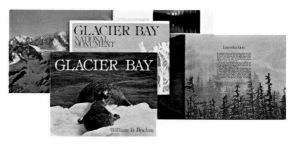

Glacier Bay: Old Ice, New Land, Vol. 3, No. 1. The expansive wilderness of Southeastern Alaska's Glacier Bay National Monument (recently proclaimed a national park and preserve) unfolds in crisp text and color photographs. Records the flora and fauna of the area, its natural history, with hike and cruise information, plus a large-scale color map. 132 pages, $9.95

The Land: Eye of the Storm, Vol. 3, No. 2. The future of one of the earth's biggest pieces of real estate! *This volume is out of print,* but the latest on the Alaska lands controversy is detailed completely in Volume 8, Number 4.

Alaska's Volcanoes: Northern Link in the Ring of Fire, Vol. 4, No. 1. Scientific overview supplemented with eyewitness accounts of Alaska's historic volcano eruptions. Includes color and black-and-white photos and a schematic description of the effects of plate movement upon volcanic activity. 88 pages. *Temporarily out of print.*

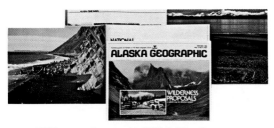

Wilderness Proposals: Which Way for Alaska's Lands?, Vol. 4, No. 4. This volume gave yet another detailed analysis of the many Alaska lands questions. *Out of print.*

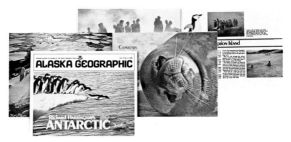

Richard Harrington's Antarctic, Vol. 3, No. 3. The Canadian photojournalist guides readers through remote and little understood regions of the Antarctic and Subantarctic. More than 200 color photos and a large fold-out map. 104 pages, $8.95

The Brooks Range: Environmental Watershed, Vol. 4, No. 2. An impressive work on a truly impressive piece of Alaska — The Brooks Range. *Out of print.*

Cook Inlet Country, Vol. 5, No. 1. A visual tour of the region — its communities, big and small, and its countryside. Begins at the southern tip of the Kenai Peninsula, circles Turnagain Arm and Knik Arm for a close-up view of Anchorage, and visits the Matanuska and Susitna valleys and the wild, west side of the inlet. 230 color photos, separate map. 144 pages, $9.95

The Silver Years of the Alaska Canned Salmon Industry: An Album of Historical Photos, Vol. 3, No. 4. The grand and glorious past of the Alaska canned salmon industry. *Out of print.*

Kodiak: Island of Change, Vol. 4, No. 3. Russians, wildlife, logging and even petroleum . . . an island where change is one of the few constants. *Out of print.*

Southeast: Alaska's Panhandle, Vol. 5, No. 2. Explores Southeastern Alaska's maze of fjords and islands, mossy forests and glacier-draped mountains — from Dixon Entrance to Icy Bay, including all of the state's fabled Inside Passage. Along the way are profiles of every town, together with a look at the region's history, economy, people, attractions and future. Includes large fold-out map and seven area maps. 192 pages, $12.95

Bristol Bay Basin, Vol. 5, No. 3. Explores the land and the people of the region known to many as the commercial salmon-fishing capital of Alaska. Illustrated with contemporary color and historic black-and-white photos. Includes a large fold-out map of the region. 96 pages, $9.95.

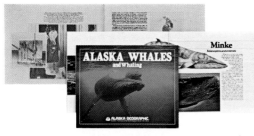

Alaska Whales and Whaling, Vol. 5, No. 4. The wonders of whales in Alaska — their life cycles, travels and travails — are examined, with an authoritative history of commercial and subsistence whaling in the North. Includes a fold-out poster of 14 major whale species in Alaska in perspective, color photos and illustrations, with historical photos and line drawings. 144 pages, $12.95.

Yukon-Kuskokwim Delta, Vol. 6, No. 1. This volume explored the people and lifestyles of one of the most remote areas of the 49th state. *Out of print.*

The Aurora Borealis, Vol. 6, No. 2. The northern lights — in ancient times seen as a dreadful forecast of doom, in modern days an inspiration to countless poets. Here one of the world's leading experts — Dr. S.-I. Akasofu of the University of Alaska — explains in an easily understood manner, aided by many diagrams and spectacular color and black-and-white photos, what causes the aurora, how it works, how and why scientists are studying it today and its implications for our future. 96 pages, $7.95.

Alaska's Native People, Vol. 6, No. 3. In the largest edition to date — result of several years of research — the editors examine the varied worlds of the Inupiat Eskimo, Yup'ik Eskimo, Athabascan, Aleut, Tlingit, Haida and Tsimshian. Most photos are by Lael Morgan, *ALASKA®* magazine's roving editor, who since 1974 has been gathering impressions and images from virtually every Native village in Alaska. Included are sensitive, informative articles by Native writers, plus a large, four-color map detailing the Native villages and defining the language areas. 304 pages, $19.95.

The Stikine, Vol. 6, No 4. River route to three Canadian gold strikes in the 1800s, the Stikine is the largest and most navigable of several rivers that flow from northwestern Canada through Southeastern Alaska on their way to the sea. This edition explores 400 miles of Stikine wilderness, recounts the river's paddlewheel past and looks into the future, wondering if the Stikine will survive as one of the North's great free-flowing rivers. Illustrated with contemporary color photos and historic black-and-white; includes a large fold-out map. 96 pages, $9.95.

Alaska's Great Interior, Vol. 7, No. 1. Alaska's rich Interior country, west from the Alaska-Yukon Territory border and including the huge drainage between the Alaska Range and the Brooks Range, is covered thoroughly. Included are the region's people, communities, history, economy, wilderness areas and wildlife. Illustrated with contemporary color and black-and-white photos. Includes a large fold-out map. 128 pages, $9.95.

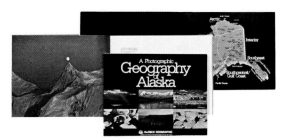

A Photographic Geography of Alaska, Vol. 7, No. 2. An overview of the entire state — a visual tour through the six regions of Alaska: Southeast, Southcentral/Gulf Coast, Alaska Peninsula and Aleutians, Bering Sea Coast, Arctic and Interior. Plus a handy appendix of valuable information — "Facts About Alaska." Approximately 160 color and black-and-white photos and 35 maps. 192 pages, $14.95.

Klondike Lost: A Decade of Photographs by Kinsey & Kinsey, Vol. 7, No. 4. An album of rare photographs and all-new text about the lost Klondike boom town of Grand Forks, second in size only to Dawson during the gold rush. Introduction by noted historian Pierre Berton: 138 pages, area maps and more than 100 historical photos, most never before published. $12.95.

Alaska Mammals, Vol. 8, No. 2. From tiny ground squirrels to the powerful polar bear, and from the tundra hare to the magnificent whales inhabiting Alaska's waters, this volume includes 80 species of mammals found in Alaska. Included are beautiful color photographs and personal accounts of wildlife encounters. *The* book on Alaska's mammals — from Southeast to the Arctic, and beyond! 184 pages, $12.95.

The Aleutians, Vol. 7, No. 3. The fog-shrouded Aleutians are many things — home of the Aleut, a tremendous wildlife spectacle, a major World War II battleground and now the heart of a thriving new commercial fishing industry. Roving editor Lael Morgan contributes most of the text; also included are contemporary color and black-and-white photographs, and a large fold-out map. 224 pages, $14.95.

Wrangell-Saint Elias, Vol. 8, No. 1. Mountains, including the continent's second- and fourth-highest peaks, dominate this international wilderness that sweeps from the Wrangell Mountains in Alaska to the southern Saint Elias range in Canada. The region draws backpackers, mountain climbers, and miners, and is home for a few hardy, year-round inhabitants. Illustrated with contemporary color and historical black-and-white photographs. Includes a large fold-out map. 144 pages, $9.95.

The Kotzebue Basin, Vol. 8, No. 3. Examines northwestern Alaska's thriving trading area of Kotzebue Sound and the Kobuk and Noatak river basins, lifelines of the region's Inupiat Eskimos, early explorers, and present-day, hardy residents. Contemporary color and historical black-and-white photographs illustrate varied cultures and numerous physical attractions of the area. 184 pages, $12.95.

Alaska National Interest Lands, Vol. 8, No. 4.
Following passage of the bill formalizing Alaska's
national interest land selections (d-2 lands),
longtime Alaskans Celia Hunter and Ginny Wood
review each selection, outlining location, size,
access, and briefly describing the region's special
attractions. Illustrated with contemporary color
photographs depicting as no other medium can the
grandeur of Alaska's national interest lands. 242
pages, $14.95.

Alaska's Glaciers, Vol. 9, No. 1. Examines
in-depth the massive rivers of ice, their
composition, exploration, present-day distribution
and scientific significance. Illustrated with many
contemporary color and historical black-and-white
photos, the text includes separate discussions of
more than a dozen glacial regions. 144 pages,
$9.95.

NEXT ISSUE

**Adventure Roads North: The Story of the Alaska
Highway and Other Roads in *The MILEPOST* ®,
Vol. 10, No. 1.** From Alaska's first highway — the
Richardson — to the famous Alaska Highway, first
overland route to the 49th state, text and photos
provide a history of Alaska's roads and take a
mile-by-mile look at the country they cross. To
members in February, 1983. Price to be announced.

Sitka and Its Ocean/Island World, Vol. 9, No. 2.
From the elegant capital of Russian America to a
beautiful but modern port, Sitka, on Baranof
Island, has become a commercial and cultural
center for Southeastern Alaska. Pat Roppel,
longtime Southeast resident and expert on the
region's history, examines in detail the past and
present of Sitka, Baranof Island, and neighboring
Chichagof Island. Illustrated with contemporary
color and historical black-and-white photographs.
128 pages, $9.95.

Islands of the Seals: The Pribilofs, Vol. 9, No. 3.
Great herds of northern fur seals drew Russians and
Aleuts to these remote Bering Sea islands where they
founded permanent communities and established a
unique international commerce. The communities
languished under U.S. control until recent decades
when new legislation and attempts at economic
diversification have increased interest in the islands,
their Aleut people, and the rich marine resources
nearby. Illustrated with contemporary color and
historical black-and-white photographs. 128 pages,
$9.95.

The Alaska Geographic Society

Box 4-EEE, Anchorage, AK 99509

The Alaska Geographic Society is a
nonprofit organization, and your $30 annual
membership brings you four big issues of
ALASKA GEOGRAPHIC®. Membership advantages
include substantial cost-savings on this award-
winning book-size publication and a guarantee
that you won't miss a single issue! Each edition of
ALASKA GEOGRAPHIC® is devoted to a single
subject, and that subject is explored inside and out,
with insightful text and beautiful photos.

*ALASKA EARTHLINES/
TIDELINES* — an eight-
times-a-year newsprint
magazine published by The
Alaska Geographic Society —
deals with a variety of natural
resource subjects for classroom study. A new volume
begins in September and
ends in May. (December/
January is a combined issue.)
Student subscriptions
generally include the 8 issues published during a
school year. **Single subscriptions** begin with the
current issue and continue until 8 consecutive
issues have been sent. Subscription prices:
STUDENT: $1.50 per subscription; minimum
order, 10 subscriptions sent to one address.
SINGLE: $2.50 per subscription mailed to
addresses in Alaska. $3.50 per subscription
mailed outside Alaska to other U.S. or foreign
addresses. (Payments to be made in U.S. funds.)
A SAMPLE COPY can be yours for $1, postpaid.
Make checks payable to The Alaska Geographic
Society, and send with your order to *Alaska
Earthlines/Tidelines*, Box 4-EEE, Anchorage,
Alaska 99509. Your canceled check is your
receipt. **GIFT SUBSCRIPTIONS** will be
announced to the recipient with a card signed in
your name.